# Taking a Stand

# Joe McVeigh

# Taking a Stand

## MEMOIR OF AN IRISH PRIEST

### MERCIER PRESS

WHAT YOU NEED TO READ

MERCIER PRESS
Cork
www.mercierpress.ie

Trade enquiries to CMD Distribution
55A Spruce Avenue, Stillorgan Industrial Park,
Blackrock, County Dublin

ISBN: 978185635 593 3
10 9 8 7 6 5 4 3 2 1

A CIP record for this title is available from the British Library

Mercier Press receives financial assistance from the Arts
Council/An Chomhairle Ealaíon

Printed and bound in the EU

# Contents

'Life is not what one lived, but what one remembers and how one remembers it in order to recount it.'

– Gabriel Garcia Márquez, *Living to Tell the Tale*

# Acknowledgements

I wish to acknowledge the help I received from the late Brian Campbell when I started out to write this book. Without his encouragement, I probably would not have written it. Brian died unexpectedly on 5 October 2005. He was a creative writer and a caring and generous human being. Brian is a huge loss to Ireland as well as to his own family. I wish to acknowledge his great contribution to Irish political and cultural life.

I would like to thank Jude Collins for his help and encouragement; people who helped and advised at various stages, including Brian MacDonald and Danny Morrison. I am grateful for the friendship of Des Wilson and Noelle Ryan and all at Springhill; Dan Berrigan, SJ, for his enthusiastic support, Silvia Calamati, Mary Madden, B.J. Ashanti, Monica Gallagher, Peter and Dorothy Beresford Ellis. Thanks also to Oistín MacBride for the photos and to Brian O'Loughlin for proof-reading. I would like to remember some dear friends, Fr Maurice Burke, SMA, Pat Kelly (Ederney), Donna Ferguson (Belleek) and Florence Dalrymple (US). I am deeply indebted to my immediate family, all my extended family, *idir cléir agus tuath*, and to all who helped me along the way. Go raibh céad míle maith agaibh go léir.

Thanks to the Gallery Press for permission to use John Montague's poem, 'After Mass', and Pádraig Standún for permission to use his tribute to Tom O'Gara.

# Foreword

Few people in Ireland, and hardly any clergy, know more about modern Ireland's struggle towards justice than Joe McVeigh. So his testimony must help fashion any future history.

He grew up in a world where there seemed little possibility of change but where, quite suddenly, change became not only possible but an absolute and realistic demand. In the north-east corner of Ireland people stopped asking for favours from the dominant political party and demanded recognition of their rights instead. That revolution happened in Ireland in the mid-1960s when other revolutions by other peoples were in the air too.

Those who were moving away from asking favours towards demanding recognition of rights were entitled to feel optimistic. They believed they must have politicians of good will on their side, universities, writers, foreign observers, and people of many kinds who, they thought, would come on their side once they knew the truth of what was happening in Ireland. The truth was that in that part of Ireland there was a regime which was unjust and often cruelly so. Some of this optimism was justified, most of it sadly not.

Catholics believed they had the great advantage of a vast and influential church to look after their interests. Some church leaders in the past, like Bishop Mageean, had spoken out with strong anger and weak influence, but oppressed people most of the time had to keep quiet and hope for better times. The mid-1960s revolution, in their thinking, was a dramatic call to people to move from enforced apathy to effective action, on the streets if necessary.

So Joe McVeigh grew up and worked in a changing world, which, unlike the world of his forbears, held real possibility of having fair government. His account, then, of what happened and why it happened, of successes and failures, has to be important.

In his account of his own life and how it was shaped by hopes and defeats, successes and surprising events, one of the saddest and most dramatic of his themes is a simple one: 'the Catholic hierarchy contributed little of value to the development of the peace process from the late 1980s onwards' (*see* Introduction). That statement is tragic for at least two reasons; because it recalls the deep and often bitter disappointment of Catholics who looked to their church for protection, and because the potential of the church was such that it could have made a great difference to the policies of governments.

And yet, what was asked of churches was simple and achievable – it was to bring conflicting people around a table to talk. There were few other bodies that could do that. And there were examples in other countries where church members and leaders intervened, sometimes dramatically, to help their people in oppression and distress. Was it a disadvantage then that Joe McVeigh could travel, and read about and meet people who did it? Disadvantage, because seeing the churches' potential for good abroad made it all the more disappointing to note their failure at home.

At a time when the vision of religion as liberation was enlightening and rejoicing so many Christians, their disappointments could be intense. Many Christian leaders chose to remain as clients in the shadow of governments rather than, as liberating theologians saw it, as free souls vitalised in the light of Christ. Joe McVeigh became part of a worldwide company of people exploring the amazing vision of religion, not just as a rule of life, but also as a vision of freedom.

Such a life's journey can be a difficult one, not least because some companions may, quietly or loudly, leave you along the way. The story is well worth telling. After all, every social change, every religious renewal, every happening which helped human beings to live in dignity began with one person, or two or a few, looking at how we are and saying: 'This is what we have, but it could be better, much better.'

However powerful the movement towards freedom through faith may become, we remember that it all began with a handful of friends for whom everything was possible so long as it was right.

Joe McVeigh sees the history of his times not just as the listing of events but as the story of people for whom God has created freedom and whose religious destiny is to achieve it. Many of those whom Joe encountered – and helped – had to confront official cruelty or negligence with blessed resilience and courage. The drama of the story is that so many of them were his friends and neighbours.

*Des Wilson*
Springhill Community House
Béal Feirste

# Preface

A bishop once said to me that the priest's mission was 'to save souls'. As far as he was concerned the priest was to be engaged exclusively with religious matters and should keep out of politics. I think that what he really meant was that priests should keep out of any kind of radical politics. I saw it differently. For while 'saving souls' is undoubtedly central to the message of Christ, it is not the whole message. Christianity also proclaims the message of social justice. I saw it as my duty and privilege as a priest to support and care for human beings in the very concrete social circumstances of their lives – and that required taking a radical political stance. As far as I was concerned it was the most Christian and spiritual thing that I could do.

In the context of the struggle for civil rights, which began in the late 1960s, I felt obliged to take a stand, to demand justice and truth, alongside the people who were demanding their rights. These people, my neighbours, were caught up in a situation where they were treated with gross injustice, treated as second-class citizens. I wanted to reach out to support real people, not merely as 'souls to be saved' but as real 'flesh and blood' people with real expectations and entitlements. This demanded acting in solidarity with the people, engaging in civil disobedience, countering propaganda from the political or religious establishment and working for justice in whatever ways I could. Sitting on the fence was not an option.

This book is a personal reflection on my life in the church and my involvement in the conflict of the last forty years in the area where I was born and raised. It tells about the events and experiences that affected me most deeply and it records my hopes for the future.

*Joe McVeigh*
2008

# Introduction

I was born in Ireland yet all the trappings of the state in which I grew up were British. The Union Jack flew over all public buildings as a constant reminder that this part of Ireland was still under British rule and we were subjects of the English crown. People with another political allegiance dominated the community to which I belonged. A colonial government in London had effectively handed the reins of power in this artificial statelet to a unionist ascendancy which lorded it over those of us who were second-class by virtue of our religion. We were trapped in this statelet and nobody much cared. While London misruled us through its proxy at Stormont, we felt abandoned by those from whom we might have expected support – the Irish government.

Partition in 1920 brought disastrous results for all the people of Ireland. As I was growing up in County Fermanagh, I became aware that the society in which I lived was divided along religious lines and that discrimination against Catholics was the order of the day. Catholics generally identified with the Irish nation, Gaelic games and Gaelic culture. Most Protestants identified with soccer, cricket and the royal family. The British government had fostered division for centuries and this resulted in periodic sectarian attacks. The decision to partition Ireland institutionalised this anti-Catholic bigotry in what nationalist Ireland described as 'the six occupied counties'.

Many of our unionist neighbours (otherwise decent people) appeared to undergo a personality transformation in the summer months. Catholic businesses with whom they dealt for eleven months of the year were avoided in July. Union Jacks hung on their houses and they went off parading in their Orange regalia.

They did this as an expression of loyalty to the crown, but for many it was also an assertion of domination over their Catholic neighbours, and routes were deliberately chosen to ensure that 'the Croppies' got the message.

Some of our Protestant neighbours were also involved in a local, exclusively Protestant, militia called the B-Specials, formed in 1920 to defend the new, post-partition statelet called Northern Ireland. I didn't yet realise that similar militias in defence of the Protestant ascendancy had been in existence in every period of conflict since 1641.

Loyalty to the Orange Order and to the crown gave Protestants some distinct advantages over their Catholic neighbours. They were preferred for government jobs. They were allocated housing when their Catholic neighbours lived in overcrowded slums. They were trusted as 'the eyes and ears' of the state.

The Orange Order was the glue that held this rotten state of affairs in place. This was, and is, an organisation committed to preserving the status quo and unionist/Protestant control and domination in all aspects of life. Protestant clergy were deeply involved in this organisation. Many served as high-ranking officers in the Unionist Party and the Orange Order. Their churches were (and are) bedecked with the Union Jack and Orange regalia during what has become known as 'the marching season'. There were, of course, individual and courageous exceptions, and often Protestant clergymen felt powerless in the face of their ruling bodies. Still, the 'special relationship' between the Protestant denominations and Orangeism has been a disturbing reality.

The system of one-party unionist government with its own political police force – the RUC – created a culture of resistance. The laws of the unionist state were repressive, giving the government the power to arrest and imprison Catholics/nationalists without a trial. In virtually every decade of Orange/unionist domination, hundreds of Irish republicans, mostly Catholic men and women

were interned either on prison ships or in grim bastions such as Crumlin Road and Armagh jails. Those brought before the courts were severely punished. The vast majority of judges were avowedly unionist and pro-British. Under the Flags and Emblems Act (1954) it was illegal to fly the Irish flag – the Tricolour. Nationalists could only watch as the democratic system was corrupted through deliberate gerrymandering of constituencies, designed to maintain unionist domination of local government. Many jobs were confined to those who took an oath of allegiance to the English monarch.

I became aware of the systemic inequality at an early age when my father and many of my Catholic neighbours could not find steady employment. Eventually, this political and economic inequality led, in February 1967, to the formation of a broad-based civil rights movement – led by nationalists, republicans and left-leaning politicians – including a few conscientious, socially minded Protestants. The demands were simply a free vote for all and an end to discrimination. The first aim of the new movement was to publicise grievances through public marches and to put pressure on the British government to bring in much-needed reforms. This was a new and exciting development inspired by the campaign for civil rights in the United States. The northern civil rights movement hardly expected the ferocity of the opposition from the RUC and the B-Specials and the latest Protestant demagogue, Ian Paisley, and his followers in the Free Presbyterian church.

The civil rights movement in the six counties lifted the lid of the corrupt statelet and exposed to the world the brutality and violence of that regime, established almost fifty years earlier by the Westminster government. The state tried to put the lid back on but could not. Censorship and repression could no longer hide the corruption. The state was rotten to the core. Some refused to look, some looked away. But with the advent of television cameras it was exposed, and politics in Ireland would never be the same again. The violent reaction to the

civil rights demands led directly to the armed conflict that lasted for almost thirty years.

By the time the campaign for civil rights had begun, I was about to be ordained a Catholic priest and was full of youthful idealism and hope that the official Catholic church in Ireland would adopt the forward thinking of the Second Vatican Council and back the demands of downtrodden Catholics in the six counties for basic civil rights. But, as had happened before in our history, the official Catholic church hierarchy took the side of the government and not the side of the working-class people.

The Catholic church in Ireland, as elsewhere, had been obsessed with the rise of radical left-wing politics, and in Ireland republicanism had been viewed with bitter hostility since its inception in the 1790s. And so it was hardly surprising when church leaders denounced 'the hooligan element' that responded with stones and petrol bombs to attacks by the B-Specials/RUC. There was no denunciation of the violence of the state, nor was there any attempt to analyse or tackle the root causes of the rioting on the streets of Belfast and Derry. A deep division within the Catholic community was evident from that time onwards. Republicans were not going to take their politics from Rome.

It was during this period that the official church lost much of its authority and respect within working-class communities in Belfast and Derry, which were otherwise deeply religious. One bishop who later brought a bit more realism to the situation was Tomás Ó Fiaich, the archbishop of Armagh, but he was very much a lone voice in the Irish Catholic hierarchy during these years. Amongst many low-points, the hostile attitude adopted towards the funerals of republican activists contrasted sharply with the welcome accorded Union-Jack-draped coffins of Catholic members of the crown forces. In the 1980s, the church bemoaned the decline in influence and political support of those described by Bishop Cahal Daly as 'natural leaders' (i.e. the SDLP) and the rise of republican

politics in the shape of Sinn Féin. Bishop Cahal Daly's refusal to even talk to the leader of Sinn Féin during this period underlined the hostile attitude of the Catholic hierarchy. Because of this attitude, the Catholic church hierarchy contributed little of value to the development of the peace process from the late 1980s onwards.

For many people of faith involved in the struggle for justice in Ireland, over the many years of conflict, it was our faith in the God of Justice, and our solidarity under pressure that has supported us through many years of intimidation, suffering and sorrow. Others found courage, strength and inspiration from different sources like the republican tradition and especially from the martyrs of 1916. People of faith in many countries like South Africa and El Salvador, Palestine, Nicaragua and East Timor all got strength and courage from their belief in a God of Justice. Out of their faith they got the courage and determination to carry on with or without the support of their church leaders or even the Vatican. Sometimes, as a result of their solidarity with the oppressed, they had to give their lives in the cause of justice.

Now that the war is over and the unthinkable has happened, Ireland can at last be an example to other peoples and nations, where there is conflict, that peace is possible given some good will and determination on all sides to make it happen.

The Belfast/Good Friday Agreement in 1998 was the breakthrough that was needed to convince republicans there was another way forward, that they could do business with unionists and continue to work for Irish unity.

Since 26 March 2007, and that iconic image of Ian Paisley and Gerry Adams sitting together with members of their respective parties (the Democratic Unionist Party and Sinn Féin), there is a sense that the long conflict in Ireland and between Ireland and Britain is on its way to being resolved by peaceful political means. The elected representatives of the people are now charged with building peace, justice and prosperity for all the people of Ireland.

There are some who do not think that this process can lead to the united Ireland which many have fought for and died for but they have not offered a viable alternative to the current strategy. I believe that the nationalist people in the six counties are now guaranteed equality and justice in law. I believe that people can now pursue the goal of a United Ireland by peaceful and democratic means. The unionist/loyalist people have accepted the principle of consent and have pledged to work the institutions of the Good Friday Agreement with its all-Ireland dimensions. As Gerry Adams, the Sinn Féin president, said on that momentous occasion, the two traditions of Orange and Green are now preparing to work together for the good of all the people on this island. Rev. Ian Paisley agreed to lead his party, the Democratic Unionist Party, into power-sharing with Sinn Féin, the main republican /nationalist party. After much soul-searching and many difficult moments, all the pieces of the jigsaw are now in place to progress in a way that does not threaten anybody.

The seeds for this settlement were sown many years before when some people urged that the only way forward was for the chief protagonists to engage in dialogue. The IRA took the war to Britain. Their members died on hunger strikes for what they believed in. It was a cruel and bitter war and terrible things happened, as happen in all wars. There was only one way to stop the war and that was to start the talking – especially to the IRA and their representatives. There were meetings between Gerry Adams of Sinn Féin and John Hume the leader of the SDLP, which prepared the way for talks with the Dublin government and the British government. The politicians in Dublin and London were persuaded that Sinn Féin was serious about making peace and building peace in a new Ireland. An Irish government led by Bertie Ahern and a British Labour government led by Tony Blair engaged with republicans and unionists to bring about the Belfast Agreement of 1998. It represented the first stage in a new settlement in Ireland between Orange and Green. After a number of hitches the scene was set for an altogether new agreement between those who had been sworn enemies.

A new power-sharing executive involving Sinn Féin and the DUP met for the first time on 8 May 2007 and elected Rev. Ian Paisley as first minister and Martin McGuinness as deputy first minister. This was a truly historic moment in recent Irish history. After so many years of conflict and violence the main parties to the conflict are pledged to work together for the good of all the people of Ireland. A peaceful unified Ireland is now a real possibility.

# 1

# The Early Years

I was born in the year 1945 in the townland of Edenaveigh near the village of Ederney in County Fermanagh. My parents were living in a rented house until our own was built on a site beside my grandparents in Moneyvriece – about a mile from the village. The local mid-wife, Nurse McCusker, was present for the birth and she remained good friends with my mother and our family afterwards. I was the first in a family of six, the last child died in infancy.

1945 was an eventful year. It was the year the Second World War ended – a war that claimed the lives of more than fifty million people. It was the year the United States air force dropped the first atom bombs on the civilian populations of Hiroshima and Nagasaki in Japan, killing hundreds of thousands. The world would never be the same again.

It was the year the United Nations came into existence. Douglas Hyde retired as president and Seán T. O'Kelly was elected the second ever president of Ireland. It was the year that the US president, Franklin Delano Roosevelt, died and was succeeded by Harry S. Truman. General Charles de Gaulle became president of France and Tito president of Yugoslavia. Before the year was out the International Monetary Fund was set up and the great tenor, Count John McCormack, died.

It was the year that Labour, under Clement Atlee, took over from Churchill's coalition government in England. This government introduced free education and the family allowance. This affected those of us living under British rule in the six counties.

It was the year that Jimmy Gralton from County Leitrim died in New York. He had been deported from his own country in 1932 by de Valera's Fianna Fáil government after a concerted effort by the local priests in Leitrim to have him removed from their midst. He was accused of spreading communistic ideas and was denounced from the pulpit. A community hall, the Pearse-Connolly hall he built for the people of Effernagh, was burned to the ground.

It was the year the first trans-Atlantic plane landed at Shannon. A Pan-Am plane crossed the Atlantic in nine hours and twenty-nine minutes. The new national airline, Aer Lingus, began flying from Dublin to London. The fare was £6.10 shillings one way. Oranges were once again on sale in Dublin for 2 pence each. Petrol was again available for private motoring, while silk stockings were once more on sale in Dublin. Aer Lingus advertised for airhostesses and received over 400 applications.

The Abbey theatre put on a pantomime in Irish. Peggy Lee was Top of the Pops singing 'I Don't Know Enough About You'. Judy Garland was singing 'In the Valley', Paul Whiteman 'Wang Bang Blues', the Nat King Cole Trio 'You're Nobody Till Somebody Loves You' and Wesley Tuttle was singing 'My Bonnie Lies Over the Ocean'. The latest film was 'Going My Way' and was very popular.

It was the year that Cork won both the All-Ireland hurling and football titles (and not for the first or last time!). More than 10,000 people gathered in Clones to see the senior footballers of Cavan beat Fermanagh in the final of the Ulster senior championship. The GAA did not recognise the border.

It was the year that more than 200 republican prisoners – men and women – who were interned in Belfast and Armagh without trial were finally released, while IRA prisoners in Portlaoise in the twenty-six counties were still struggling for the right to political status.

It was the year the cardinal archbishop of Armagh, Cardinal MacRory, died. Cardinal D'alton succeeded him. It was the year that the 'Irish Anti-Partition League', led by a number of parish priests and nationalist politicians in the six counties, was formed in Dungannon, County Tyrone.

Life was tough but simple in those days, where we lived near the Fermanagh/Donegal border, during and after the war. There were few cars, only bicycles for getting around. Money was scarce. A few young men from the locality joined the British army. Others emigrated. Country people visited each other's houses at night during the winter. They helped each other with the hay and turf in the summer. They had their own ways of socialising and their own forms of entertainment.

My father, Michael McVeigh, was a young man of about twenty when he first met my mother, Marie Leonard, who was a few years older. They met at a dance in a small parish hall in Lettercran about five miles from Ederney in County Donegal. It was some time in 1942. Neither the Second World War nor the artificial political border that was drawn in Ireland in 1920 curtailed the social life of the people around Pettigo and Ederney. The locals had a song at the time, 'South of the Border down Pettigo Way', a variation of the Jimmy Kennedy song. They made up the words to suit the occasion: 'South of the border/down Pettigo way/That's where we get sugar to put in our tay'. During the war, sugar and other food-stuffs were rationed in the north. Smuggling became a way of life in border areas.

My parents were married in the Catholic church in Bundoran in 1944. It was a small family wedding. A photograph of them on their wedding day shows a young, happy, smiling couple. My mother was twenty-four and very attractive and my father was a handsome, strong looking young man of twenty-one. Both their families were proud of them on their wedding day. They went to Sligo on their honeymoon.

My mother, Marie Leonard, was born in County Donegal in 1919. Her parents had just returned from America with their children. Her father, James Leonard, came originally from the Mulleek area, of County Fermanagh. He emigrated to America where he met his future wife, Ellen Maloney from near Mitchelstown, County Cork. They wrote to the parish priest in Belleek/Pettigo asking him if there was any property for sale in the parish at the time. He wrote to them about a farm for sale near Pettigo in County Donegal. They purchased this farm and returned to live in County Donegal in 1918 at the height of the Tan war and just two years before the British government partitioned Ireland.

My father's parents, Joseph and Teresa (McGrath), came from County Tyrone – from the Drumquin area, about five miles from Ederney. They had come to live in the townland of Moneyvriece in 1912 after they married. My father was born in 1923 and was the youngest in a family of five – three boys and two girls. He left school in 1937 to help with the farming at home. During the Second World War, he got his first job, with the air ministry based at Castle Archdale near Lisnarick, as a lorry driver and doing maintenance work. He also worked at St Angelo air base near Enniskillen. That job finished when the war ended in 1945.

I spent the first four years of my life in the townland of Edenaveigh. We lived in a two-storey house situated on a gentle hillside over-looking a wide-open valley – the Glendarragh valley. From the top of the hill, behind our house, you could see Lough Erne – up to five miles distant.

My memories of my early years in Edenaveigh are happy ones. I was often reminded by my mother that when I was just two years old I nearly lost my life in the 'big snow' of 1947, when I left the house on the hill on my own and stumbled down to the road. It was lucky that my father found me before I had gone too far. I was a bit restless and adventurous even when I was two years of age!

I remember Irish music in our house in those early years, fiddle playing on occasions, when my father would take down his fiddle and also when my father's cousin, Seán McVeigh, from the nearby village of Dromore in County Tyrone, came to visit. He was regarded as a good fiddler and played in a local band called 'The Moonlight', which mixed céilí and old-time music, popular for dancing at that time. But there was no money in the dance bands then, so he left Ireland and went to New York to find a steady job. I do not remember much music being played in our house after that. On an odd occasion my father would play the fiddle; one regret I have to this day is that I did not learn to play the fiddle when I was young.

I spent a lot of time outdoors playing with my cousins, the McGraths, who lived beside us. We invented our own games and had fun imitating clucking hens and building outdoor houses. We learned to dig and to 'drive' using the lids of pots. We learned to climb trees. My family did not have a car, but our cousins had a van and we travelled with them when we had to go anywhere.

In 1949, when I was going on four years of age, we moved to our newly-built house about a mile away in the townland of Moneyvriece – nearer to the church and school. I don't think I was very happy about moving house as I felt I was leaving my friends behind. I remember the lorry, belonging to a local shop-keeper, coming to move whatever furniture we had. It was a much smaller house than the one we had lived in during my first four years, but it was new and it was our own. My father had pur-chased most of the concrete blocks and the sheets of corrugated iron for the roof from the air ministry when they were leaving Castle Archdale after the war. The three-roomed house was big enough at the beginning but was a bit small as more children arrived.

Our new house was situated near the roadside, which went along a low-lying valley surrounded by a number of small hills. There was a small hill like a drumlin in front of our house and a lane going across the side of it to Mulligans' house. My grandfather's house was situated on that lane almost on top of the hill and was clearly visible from our front room. It was built beside an ancient rath or ring fort. There are a large number of ring forts and ancient stone monuments in the area, indicating that people lived in this part of Fermanagh for thousands of years before the Christian era. From my grandparents' house there was a good view of the local village and of Lough Erne. There was another hill behind our house and a large area of bogland with all kinds of trees and foliage, which I liked to explore. In the distance looking eastwards towards the village of Lack you could see a higher mountain range called Tappaghan, where there is a wind farm generating electricity. It was a well-populated area when I was growing up and you could see the lights of all the houses for miles around, especially during the winter nights.

In the late 1940s and early 1950s after the Second World War, my father, like most young men from a nationalist background in that area, found it difficult to get steady employment. Many of the young people were forced to emigrate to America, England or Scotland in search of a job and money to send home. However, my father managed to get enough paid work to keep us going. In spite of the scarcity of money, I do not remember that we lacked for any of the necessities of life.

Throughout the 1950s, my father worked part time as a farm labourer for a local farmer who was a Protestant and in my father's words 'a decent man'. He also worked as a lorry driver for a local shopkeeper, P. J. Monaghan. He was also involved in buying and selling cattle. It took it all to make ends meet in our home.

The highlight of our week was when my father brought home the groceries on a Saturday night after he was paid. We children got a treat – but only if we were good the previous week! That was the way they kept discipline in our house. He did not go in for luxuries for himself. He wanted the best for his wife and family and worked hard to provide for us. He cut turf to keep the fire going in the Stanley range during the winter and made hay for the livestock. I never remember him going on a holiday or taking a day off work.

My mother was a strong-willed and proud woman, proud of her family – the Leonards, proud of her Cork connections – the Maloneys and the Hennessys. She was also proud of her native County Donegal. Her father died when she was only four years old, leaving her mother to rear the five surviving children on her own. She liked the national school in Lettercran and often talked about her kind teachers Miss McMeel and Master Gaffney and those who were her friends at school. She left school at fourteen years of age and went to work in her sister's drapery shop in the small border town of Pettigo around 1937. In her late teens, she left that job and went to work as a receptionist in the Tonic cinema in Bangor, County Down. One of the perks of the job was that she saw all the latest films of the time. She often talked about them and about her favourite actors, Janette MacDonald and Clark Gable.

My mother was a good conversationalist and had all the time in the world to sit and talk. The kettle was always on the boil, she made tea many times a day and whoever happened to be pass-ing along the road was called in for a cuppa. She worked hard at home-making and took great pride in keeping the house clean and freshly painted. She had a good interest in farm animals, coming as she did from a farming background. She remained very close to her sisters, Anna (Moss) and Eleanor (McGrath), both of whom died before her. She also remained close to her two brothers, Maurice and William Leonard, who were well-known cattle dealers in south Donegal. She like nothing better than get-ting out on her bicycle and cycling all the way to Lettercran to visit them – a round trip of about twenty miles. On a few occasions, I went with her when I had learned to ride a bicycle. I can tell you I slept soundly after those trips. It was probably on these trips that I first became conscious of the artificial border dividing our country.

As well as being a good talker, my mother was a thinker and a questioner. She took a stand on things she regarded as unjust or just downright stupid. She would never criticise the clergy but spoke about the need to introduce changes in the mass – like taking communion in the hand. She was a much more dominant personality than my father, who was quieter and more accepting of things as they were. My mother had a different life experience, with the death of her father when she was young and the death of her mother in 1940 when she was twenty years of age. I think it was because of that experience of loss and bereavement at a young age that she had such an understanding of life and compassion for those in need.

Both my parents came from strong Catholic families and this Catholic identity was very visible in their new home. The symbols of the Catholic faith were in every room in our house – the Sacred Heart picture and lamp, the statues and pictures of the Blessed Virgin, the Child of Prague and the holy water font hanging on the wall near the door. There was usually a picture of whatever pope happened to be in office. All of this added to our sense of belonging to a particular religious or faith community. I suppose it gave us a certain security in a world of great insecurity and fear. My mother found great comfort in her faith and was often saying her novenas and private devotions.

In my memory, my mother was in bad health for most of her life. She suffered from high blood pressure and was on medication to keep it under control. She was not overweight, so it must have been something she inherited as well as the effects of childbearing. Her sisters suffered similarly. I was often sent to bring out the doctor or to go to the chemist for her medication. I do not remember my mother ever taking a holiday – except the two days' pilgrimage to Lough Derg for as many years as she was able. That was her annual 'holiday'.

My mother's sister, Eleanor, was married to Hugh McGrath, who lived near us. There were eleven children in their family, three girls and eight boys. We went to school together and as youngsters we travelled in the back of their Ford van to the seaside at Bundoran during the summer holidays. When we arrived in Bundoran, having been stuck in the back of a van for an hour, we were excited and crazy for action – in the sea and in the amusements arcade. How we all survived these trips to the seaside amazes me. Our favourite stop when we arrived in Bundoran was the bumping cars. This is where we learned to drive! It was then off to the amusements where we learned to smoke the cigarettes we won in the machines. We always enjoyed our trips to Bundoran.

Our two mothers were very close and would spend hours in conversation almost every other day. I often wondered what they had to talk about. I knew they took a great interest in what was going on in the community and in their own native parish of Pettigo. Then there were the antics of all of us, which gave them plenty to talk about! We were fond of devilment, like climbing trees and going off on bicycles to rob orchards. There were many accidents and cuts suffered during these escapades.

My mother and her sister, Eleanor, were very friendly with two Protestant sisters who came from the Pettigo area to live in our locality. Even though they were Protestants, they were opposed to the Orange Order and to all kinds of Orange bigotry. They often came to visit in our house and a great fuss was made for Edith and Muriel. They were two lovely people. They eventually had to move away from our area. I would say they were not too popular in most unionist circles – for it was well known that they did not toe the party line.

In 1950, my formal education began in Moneyvriece primary school. It was, at first, a bit intimidating – being in a room with a large number of complete strangers and being asked to do things like writing and reading. I was looked after on that first day by a neighbour, Pat Kelly, who was a few years older, and also by my older McGrath cousins. Like most other children I was shy at the beginning, but the teacher in charge of the first year pupils, Nora O'Neill, was kind and soon made us feel at ease in our new surroundings. I liked learning to write and learning to read. A new world was opening up – the world of imagination.

My next teacher in the primary school was Eileen Cassidy (nee Clarke, a native of Lisnaskea, married to a local man, Jim Cassidy) and as well as keeping us at the books she taught us to knit. We knitted teddy bears to make money to send to the missions. This teacher was ahead of her time in encouraging boys to do work traditionally associated with women. And she was also ahead in making us aware of those in our world who were not as well off as us. She encouraged me to read and told my mother that I was lazy and needed to be pushed. When Eileen Cassidy was on maternity leave, we had Mary Hughes from Dromore and Marie Lilly who came from Trillick. Miss Hughes was young and attractive to us young boys. I was not the only boy to have a crush on her. One boy used to come into her class from the senior room for the roll book and made excuses to hang around. She used tell him to buzz off, at which he would make the sound of a bee – buzzzz – and make his way out of the room rather smartly. These were exciting days at school, a time of discovery, growth and happiness.

One of my earliest memories is of going with my father on the bar of his bicycle to get my hair cut in the local village. Frank McGee was the barber and one of his girls was the same age as myself. There were altogether five girls in the family. All the McGee girls were good-looking and many of the boys fancied them. My mother took me to be fitted for new boots in Maguires, the drapery and shoe shop, and I recall the excitement of fitting new boots and clothes. Fashion conscious, even though I had not reached ten, although there are those who would disagree!

I was the oldest in my family. There were five children born after me, one almost every year. I remember when my mother would have to go to hospital 'for the new baby'. I, along with a cousin from near Drumquin, would have to 'look after' the others in the family. That was an annual event for five or six years. It was always a source of joy and wonder when the new baby came home and there were plenty of visitors to see the latest arrival. After me came two girls, Teresa and Pauline. Then there was my brother Michael, followed by two more sisters, Helena and Brigid-Marian. The last baby, Brigid-Marian, died in infancy. That was a sad time for my parents. We were too young to understand but I was old enough to realise that this loss had a profound effect on my parents. It was my first real experience of grief.

As the eldest in the family, I was charged with looking after the younger members and playing with them when our mother was busy. We played outside when the weather was fine. I used to entertain them with concerts like those we saw in the parish hall or the travelling shows like 'The Clarrie Hayden Road show'. We would act out little plays and sing songs we had learned. As we grew older we learned other games like draughts, ludo and snakes and ladders.

There were always neighbours ('ceilidhers') who gathered in our home – especially during the winter nights – to talk and tell stories. They told stories about 'adventures' they had or that others they knew had along the border. These local men arrived around nine o'clock and stayed until about eleven. My mother would always give them tea and homemade bread. One of them, Johnny Beacom, was a Protestant who lived on his own just down the road from us. He always arrived as soon as the rosary was finished. Our house was that kind of home where all the neighbours were made welcome.

I was usually busy with the school homework and had to go to bed early to get up early for school next morning, so missed most of this 'adult' conversation. Sometimes, when I had no homework, I heard Johnny Beacom telling ghost stories and tales of his time working in Scotland farming with Clydesdale horses. He was a great man for horses and kept several himself. Every day Johnny and his horse-drawn cart drew the milk from our townland, and the surrounding townlands, to the creamery in Kesh. When he met us on the road coming from school he would always say, 'how many slaps did you get to day?' That was his idea of school! Mind you, corporal punishment was practised in all schools in those days, but our school was far from the worst. I was slapped on at least one occasion for misbehaving. I bribed my sister with my lunch money (a penny halfpenny) not to tell my mother in case I would get another slap when I got home. Many others at the school were slapped. It was horrible to watch people being caned. I always thought it was disgusting to see an adult beating a young person. It was good to see that barbaric practice made illegal.

During the holidays, I sometimes went with Johnny Beacom on the horse-driven milk cart to Kesh, about four miles away. This was a great experience to mix with adults and to see how they processed the milk. On the way home from the creamery, he might stop for a pint in the local pub in Ederney along with another man, Mick Muldoon, who also drew milk to Kesh. The horses were so familiar with the road that they knew the way home. One day while the two men were in the pub some pranksters switched the horses in the carts, which were parked a little bit down the street. But when the horses refused to go in the usual direction home the owners realised there was something wrong. There was a good bit of scolding and wishing bad luck on the scoundrels who would do such a thing. In those days, pranks were a common source of amusement – especially at Halloween.

Other neighbours who ceilied in our house were Jimmy Monaghan and Mick McGarrigle – both long since departed. Jimmy told stories about cattle smuggling and some of his escapades with the customs and excise along the border. People who engaged in smuggling knew that they were taking risks and that the penalty if caught was either a hefty fine or a term in prison. Risks were taken. Men were sometimes lucky and sometimes not so lucky. Jimmy was caught smuggling one time and ended up in court in the village of Kesh. During the trial, the judge dropped dead and Jimmy seized the opportunity to escape from the courthouse and across the border. He got a job in Finner army camp near Bundoran, working as a cook!

We lived on a very small farm of less than ten acres. Some of it was used for planting potatoes and vegetables. I learned early on in life how to sow potatoes and vegetables. We kept a few cows, some pigs and hens and I learned how to tend to these. During the summer months, I had to help both my father and the neighbours making hay and saving turf. Some of the neighbours I worked for were Protestant and they paid me well for my labour. I did not mind too much using the wooden rake and pitch-fork to gather the new-mown hay, especially when my hands hardened. One or two of the neighbours provided a helping hand, in the old 'meitheal' tradition of neighbour helping neighbour with the crops. This was common practice until recent times when farming became mechanised. We did not have much of the luxuries of life, but we had enough wholesome food and fresh vegetables. From an early age, I experienced a sense of belonging and a sense of community in our parish that I found to be enriching and character forming.

I loved the fields and meadows and the bogs and the drains, the trees and woods where I lived. We gathered nuts and raided orchards for apples and plums. We fished a bit in the rivers and the lakes. I remember the sound of the corncrake early in the summer evenings across our fields. Regrettably, that sound is no longer to be heard, the disappearance of the corncrake in some ways symbolic of the many changes that have come over rural Ireland since my childhood.

I learned about cows calving. I used to have to take the cows to the bull for one of my neighbours, Hugh Rushe, a well-known traditional singer and musician in the area. The farmer who owned the bull lived about three miles away, so I had to drive the cow and make sure it did not get through any gaps along the way. I used get a half crown for this task. The more often the cows had to go to the bull the better for me! Of course, this job also brought me into contact with the world of reproduction. My first sex lesson! The farmer – or his daughter, if he was not about – would bring out the bull into the enclosed yard and after about ten or fifteen minutes of introduction the bull impregnated the cow. The AI (artificial inseminator) man put paid to such romantic encounters.

Hugh Rushe was a wonderfully eccentric and charmingly inno- cent local character who lived with his wife, Annie, whom he mar- ried late in life. Hugh, as well as being a well-known traditional singer, also played the tin whistle and the fiddle and had a great store of old tunes he had learned as a youth growing up in Ederney. Hugh would play music at any time of the day or night. Donncha Ó Dulaing, the broadcaster, recorded him talking and singing for his popular radio programme, *Highways and By-ways*. Other well- known musicians like Cathal MacConnell came to learn some of his old tunes.

In those days, the parish priest lived in a huge house beside Hugh Rushe. It struck me as a bit odd that he should have such a large house for himself while our family and some other families around about had very much smaller houses. It was built in the early 1900s at a time when the parish priest was regarded as the most important person in the parish. He replaced the landlord in the pecking order in society. One of my earliest memories is going to this big house when the old parish priest, Fr McCarney, died. I was about eight years old and it was my first ever wake. I went with my older cousin, Colm McGrath, and we both knelt down and said prayers – like everybody else was doing. It was the first time I had ever seen a corpse and this amazing experience gave us a lot to talk about afterwards.

Down the road from us towards Drumquin were Johnny Beacom and the Curtis family, the Walshes, the Ingrams, the Reids, the Pattersons and old Maggie Noble. Across the fields to the front of our house in the townland of Clonee lived the Kellys, the Cullens, the Ginns and the Maguires.

When I was young, just after starting school, my mother sent me to Irish dancing classes every Saturday in the parish hall. The travelling teacher, who lived in Enniskillen, also taught us Irish songs, like 'Boolavogue' and 'Kevin Barry', some of the most beautiful songs I ever heard. These songs were part of my formation as an Irish nationalist. We did not learn any of this at primary school. We never heard anything about our Irish history, 1798 or 1916 or, indeed, Black '47. When I heard about Fr Murphy leading the Irish against the crown in the song 'Boolavogue', I was already learning something about our history. Only later did I learn that Fr Murphy was an exceptional priest and that most of the Catholic clergy sided with the English crown against the rebels.

My mother had learned some Irish at school and used some words and phrases unconsciously now and again. She would urge me to say *ma's é do thoil é* (which she pronounced 'mar-shay-de-hilly') for 'please' or *dún an doras* ('close the door'). She also taught me the Hail Mary (*Sé do Bheatha a Mhuire*) and the Our Father *(Ár nAthair)* in Irish. I liked the musical sound of the Irish language even then. Although we did not learn Irish in primary school, I think that it was from my mother that I first developed a love for the Irish language.

In our final years at primary school, when I was about ten years of age, we moved into the master's room. When we were in his class, we had to go to the technical school in Irvinestown one day a week. I loved that experience. Irvinestown, five miles away, was the biggest town in the district. The boys went there to learn woodwork, the girls to learn cookery. Women did not do carpentry and boys did not cook in those days. I liked carpentry and thought, maybe, I was going to be a carpenter like my grandfather. I wanted to be something.

My mother and my uncle Jim encouraged me to work hard for the 11-plus examination, the test that would decide the future education of children in the six counties for decades and is only now to be dropped (and not before time!). My family knew it was the only way I could get further education, for we could not afford to pay for it. Thankfully, I was accepted into St Michael's in Enniskillen.

I loved growing up in Ederney, like most people have a love of the place they come from. There were great people there, Catholic and Protestant, and by and large we got on pretty well with one another. But there was an undercurrent. We had occasional rows with some Protestant children on the way home from school. These hostilities happened only on rare occasions. We were off school during July when emotions ran a bit high with the commemoration of the Battle of the Boyne, when the Protestant King Billy (backed by the pope, no less) defeated the Catholic King James. The old sectarian refrains were chanted and we came to blows on a few occasions.

We were very friendly with our Protestant neighbours, the Curtis family and the Beacoms who lived a short distance from us. Fred Curtis had come from County Cavan and married a local woman. They had three boys and a girl around my age. I used to play football and even cricket with the boys some Sunday afternoons. The oldest boy, Brian, was a terrific cyclist and won in competitions all over the county. He then took up motor-cycling and was killed in an accident near Enniskillen. We were all deeply saddened by his premature death.

In spite of our friendships, I sensed that there was a barrier between us. After all, they went to a different school and a different church. It was not always possible to talk freely. I suppose as I grew older I found it was easier to be friends with those neighbours from within my own religious community. We played Gaelic football and went to the same school and church. Because of the political alienation, Catholicism took on an added significance for those of us living on the wrong side of the border. It became our main badge of identity.

So it was early in my life that it became apparent to me that all was not 'normal' in this part of Ireland. As I said, most of our unionist neighbours put up Union Jacks on their houses around 12 July. Some of the I worked for at the hay were part-timers in the B-Specials – an exclusively Protestant militia that was detested by us Catholics. I saw them going off in the evenings in their uniforms with their guns on their backs to carry out border duty. They would spend a few hours checking people and vehicles coming and going across the border and had a reputation for being hateful towards Catholics – even their neighbours.

This sectarian force, along with the RUC, created a climate of fear and suspicion in the community. In the days of the smuggling, some of them were suspected of acting as informers. Indeed, a cousin of mine strongly suspects that a B-man was responsible for his father ending up in court and his uncle in jail, both on charges of smuggling!

The older people in the community had seen many changes. Some of them had lived, before partition cut them off from their families and neighbours across the border, in another state. Some remembered the first motor car arriving in the district. Some homes had an old-time radio set or a gramophone for entertainment. These people had a deep religious faith and lived their lives more simply and frugally than today. The people were faithful to their prayers and devotions. They had a strong sense of the sacred; they could adjust to the sorrows and tragedies of life and to the deaths of their family members and neighbours with a conviction that this life was a preparation for the life – the really important life – to come. They were people of sensitivity who cared for each other like members of one family. This was my community, and even though I left for school in Enniskillen and further to May-nooth and life as a priest, I suppose that I never really left my Ederney roots.

# 2

# Growing up in the 1950s

When I was growing up in the 1950s, mass on Sundays was the high point of the week for most of us Catholics. Apart from being a church obligation, going to mass was seen as an important social occasion as well as a religious moment. Some men would meet up beforehand to catch up with the latest news and hang around afterwards for a chat about football and the price of cattle. It was also where the politicians came before elections to address the people. This scene is well remembered in a poem by John Montague called 'After Mass':

Coming out of the chapel
The men were already assembled
Around the oak-tree,
Solid brogues, thick coats
Staring at the women,
Sheltering cigarettes.
Once a politician came
Climbed on the graveyard wall
And they listened to all
His plans with the same docility;
Eyes quiet under caps
Like sloped eaves.
Nailed to the wet bark
The notice of a football match;
Pearses vs Hibernians

Or a Monster Carnival
In aid of church Funds
Featuring Farrell's Band.

I think that the reference to the men outside the church having listened to the politician with 'the same docility' captures the mood of the time, a certain resignation with the way things were. The religious preaching of the time would have only reinforced that 'docility'.

As I remember it, the women, including my own mother, also assembled after mass in another group, separate from the men, around the candelabra, lighting candles for all their different intentions. They would chat there or at the church door and catch up with all the local news, mostly about their families and how each one's children were doing at school.

For Catholics who lived in the six counties, going to mass (or going to the chapel, as we called it) was also a political statement. The Protestants went to 'church'; we went to 'the chapel'. Identifying so closely with the Catholic church gave those who were cut off from the rest of Ireland an identity. It also gave people a sense of belonging to a worldwide movement as we were often reminded of the foreign missions and of the suffering church in countries like Hungary and Poland. We often prayed for the church behind the 'iron curtain' and for the conversion of Russia. Mass was said in Latin in every country in those days before the Second Vatican Council, which was another example of the universal nature of the church. I was an altar boy and had to learn the responses in Latin, even though I did not have a clue what they meant. They sounded good: *Juventutum meum, Dominus vobiscum, Et cum Spiritu Tuo, Ora pro Nobis*, etc. This was the beginning of my classical education! The Latin went out with the introduction of the vernacular in the liturgy as directed by the Second Vatican Council.

The parish priest in Ederney in my young days was Fr Felix

McKenna, a slightly built, bony man, full of energy. He was a great character and a holy man who was very much involved in the life of the parish. He came to our parish in 1945 and was there until he died in 1962. He was a down-to-earth man who befriended everybody irrespective of their religion. There were two young curates as well – Fr Tom Marron and Fr Gerry Timoney. No wonder we had so many devotions with three priests in the parish. They did not have much else to do. Devotions at home and in the church were very much part of our young lives and part of the Catholic culture of the time.

The devotion to the Virgin Mary and the rosary was second to devotion to the Blessed Sacrament and the Sacred Heart. The red-globed paraffin oil lamp was always burning in our house, under the picture of the Sacred Heart. We knew the divine praises – Blessed be God, Blessed be His Holy Name – off by heart! And the litanies! They were funny, the pronunciations, I mean, but they were our first encounter with poetry – Tower of Ivory, House of Gold, Tower of David, Ark of the Covenant, Gate of Heaven, Morning Star, etc. – all different ways to describe the Virgin Mary. Sometimes, when the words were not pronounced properly, somebody would start laughing during the rosary or the litany and break the hypnotic effect of the repetition. The laughter was contagious. We would be reprimanded afterwards for being disrespectful at our prayers. Sometimes the wrong person was blamed for starting the fits of laughter and that would cause another row.

Our family were not religious fanatics. We were a normal 'run of the mill' Catholic family at that time. Maybe others did not take their religion so seriously but most of the people I knew did take it seriously and were committed Catholics. I remember people in the mid-1950s coming to early mass on a Sunday morning by pony and trap while others walked three or four miles in all kinds of bad weather. They were devout Catholics.

In the local church, we had the holy hours, forty hours and

adoration of the Blessed Sacrament. Most of these devotions dated back to what is called 'the devotional revolution', in the period after the Great Famine (1845–50). The Jesuits were at the forefront in promoting many of these devotions, as were some of the other religious orders that gave parish missions. At that time, I thought they dated back to the New Testament! Pope Pius IX and later Pope Leo XIII introduced this new form of sentimental piety. It had a particular appeal for the people at the time and, in its favour, presented a softer, more loving image of God.

For me, the evening devotions were an excuse to get out with my cousins who lived up the road from us. There were the 'May devotions' to Mary (followed by football), the 'October devotions' to St Joseph and the 'miraculous medal devotions'. There was devotion to the Sacred Heart every first Friday. There were special masses on the first Friday and in Lent and November. Looking back on it, we were quite preoccupied with our religion and with going to chapel. I was an altar boy for about five years when I was at the primary school in Moneyvriece. Being an altar boy had its rewards. It gave you confidence and made you feel important in the community. There were also 'the tips' at weddings and the annual outings, usually to Donegal. I think the girls were annoyed about this preferential treatment!

We were together in the choir and we learned new hymns especially for big occasions. I liked the sound of the organ music and when the old parish priest gave my father an old one from one of the churches I spent many long hours practising. I took some lessons from a Miss Johnston who came to our house on a bicycle but I did not have the patience to stick at it. We learned all the traditional hymns and all the Christmas carols. We went carol singing in the villages round about.

The catechism at school was regarded as the most important subject. The religious examiner, a diocesan priest, came around once a year and for weeks and, maybe, months, all we ever seemed to study in school was catechism and bible history. When the religious examiner came to visit the school, he used ask us rather predictable questions which did not challenge anybody too much. He asked my friend 'Where is God?' and he answered 'God is everywhere'.

And then he asked him, 'Is he in your pocket?' and my friend said no, he wasn't.

'Why not?' asked the priest.

'Because there's a hole in it,' said my friend – and we all split our sides laughing at this smart answer!

The religious inspector was a quiet gentle person and did not want to embarrass anybody. All you had to do was learn the answers 'by heart'. The answers to every question under the sun were in the catechism. Such was religious education in primary school. I enjoyed the bible history but the questions and answers in the catechism never made much sense to me. They introduced me to some new words like 'sanctifying grace' and 'original sin' and 'transubstantiation' – words or concepts I did not understand and could hardly pronounce.

While there was much to criticise about the Catholic church at that time there were some good things about the faith we grew up in and the education we received, not just in the school but also within the community. It contained much that is good in Catholicism, the community spirit, the mystery of the mass, the sacredness and solemnity of processions at Corpus Christi and Holy Week. There were also the special occasions like the celebration of the sacrament of confirmation and the celebration of marriages in the local church. It brought us into a real living community and created a bond with local people that was very strong. The closeness of the people in the community was especially evident at wakes and funerals.

On the negative side, most of the older people I knew did not question either the religion as it was taught to them or the political situation in which they were clearly treated as second-class citizens. They were 'docile' or passive about the political and economic situation. Many were passive about the authoritarian attitude within the church itself. They were very accepting of the way things were and felt powerless to do anything about the unjust situation in which they found themselves. The attitude seemed to be, 'Ach, sure things will never be any different here'. Some of them also knew from their history that it could be costly to step out of line. My grandfather never said much about the political situation. He depended on all creeds and classes to get work. My father followed his example.

There was a strong attachment to the 'valley of tears' theology and the notion that life was always a struggle. Everything was God's will – when somebody died in an accident or died in an earthquake. In the Catholic thinking of the time it was the next world you had to think about more than this one. It was the job of the priests to remind people of this and it was the theme of the annual parish missions given by the Redemptorists or Passionists. I suppose we should remember that the thinking of the people had been formed by their life experiences of deprivation, poverty and war and by the preachers and teachers of the day. There were many 'fire and brimstone' preachers warning people of the grave danger of losing their souls and going to hell for all eternity. Most people did not take them too seriously – but some did with terrifying consequences.

From an early age, about fourteen years, I discovered that Catholic morality was obsessed with sex and 'sins against the sixth commandment'. Mortal sins, venial sins, purgatory and hell were all there and they instilled a certain amount of fear and foreboding. The sixth commandment covered many more 'sins of the flesh' than adultery, like masturbation, 'bad actions' and even 'bad thoughts'. This obsession with sex goes back into church history. It became an obsession in Ireland especially after the Great Hunger in the 1850s.

There was very little talk about justice except a very narrow notion which could be summed up as 'doing an honest day's work for an honest day's pay' – this at a time when many had no work or had jobs that did not pay a just wage. There were no sermons, that I can ever remember, about state injustice and the sinful actions of employers who exploited the workers.

There was not much talk about the loving and the merciful God but rather more about the strict judge-God who punished people severely for even the most trivial sins and especially for 'sins against the sixth commandment'. This negative legalistic kind of religion around the subject of sexuality was talked about in the context of confession. It often depended on which priest you got in the confessional; some priests were gentle and under-standing but some made life difficult by asking stupid and embar-rassing questions. This was, partly, a result of a very conservative and legalistic theological training in Maynooth. However, many individual priests were more sensible and showed great compas-sion towards the people in confession and in the parish.

The negative kind of religion was evident during the occasional parish mission where the preachers preached 'fire and brimstone'. They preached a lot about 'the fires of hell and the Day of Judge-ment'. This contributed to the creation of a culture of fear within the Catholic church, which remained until recent times. I have to say that I did not experience much of the harshness from priests that some people have written about. I knew they existed and there is plenty of evidence for their existence. There were other priests who were not like that and I was lucky to meet some of them. They helped to keep the Christian faith alive and who witnesses to the compassion of Christ in the real world. These men planted the idea of a vocation to the priesthood in my young mind.

However, I did discover at this time something of the authori-tarianism of the institutional church at the official level. The bishop would come to the parish for the sacrament of confirmation with a lot of pomp and splendour and give out about something or other. He always seemed to be in bad humour and was always giving out. Most people did not pay much heed to him. They came into regular contact with the institutional church through the local priests. When I was growing up, the priest was an important member of the community, along with the doctor and the teacher. The priest was looked up to and sometimes placed on a pedestal. I discovered early on in life that it was dangerous and stupid to put a priest or anybody else up on a pedestal.

There was a priest in our parish around 1960 who went off with a woman with whom he was having an affair. It was the talk of the country but most people took it in their stride and were not all that shocked or scandalised. However, the bishop at the time made a big issue about it and came to the church in Ederney to read the riot act from the pulpit blaming the people for not reporting the matter sooner. I understand that he was also critical of the other priests in the parish for not confronting him earlier. The Ederney people were not pleased with Bishop O'Callaghan's outburst on this occasion. The story about the priest from Ederney and the woman filled columns in the local unionist weekly newspaper. That priest and his woman friend went off to England, married, and reared five children.

The same bishop, Dr Eugene O'Callaghan, made the national news on a few occasions. Once he announced that nobody in the diocese of Clogher could go dancing after midnight or organise dances that ran past midnight. If they did they would be excommunicated. Most people did not take him too seriously. Some went to dances outside the diocese in Donegal or Cavan where there were no church rules about dancing after midnight. It sounds funny now but this kind of attitude made the church a bit of a laughing stock and made it difficult for people to take episcopal pronouncements seriously.

Some priests took an authoritarian line in their parishes. In my home parish, there was a man (William) one time who went to the old parish priest – before Fr McKenna – to get the use of the parish hall for a dance to raise some money to build a new laneway. The parish priest told him he could have the parish hall, but only if he could guarantee that there would be no sins committed, mortal or venial, during or after the dance. Willie said that he could not guarantee that and so he did not get the parish hall. Incidents like this happened in our parish and in parishes all over the country but the faith and loyalty of the people survived.

When rock'n roll came to Ederney in the early 1960s the new parish priest, Fr Clancy, who succeeded Fr McKenna, came to one of the dances in the parochial hall and when he saw girls swinging and jiving and throwing up their legs and their skirts he stopped the music and the dancing and said that would be the end of 'the pagan dancing'. The Claxton Showband who were playing at the dance decided to go for their tea, which was customary after the dance. When they came back, the parish priest had gone home to his bed, so they started up again and they rocked around the clock all night. This was the era of Bill Haley, Elvis and the Melody Aces and the Clipper Carlton from Strabane. It was an era that the church, even at a local level, was not going to come to terms with too easily. If that long-deceased parish priest were to come back to a nightclub nowadays, he would be carried out on a stretcher in a state of great shock.

A big social event in our parish each year was the parish bazaar, which ran for a week or two, as long as the prizes lasted. Prizes were donated and raffled. It was organised each year throughout the 1950s during the Christmas holidays by Fr Felix McKenna and his team of helpers to raise money for the new chapel. At the parish bazaar there was the rickety wheel, a roulette table and a shooting range. I used to spend all my pocket money on the roulette table. 'Two to one the black, five to one the red', John McPhelimey, the local bicycle dealer, would shout over and over again until it stuck in your brain. This was long before we ever heard of Las Vegas. After a number of years, I became old enough to sell tickets at the bazaar and we used to compete to see who could sell the tickets the fastest. Frankie McDonagh, who lived in High Street and was at school with me, was the fastest ticket seller in the hall. He was also the best footballer on our team. Unfortunately, he emigrated to England like so many others. The annual bazaar certainly provided a great sense of community and was an enjoyable function for many years in my early teens. I am sure the parish made some money out of it. They certainly made some out of me (or rather out of my mother) on the roulette table.

At Halloween, we used to dress up as mummers and go around the countryside acting a drama (which dates to the twelfth century) on the kitchen floor and collecting money afterwards. Colm McGrath, my cousin, was usually the leader. Colm was a bit older than me and was always ready for adventure. We wore false faces, which, at first, we made ourselves out of cardboard boxes, and strange costumes tied with rope, so that the neighbours did not recognise us. I am almost ashamed to say that the money we collected was for ourselves and it was divided as evenly as possible among the eight of us at the end of the night.

My Christian faith and religious upbringing involved not just going to mass and devotions but it also required sensitivity towards those who were poor or marginalised. In those days the travelling people were called 'the tinkers'. They used to go around the country looking for old pots and pans to mend. My parents were always kind and welcoming to travellers and often gave them pots and cans to fix. My mother was devotional and prayed her novenas and rosaries. Even though she was a traditional Catholic, she was forward thinking and outward looking. My father was more of a practical Christian, visiting people, attending wakes and funerals. They welcomed the stranger and the traveller and

the neighbour no matter who they were or what religious affiliation. Even though they did not have much they were always ready
to share what they had.

I have to say looking back that I was influenced most of all
by the attitudes of my parents to the Catholic faith and practice
– especially their commitment to the mass and religious devotions.
For them commitment was the big thing. I was influenced by their
hospitality to the visitors and the strangers who called to our house.
I was also deeply influenced by Felix McKenna, our parish priest
when I was growing up. He showed us great kindness and generosity. He was an exceptionally kind, humorous and compassionate
person. He was humble and caring. He wanted the best for our
parish community and so he set about building a new church. That
was quite an undertaking in the 1950s, in a parish where money
was very scarce. I was also influenced by my father's cousin who
was a priest in the Salesian order in England. He came to visit us
every year and he always seemed to be happy and good-humoured.
I thought it cannot be too bad a life, if there are so many that I
know who are so happy in this work or vocation.

The priests were in those days like community leaders, involved
in the lives of the people from birth until death. They played a major part in the social, community and religious life of the parish.
Some of the priests in my parish made a great impact on us as
young fellas. They trained us to be altar-boys, took us on outings,
trained us for football and took a general interest in our progress
in school. The only abuse I got was a clip on the ear from a local
curate when somebody reported me for carrying on in the bus to
school.

I was aware from a young age that there was a political border
in our country. I was also becoming conscious by the age of about
ten or eleven that there were two classes in our society, even within the Catholic community – the well-off and the poor; 'the haves'
and 'the have nots'. I felt it in the early days when my father was

sometimes unemployed, when I saw the big houses and the cars that some people owned, when I heard the collection being read out at mass and the large sums being paid by a few compared to the small sums of the majority. It's not that we were wanting for food or clothes but I did feel that there were people who seemed to be a lot better off than we were, people who had money and property. There were a lot of families in the parish like our own who were finding it hard to make ends meet.

# 3

# A Time of Discovery –
# Lady Chatterley and the IRA

There was no running water in our house or in many of the country houses when I was growing up. It was one of my tasks to go to the well in a field belonging to my grandfather, across the road from our house. This was a daily chore. I would bring home a bucket of water for drinking and making tea. I used to like going to the well for the water because it was always an excuse to visit my grandparents' house (my father's parents) and get the best home-made bread and good strong tea and sometimes a shilling or two from my grandmother. To reach their house I had to climb a fairly steep brae. Their house was situated higher up than ours – on the top of a small hill or drumlin beside an ancient rath or ring fort.

The well had always been an important resource in country areas; several families would use it for their drinking water. It was important that it was sheltered and kept clean. The owner of the well was responsible for cleaning it out and keeping it clean with lime, a couple of times in the year. My grandfather used to pay me to clean the well during the summer months. The water from the well was good to drink and good for the thirst – especially when we were working at the hay in the warm weather. Water for washing clothes was collected in a barrel at the gable of the house. This barrel was nearly always full for there was no scarcity of rain in Fermanagh.

As I entered my teens, I started to see a girl from up the road whom I fancied and the well was a handy meeting place. She was a few years older and we were both at the stage of discovering our sexuality. Our encounters were mostly innocent – holding hands and fumbling. I thought she was a very funny girl with a lovely smile and a hearty laugh. On one occasion, I stayed too long and my mother, thinking I might have fallen into the well, came out to look for me. Well, that put an end to meeting at the well – and to our short-lived courtship. My mother thought she was a bit too old and too 'old-fashioned' for me.

I still had to go to the well for a good few years after that. Soon, I discovered I was able to carry two buckets, and it was just as easy as one balanced the other. I used to stop a few times, to rest on the way home and talk to whoever was walking or cycling along the road. There were some rare old characters from further down the road towards Drumquin like 'Big Mick' McCrea – a councillor in Omagh – and Felix McElholm, who said that you were not safe walking on the road with the number of cars driving up and down. This most innocent of men walked our roads until he died. Then there was 'the wooden cubs' – the two McCanny brothers. I think it was because they stood up so straight that they were given that nickname. There was also the McKennas, Fonsie, Peter and Patsy, and the McGoverns, who came from Cavan about 1956. Shortly after they arrived one of the McGovern boys aged about fourteen was stopped by the RUC one day while riding his bicycle home from school. He was carrying not just one but two young Mc-Grath boys on the bar of the bike. They were all summoned to the court in Kesh and fined a shilling each! It was great to have such a vigilant police service in the community.

The mountain lough, which supplied the water to the village of Ederney, was nearer to our house than the houses in the village but the water was not piped to our house until 1970 – many years after the people in the village had it piped. It was years after that when we got the electricity. I often thought about that, even in my young days, and I felt indignant about the fact that we were deprived of these basic necessities, which were available to some and not others – certainly in this part of the world. Being deprived of running water and electricity added to the hardship endured by my mother trying to wash and dry clothes. People who lived in the rural areas were deprived of these conveniences which many others in the towns and villages had for years.

I was aware from an early age that, even though the queen of England and her majesty's forces ruled us, and even though a section of the population, mostly Protestant, thought of themselves as British, our family and the Catholic families who lived near to us were not British. This was the 'Protestant state for a Protestant people' as described by the unionist leader Craig in the 1930s. I soon became aware that it was not that easy for a Catholic in Fermanagh to get any kind of job in the public sector nor was it easy to get houses, which were allocated by the unionist-controlled county council. I was not yet aware of the way the electoral boundaries in the county were gerrymandered to favour the Unionist Party. In many nationalist areas like Fermanagh where there was a nationalist majority in the county, the unionists held twenty-two seats and the nationalists eleven seats. The unionists were in absolute control and were determined to keep it that way.

The British royal family and the Westminster government held sway in the six counties and we were never allowed to forget it. I remember when the new queen of England was being crowned in 1953 we all received some kind of chocolate sweets with the queen's head on them. I actually ate these chocolate sweets with the queen's head on them! That's how I was first introduced to her majesty the queen of England. I was about eight years of age. I suppose I should have been thankful that I did not have to learn

'God Save the Queen' or sing it! But we heard it often enough. We also heard 'The Sash Me Father Wore' – the signature tune of the Orangemen.

Visitors from outside of Ireland did not understand the Orange Order with their many parades and their colourful dress and decorations. There's a story by Tony Gray in his interesting book *The Orange Order* (published in 1972) which illustrates the way our unionist neighbours saw themselves and their culture. An Englishman was in Belfast when he noticed a large parade and much drum beating. So he stopped to ask a wee man, who was completely absorbed by the parade, what was going on. The wee man did not take his eyes of the parade and said through the side of his mouth, 'It's the Twelfth'.

The Englishman was none the wiser so he asked him again.

The wee man says, 'Did you not hear me, it's the Twelfth.'

The Englishman says, 'I know the date is the Twelfth of July, but what's all this marching and beating big drums about?'

The wee Belfast man turns round for the first time, looks him straight in the eye and says, 'You don't know what this is about? Away home and read your bible.'

For most unionists the Orange Order existed to defend their religion and way of life. It was 'a bastion against popery'. The Orange Order was an important force in propping up and maintaining the six counties as a separate political entity though I was not fully aware of its influence when growing up. It was only later on that I realised how influential it has been in maintaining unionist power and control.

In the north, some Catholic bishops made periodic statements about the discrimination against Catholics in jobs and housing. However, apart from Dr Mageean in Down and Connor it would seem that none of them was going to cause the unionists in Stormont or the British government many sleepless nights. There was a parish priest on the other side of Fermanagh, in Newtownbutler,

Canon Tom Maguire, who made the headlines in 1954 when the RUC removed the Tricolour that was flying from his house. The following year the RUC used a water cannon for the first time in the six counties on the aged Canon Maguire and those attending the *feis* in Newtownbutler 'Cannon used against Canon' might have been the headline in the local paper the following week! This incensed the local people and caused a riot against the RUC. Basil Brooke (who styled himself Lord Brookeborough) was the prime minister in the six counties since 1943 and once boasted he had not one Catholic working for him on his huge estate and did not intend to have any. He certainly was not going to tolerate an uppity parish priest in Fermanagh challenging the political status quo in his beloved 'province of Ulster'.

The state forces of the RUC and the B-Specials seemed to be firmly in control of things at this stage of the game but there was a new, defiant mood in the nationalist community and change was in the air. Some people were beginning to talk about the denial of civil rights and the abuse of power by the RUC and B-men. Local papers published facts and figures about anti-Catholic discrimination. Nationalist politicians in the north continued to criticise the unionist Stormont government. Unionists were fearful of making any changes or concessions.

When I went to school in Enniskillen, there were other young people from unionist families on the bus. We got on well, most of the time. There were occasional fights between the nationalist/Catholic boys and the Portora boys who were from unionist backgrounds. I could not be sure who started the fights. Anyway, I stayed out of them; it was a kind of macho thing at the time. I got on well with the collegiate girls who were then from a Protestant background; I formed a close friendship with one girl from Kesh. It was almost a status symbol to have a collegiate girlfriend!

The politics of the situation complicated the relationships we formed because our neighbours had totally different loyalties, played different sports, went to different schools and socialised in different places. I was aware that a deep political divide existed even though we could be the best of friends when we met on the bus and even though some lasting friendships were formed.

In those days before the Second Vatican Council, Catholics did not go to Protestant church services. The church authorities did not encourage this. Some would go to funerals but usually stood outside the church, while Protestants did the same at Catholic funerals. Most of the Protestants I knew felt strongly about their Britishness and their loyalty to the crown.

Some people have argued that it is the separate schools that divide the people in the north. However, it must be said that partition and the existence of a separate statelet in the six counties divided us along religious lines. In the towns and cities, the unionist policy of housing people of the same religious persuasion for voting purposes was so arranged that people were segregated from birth.

There were those among the Orangemen, in leadership positions, who wanted to exaggerate the differences and instil fear, hatred and distrust of Catholics or 'papishes'. This was very obvious at the Twelfth of July parades when some Orange preachers and unionist leaders would appeal to the baser instincts of their own people and urge them always to be on their guard against those great enemies of the state, the church of Rome and the Dublin government, which they believed was run by the Roman Catholic hierarchy and the IRA.

These were real displays of their so-called Britishness. It was 'in your face' supremacism and was the result of a siege mentality. It was not very nice, but there was not much we could do about it except develop our own cultural heritage and show it off in a kind of defiant spirit. This situation made me feel stronger about my Irishness. In a peculiar way, I came to realise that my neighbours were also Irish even though they professed a strong loyalty to the British monarch. I was beginning to hear stories about the

United Irishmen and Tone, Emmet, Davis, Russell, and Henry Joy and his sister Mary Ann. I began to question the assumption that the Protestants were all monarchists and the Catholics all republicans. Through the years, I have discovered from reading our history that some of the great leaders of Irish republicanism and nationalism – Tone, Davis, Parnell, Childers and Hyde – belonged to the Protestant tradition and some of the staunchest defenders of the English connection have been Catholic businessmen and Catholic churchmen.

The border was always a factor in our lives and was often a subject of conversation. There were all kinds of customs and excise regulations and checks on people crossing back and forward to find out if they were smuggling contraband like tobacco, cigarettes or sugar. There were many stories about smuggling – about sometimes being caught but most often about getting away. These were almost like hero tales in my young days. There's one story about one man from Belleek who crossed 'the border' every month on a bicycle with a large bag on the handlebars. Each time the customs searched the bag and each time they found a few bits of turf in the bag. The man was smuggling bicycles.

The main political issue for nationalists and republicans in those days was still partition and it featured very much in the 1956 election. Fermanagh nationalists felt really hard done by. It was always an emotive issue. They were cut off from the southern neighbours by the border. I have a vague recollection of hearing about the Sinn Féin victory in Fermanagh/South Tyrone in 1956. There were victory parades in the nationalist towns and villages throughout the county. However, the victory celebrations were short-lived when the British government overturned the election result because the successful Sinn Féin candidate was in jail.

When I went to St Michael's college in Enniskillen in 1956, a completely new world opened up for me. I began learning subjects like history, geography, mathematics and new languages like

French and Irish. There was great emphasis on sport, especially Gaelic football, and also on religious education. I was making new friends from different parts of Fermanagh and Tyrone and learning more about local and national politics. My favourite subjects were Irish and history. We had some wonderful teachers as well as some tough guys. Fr John McElroy was a great teacher of Latin and if we had him last before lunch or at the end of the day he would stay on for a half an hour debating some subject or other about school or politics or religion. Colm Gillespie from Derry taught us English literature and French and insisted that, to brush up on our English, we should read a quality Sunday newspaper like the *Observer* and, to improve our French, we had to read a French magazine called *Paris-Match*. The principal of the school was a young priest called Patrick Mulligan, a native of Lisbellaw, County Fermanagh who later became bishop of Clogher and was a big influence on my life.

St Michael's college had just opened as a diocesan college in 1956 – the year I started. It was situated in Belmore Street, where the bomb went off in 1987. Before that, the Presentation Brothers ran the old St Michael's. The bishop of Clogher at the time felt that too many Fermanagh students were going to colleges in other dioceses and those who decided to be priests opted for the diocese in which they went to school. To promote vocations for the home diocese he opened St Michael's in Enniskillen and sent five or six Clogher priests to teach there and to encourage young fellas to think about going for the priesthood in the diocese of Clogher.

There was corporal punishment in this new school as a matter of course. Some teachers used the strap or stick or even a thick board. I remember once when the whole class got a severe beating with what looked like the leg of a chair. We were beaten when someone mixed some acids in the science lab and the boy who did it would not own up. The whole class was punished. Such was justice in this Catholic school!

Pupils could be expelled for breaking the rules – especially the rule about smoking. I was caught smoking and was threatened with expulsion. The principal relented and sent a letter to my parents. They were not pleased. I was caught scheming school once by the school inspectors; I suppose I was glad I was not expelled. Violence in schools was acceptable then and was carried out by men who did not seem to realise the harm they were doing to young people.

I was, like many young boys at the time, acting grown up. I started to smoke cigarettes. We could buy cigarettes in ones or twos in 'Elsies' – a shop in Water Street in Enniskillen – while we waited for the bus in the evening. That was one of the worst habits I ever developed, and it took me years to get off them for good. We had an hour to wait for the bus home to Ederney every evening, so we often spent it hanging out on the Diamond in Enniskillen. There was the odd fight between boys from different areas of the county, or boys from different schools. I was not much interested in fighting, so I used to spend much of that time in the county library. I think it was there I developed my love of books. I still buy a lot of books, many of which I have not yet read.

In my early teens, I turned a bit rebellious, as some boys do at that stage in growing up. I am sure I caused my mother a certain amount of anxiety and worry. I was just being contrary a lot of the time and trying to assert my independence. I started to wear the style of the day, a kind of Teddy boy style – drainpipe trousers, suede shoes and long hair, combed back with plenty of oil or Brylcreem. I remember wearing a flamboyant tie we got one year in the parcel from America. The tie was a silky white or cream with a beautiful horse's head impressed on it. The trick was to tie the knot in the right place to show the horse's head clearly. The first time I wore it to school, the French teacher, Mr Doherty, embarrassed me: 'McVeigh, where did you get the tie?' he asked during the class.

'From America, sir.'

'I was thinking. I never saw a tie like that before.'

I suppose, in a way, I was looking for attention at the time, but not from the teachers. It is no wonder they introduced school uniforms shortly after that!

I was encouraged at home to study and to stick at my homework but I was easily distracted. I would spend too much time listening to music on Radio Luxembourg, playing an old pedal organ that the parish priest gave my father or just simply daydreaming. Homework was a bit of a chore. I looked forward to the long summer holidays. My mother urged me to concentrate on my schoolwork because, as she often said, a good education was the necessary ticket to getting a secure job and personal advancement. Her older sisters and brothers also shared this view. She never once mentioned priesthood to me. My father did not interfere in these matters at all. His attitude seemed to be, *que sera sera* (what will be, will be). However, his brother, my Uncle Jim, took a keen interest in me and in my education and was always encouraging me to stick at the books.

During the two-month summer holidays, I worked in Cassidys' shop in Ederney. They sold all kinds of groceries and animal feedstuffs. We used to bring the meal for the animals to the local farmers – in the main Catholic. Most of the Protestant farmers dealt with another grocer in the village, who was Protestant. But there were always some who did not stick to this custom. The Cassidys had a mobile shop and I went out on it with one of the owners all around the countryside on different days of the week. In that way I came to know the people of the locality very well. I also got to know the geography and townlands very well.

The summer holidays meant freedom, football, and trips to the Donegal Gaeltacht for a few weeks to learn how to speak Irish. I helped at saving hay and turf for my father and for the neighbours. So there was not an idle moment.

All this time I was enjoying life to the full. The showbands were all the craze. (At one time they say there were 600 showbands in Ireland!) Any chance we got, we were off to the 'Silver Swallow' in Enniskillen, to Castlederg or to the Patrician hall, Carrickmore. I remember being at a dance in Carrickmore one night in 1964 when it was announced that Jim Reeves was killed in a plane crash earlier that day. There was shock and stunned silence among the thousand-plus dancers.

Parish carnivals were popular in those years (1960–64). Before the dances most evenings there was a football match. The Ederney tournament attracted teams from Omagh, Letterkenny, Sligo and Leitrim as well as Trillick and Dromore. It was an amazing competition – the main prize one year was fifteen transistor radios. I was part of the winning team and was the proud owner of the latest model of transistor radio. After the football match there was the opportunity to go dancing in the big marquee – hired for the carnival. I can never blame my parents for not allowing me out, though my mother would make sure that I was with some of my older cousins, the McGraths, who she trusted would look after me and bring me home safely. It was during this time in my life that I was discovering more about girls and about my sexuality. We had not much formal education about sex either at home or at school. I have to say we learned most of it in the back of the bus from the older people on the way from school.

One of my unionist neighbours used to go to Scotland for a period each year. I was left to look after his house when he was away. I remember at this time there was a controversy about a novel by D. H. Lawrence, *Lady Chatterley's Lover*. It was banned by the censors – even in England! One day, I noticed a paperback book sitting on the table of my neighbour's kitchen and out of curiosity I picked it up and to my astonishment it was *Lady Chatterley's Lover* – the most talked about and wanted book in Europe! I don't know how he got his hands on it though I suspect he got it on one of his trips to Scotland. It was definitely not available anywhere in Ireland at the time. I might have been only the second person in Ireland to read *Lady Chatterley's Lover*! I could not resist picking it up and opening it at random. I was entranced. I had never read anything as explicit about sex as this before – about Lady Constance Chatterley seducing and making love with her husband's gamekeeper, Oliver Mellors. I had heard that there were no morals in England and this confirmed it! It was a further instalment in my education. I had not read enough to realise that D. H. Lawrence was one of the greatest writers of the century and a deeply spiritual man as well.

Though I was not aware of it then, many Irish writers in the twenty-six counties suffered the same fate as D. H. Lawrence. The Dublin government had introduced strict censorship laws. Marvellous writers like John McGahern, Benedict Kiely and Edna O'Brien had books banned because they were 'in general tendency indecent and obscene'. It all seems so ridiculous now but that was the narrow-minded culture of the time supported by the all-pervasive Catholic church – especially during the reign of John Charles McQuaid in the archdiocese of Dublin. Fortunately for posterity, these writers were not deterred and continued to write and publish their work.

In my young days, I used to go on summer holidays to my cousins in Donegal – the Leonards and the Mosses – who lived near Pettigo. On fair days, the young people used to gather the sheep and cattle for the fairs which were popular in the 1940s and 1950s and into the early 1960s. We used to go to Glenties, Westport and Dungloe with my uncles and cousins. It was another world. The cattle-dealers had their own sign language and their own way of clinching a deal, in the days before the cattle marts became popular.

I remember in 1961 when President de Valera came to Pettigo on his way to the pilgrimage centre in Lough Derg. I was fifteen years of age. I did not know much about de Valera, except that he had been a military leader in the 1916 Rising. He was prominent in the anti-Treaty side after 1921 and during the Civil War. He was the founder of Fianna Fáil – having broken away from Sinn Féin. For some Irish people he was a hero, while for others something of a villain. His visit was a big day for Pettigo, which was packed full of people from the area, and we all waved and cheered as he passed by in his motorcade.

While at St Michael's, I was beginning to learn something about the politics of the six counties – not from any books but from the stories I heard from some of the other students. In the years 1957–60, I heard about the antics of the B-men in other parts of Fermanagh. We heard stories from one of the teachers who lived in the border town of Belcoo. The IRA had launched a border campaign in 1954, bombing customs posts and attacking RUC and B-Specials. I had not much of an idea, at this time, what the IRA was or what it was hoping to achieve by the dangerous actions that were reported in the papers and talked about at school. My unionist neighbours in the B-Specials were once again enlisted by the Stormont government to carry out vehicle checkpoints and searches along the border.

In early 1957, when I went back to St Michael's after the Christmas holidays, there was a lot of talk about an ambush at Brookeborough RUC barracks in Fermanagh on New Year's Eve. This attack resulted in the deaths of two IRA volunteers, Seán South from Garryowen in Limerick and Fergal O'Hanlon from Monaghan town. These two men are now part of republican folklore. Little did I know then that I would in years to come be living opposite Fergal O'Hanlon's home in Monaghan and become friendly with his family.

In July 1958, Patrick McManus from Kinawley was killed while on active service for the IRA. He had two brothers in St Michael's: Seán, who was in my class, became a priest with the

Redemptorists and was a founder member of the Irish National Caucus in America, while Frank was active in the civil rights campaign and was elected MP for Fermanagh/South Tyrone. The incident in which Pat McManus lost his life made me more aware of the seriousness of what the IRA was about, as, like many before and since, they were prepared to give their lives in the cause of Irish freedom.

My parents did not talk much about politics or the IRA campaign along the border during the 1950s. I would say they were just too busy helping us to survive. I don't remember them ever talking about voting or supporting any party. Perhaps they were conscious that we had too many unionist neighbours and they did not want us getting into any trouble with them.

In the rural parts of Fermanagh, there was not the kind of segregation and bitterness that you get in a city like Belfast or in the larger towns like Portadown or Ballymena or even Enniskillen. Like in the southern states of the United States there was far more interplay between the people in the rural parts than in the cities or towns. In Belfast, the British government and their civil servants systematically engineered a definite segregation for political purposes. In spite of the segregation, some people from different religious denominations continued to mix socially and inter-marry. As Des Wilson remarked:

> The people of Belfast, and of the six counties as a whole, are normal. But thousands of halls, lodges, associations, interest groups, clerical and political factions not only kept enmity alive among them but even resurrected it when citizens by the normality of their lives had allowed it to die.[*]

AT ST MICHAEL'S there were some boys who were sons of large farmers or business people as well as many boys like myself who came from poor enough families and who struggled to put their

---

[*] Des Wilson, *Democracy Denied* (Mercier Press, Cork, 1997), p. 9.

sons through secondary school. I suppose we were the first generation of young people from a poorer working-class background to get a secondary education. By the time I finished in St Michael's I was fully aware of this great social divide within the Catholic community. It seemed to me that there were two classes in society and those who belonged to the working-class/unemployed never got a fair deal. The awareness of this great division has stayed with me all my life. It has influenced the way I think and all my political and theological instincts and inclinations.

However, when I was growing up in the 1950s and 1960s, it was the religious divide, not the social/economic divide, that was most emphasised in the six counties. With a few exceptions, Catholics were regarded as Irish nationalists and Protestants as pro-British unionists. I know that this can be misleading in trying to understand the conflict, but that was how it was in practice. I should say that was how the colonial masters in London designed it. It was the classic policy of 'divide and conquer'. The only way to deal with this was through radical political thinking and strategic action aimed at undermining the colonial power. Even though two-thirds of Ireland achieved independence of a kind from British rule in 1921, nationalists in the six counties were isolated and still subjected to British colonial and military rule in an undemocratic state.

My family did not seem to bother too much about what politicians said in those years. They were busy surviving. That seemed to be the way with most Catholic families in my area. There was a kind of grudging acceptance of the situation, a sense that things would never be any better or any different – that we were condemned to second-class citizenship and there was not much the people could do about it. Those in power in the twenty-six counties did not care and there was no point in appealing to the American government, Britain's close friend and ally since the Second World War.

In St Michael's college, where there was a strong emphasis on learning the Irish language, I was beginning to develop an appreciation of our Irish culture and heritage and a working knowledge of the language. I had a very strong awareness of my Irish identity at that time but it was not going to be easy to express that identity in the state in which I lived.

It was also the 'swinging sixties' when the Beatles and Radio Luxembourg were all the rage. Some homes had television. We did not, as we had no electricity. John F. Kennedy had become the first Catholic president of the US and the name of Martin Luther King Jnr was becoming well known – not just in America, but all over the world. Ireland too was beginning to be influenced by world events and the changing western culture.

In March 1963, Lord Brookeborough resigned as prime minister and was succeeded by Captain Terence O'Neill. In June that year, President John F. Kennedy visited Ireland – and thousands came out to greet him in Dublin. A few short months later, he was killed by an assassin's bullet while travelling through Dallas. The world stood still. Everyone in Ireland was shocked that such a thing could happen. I was a boarder in my final year in St Michael's and I remember well the night when the news of his assassination was broadcast. I thought there could be a world war after that if the Russians were involved in his murder.

It was during those final years in St Michael's that I first came to understand the Catholic faith and the gospels in terms of a commitment to justice and not just to being charitable. It was a time when I was discovering a new way of understanding God – the God of Justice and the God of Jesus who took the side of the downtrodden. That understanding made more sense to me than believing in an abstract God whose existence, according to the religious book on Apologetics that we studied, could be proved in many different ways to anyone but the most ignorant or hard-hearted. I read something that Pope John XXIII had written about social justice and was impressed. Pope John XXIII was a lot different from the rather stern-looking Pope Pius XII who had been in office all during my life up until then. I was impressed by his humanity and his humility, his intelligence and his commitment to justice in the world. I was greatly impressed by the compassion and concern expressed by this pope in his letters and statements. It was Pope John XXIII who called the Second Vatican Council in October 1962, which introduced so many of the much-needed reforms into the Catholic church and was intended to set the church on a new course of engaging with the world and with social issues. It was an exciting time to be a Catholic and there was great hope that this was the beginning of a new era in the Catholic church.

While in my teens, as well as going to dances and to the Adelphi cinema in Irvinestown, a few of us from Ederney began to go to Lough Derg each summer for two days of fasting and praying. I must confess that my motives for going on pilgrimage to Lough Derg were not entirely spiritual. I was not just going to do penance, it was another opportunity to meet the girls from the convent. I must emphasise though, that nothing other than talking took place while on Lough Derg.

During my final years at secondary school I was unsettled and I spent a long time off sick with an asthmatic condition. I do not know whether it was stress-related or due to the weather, but I have since discovered that so many illnesses are related to stressful living. It was one of the worst periods of my early life. It taught me early on about having to take the rough with the smooth and that life is not always plain sailing. I did not do as well as I had expected in the 'O' level exams, so I had to repeat some of them. That was another lesson about the need to deal with what life has in store. After that, I went as a boarder to St Michael's, Enniskillen for the final year and I just had to keep my head down in the books.

Given the part that the Catholic religion played in my early life and in the life of the community when I was growing up in the 1950s, it was hardly surprising that I would seriously consider the priesthood when it came to choosing what to do with my life. We were often reminded about the need for priests if the church was to continue its mission. We were told about the idealism and commitment involved. It sounded like a worthy way of spending your life doing good for others. Some priests – usually home from the missions – came to talk to us in school and described it as a generous way of living your life. The key thing for me was to live life in as generous a way as possible. It was a kind of idealism and the priesthood seemed to me to be the best way to live a generous and fully self-expressed life.

I had a sense in the final year (1963–64) at St Michael's that I was moving into a new phase in my life. I had had enough of secondary school. I was going to try the priesthood. I told my parents and assured them that if I did not like it I could leave. They assured me that if I ever changed my mind that it would be all right. My mother even asked me a few times, 'Are you sure you want to do this?' I said that I wanted to give it a go and see what happened. I think she was satisfied that I had given it a good bit of thought, it was what I wanted to do and that I was not trying in any way to please her or anyone else in making this decision.

I discussed the possibility of going to study for the priesthood with some priests in St Michael's college. The choice that I had to make, and which had to be accepted, was to go for the missions or for the home diocese of Clogher. Traditionally, most priests who went for the diocese came from fairly well-off families. I did not belong to one of those.

When I got my A-level exam results, which were good enough to get me a scholarship, it was time to make some final preparations. I had to make a very definite decision about the future. A big concern for me about going to Maynooth was the college fees.

The scholarship would pay for my tuition for the first three years in Maynooth, and the diocese paid the rest of the college fees. I went off to buy a black suit and a black hat and then reality began to sink in. During the summer of 1964 I was having a good time at the dances and went out with a few girls. I knew it could never be too serious as I was already packing my bags for Maynooth.

Looking back it is an odd decision for a young man of eighteen to make, knowing that it involves celibacy. It was one which did not make sense outside the context of faith in Christ as seen in the gospel story about the calling of the first apostles. The gospel states: 'And they left everything and followed him.' I'm afraid that I can only understand my decision as the Jesuit writer, William Johnston, has explained:

> Sometimes people have asked me why I entered the Society of Jesus. The fact is that authentic vocation is mysterious. It comes from the true self, from the depths of the unconscious where we are in touch with the Absolute. Perhaps there is no reason for vocation. Perhaps it is an irrational (or should I say supra-rational?) awakening.[*]

I knew you did not have to be perfect or a saint to go for the priesthood. Just as well, as I did not want to be turned down because I was not good or holy enough! It used be said in some quarters that to be a priest you had to be holy, healthy and learned. I preferred the Benedictine rule that the best person to make a priest was someone not too smart, not too holy and not too healthy. I fitted into that bracket. I opted for the diocese of Clogher. I thought that I would enjoy the challenge of working on the home mission like the priests I had known growing up in Ederney. As well, I thought that I would go to Maynooth and get a degree and if it did not work out I could always turn to teaching.

I knew that it involved a big sacrifice – but I was prepared to try it. I accepted the rules and I kind of understood it in the con-

---

[*] William Johnston, *Mystical Journey: An Autobiography* (Orbis Books, New York, 2006), p. 25.

text of making a sacrifice for a special cause. Within that context, the rule about celibacy made some sense. As the years went by I began to question the whole idea of compulsory celibacy and discovered that the longing for intimacy and friendship did not go away. It has taken me all my life since then to come to terms with that longing and the basic human desires of being a single man.

I was choosing to be a priest at a time when there was great optimism in the Catholic church. It was a big decision to go to a seminary but I felt I would get advice along the way and that I would have time to reflect before making any final decision. Was I a suitable candidate? In some ways, I thought I was a good candidate. I had a strong religious background. I had seen and experienced a good bit of life. My father's first cousin was a Salesian priest in England. He used to visit us every year when he was home on holidays and he seemed like a very happy, normal man. I had seen many priests who were happy and fulfilled in their lives.

In a very real sense I feel that the vocation to the priesthood comes not just directly from God but from the local faith community. During the years of preparation, I felt the support of the community in Ederney willing me on, and showing a strong interest in my journey. I felt they were in solidarity with me and would continue to be when I was ordained. Without that kind of community support, I doubt if I could have gone ahead with this demanding way of life. Those who do not understand that sense of community and solidarity would not understand the commitment a person makes to the priesthood or religious life.

I read stories about other people's call to the priesthood. As I reflected on their unique stories, I realised that the things we have in common are our doubts, our fears and anxieties, tensions with authority and our need for friendship. Good and close friendships are of the utmost importance in this vocation, as in all of life.

# 4

# Maynooth – The North Erupts

Leaving home in September 1964, when I had just turned nine-teen, was the first big break with my family and friends. I would not be home again until Christmas, and would miss the football, the cinema and the friends. I cried my eyes out when that reality hit me a few days before departure – but it was time to move on.

My father's older brother, Uncle Jim, along with a priest native of Ederney, Kevin Cassidy, took me by car to Maynooth. When we reached Lucan, a few miles from Maynooth, we went for a meal in the Lucan Spa hotel. I had a large mixed grill since it was suggested that it might be the last good meal I would enjoy until the holidays at Christmas. We then proceeded to the college with my luggage. All the new students – about 120 – from all over Ireland assembled in a large hall and we were each allocated a room. Some expressed curiosity about 'the ghost room' in one of the buildings. I did not want to be anywhere near that one. There was one other student from St Michael's – Michael Haran. He was the only person I knew in our class, although there were a few older students in Maynooth whom I had known in St Michael's.

The college buildings were impressive at first sight. There was two sections – one for arts and one for theology students. The main living quarters were built in the form of a rectangle with a large square in the centre with shrubs and flower-beds. As it was September there was great colour everywhere. The buildings, some covered with ivy, were hidden from public view behind high walls. Within the walls, there was plenty of space for walking along tree-lined avenues. The college was built in the 1790s, with funding from the British government, on the best farming land in Ireland. There was a large farm attached which provided much of the food for the staff and students. I could not believe that there was land so rich and productive anywhere in Ireland. I was used to the damp meadows and hills of Fermanagh and the rocks and mountains of Donegal. There was a beautiful chapel and an aula maxima used for plays, concerts and prize-giving ceremonies.

Maynooth at that time was a different world – a world of black suits, white shirts, black ties and round Roman collars and long black coats. We even had to wear a black hat. Inside the college, we had to get used to wearing long black soutanes, birettas and surplices for religious ceremonies. It was all dreadfully formal. I felt from early on that the whole thing was too regimental – the dress code and all that. As far as I was concerned what mattered most was the person and the person I was becoming. I was not going to change my personality but I had to grow up and understand something about life – the reality of the world outside. I loved music, films, sports and books. I loved to travel and I used to imagine what it would be like to be a priest. I thought that I had a lot of experience of life and that I had been blessed with really great opportunities for education and recreation. I was becoming accustomed to the idea of leaving home. My cousins and some of my friends had gone to work in England. That was a big move for young men in their teens who were the same age as myself. My move to Maynooth was a big one but I was going to be living in Ireland.

It was a most exciting time and yet an emotional period in my life. It was like setting out on a great and exciting adventure. I had to deal with the reality of different emotions, the reality of sexuality and the reality of growing from a boy to a man during the first years in Maynooth. Some of my school friends were already getting married and becoming parents! I was setting out on a completely different journey. At least ten students from my year in St Michael's went to various colleges to study for the priesthood and most of them became priests.

The students in Maynooth college, at that time, were cut off from the outside world. We were not allowed to leave the college except with the express permission of the president and then only for a very serious reason – like a funeral of a family member or to go to hospital. Even footballers or hurlers picked to play in the All-Ireland final had difficulty getting out. The daily routine was like the boarding school where I spent the previous year. Morning prayer at 7.30 a.m. followed by mass at 8 a.m. followed by breakfast and then class at 9.30 a.m. The dean, who was the first member of staff we met, was strict about punctuality. Anyone who was consistently late for mass or class had to provide an explanation, and if things did not improve he might be told to think about a different vocation. We had newspapers and television, which had been a recent introduction, and we received letters from home. My mother was a good letter-writer, and kept me informed about all the local news. When I got down to study, the time went by quite fast.

I settled in surprisingly well with the other young students from all over Ireland. Every one of the Irish dioceses had at least a few young men who had decided to try it. Cork diocese had, by far, the most new students. I was placed between two Corkonians for meals. This was a permanent kind of arrangement right through all the years in the college. Students were known according to a seniority list. I do not know how they picked it. Anyway, at the beginning, I could not understand a word the two Cork students were saying nor could they understand my northern accent. We would have needed an interpreter for the first year or so. There were over 500 students in the college in 1964. Maynooth, at that time, offered a wide variety of courses and activities. As well as the academic, there was drama and concerts, football, snooker, swimming and numerous societies like the debating society and the Irish language society.

In the early days we associated mostly with other students from the northern dioceses. I hope this does not sound partitionist but I must stress that the diocesan boundaries dating back to AD 1111 were not affected by the artificial political border in Ireland, which was drawn up in 1920. The deans of discipline in the college used to snoop around the corridors and pay unexpected visits to our rooms. I was challenged early on by the junior dean: 'Do you have trouble conforming, Mister McVeigh?' he asked. (You were always called 'Mister' in those days – not your Christian name!) I said I did not think so but I did not really understand the question. He said that I was wearing a soutane (a long black garment like a long coat to the ankles), which was slightly different to everyone else. I had mine made by a dress-maker at home, as it was cheaper than to buy in the shop, and there were buttons showing on the outside, down the front, that were not on the others! Maybe, I was trying to make a statement. It is difficult to know what the unconscious or subconscious is up to, sometimes.

This was to be my first brush with church authority, but not my last. I suppose the general theme of most of these 'brushes' was 'conformity'. This was the most prized quality in a student for the priesthood and, of course, for the priests afterwards in their parishes. If, as students, we showed any signs of non-conformity, we were going to be challenged and perhaps told that we were not suitable material for the priesthood. It never came to that for me.

During the first three years in Maynooth, we studied for either an arts or a science degree. I studied history and Irish for the bachelor of arts degree. The main teachers were Tomás Ó Fiaich from Armagh and Pádraig Ó Fiannachta from Kerry. Tomás, who was always in good humour, was both enlightening and entertaining in his presentation of history both Irish and European. Pádraig was a man with an obvious love of the Irish language who used to laugh a lot. I got through the first year; in fact it seemed to pass very quickly. I spent the summer holidays in the Donegal Gaeltacht or travelling around Ireland. The next two years also passed quickly. I then moved into the theology course. Some of the fellas left having obtained their arts or science degree to pursue all kinds of different careers.

I must confess that at that stage in my life I was not yet aware of the negative political influence of Maynooth and the Catholic hierarchy in Irish politics since its foundation in 1795 by an act of the British parliament. It was only later, after I had left the place, that I learned more about the role of Maynooth and the Irish bishops (with one or two exceptions) in the political and social life of the country. They had given support – directly or indirectly – to the British government since the foundation of Maynooth and especially after the Act of Union in 1800, which abolished the Irish parliament. The main issue for the Irish hierarchy was the advancement of the Catholic church and the increase in power and control of the bishops and clergy.

I was fairly sure that Maynooth was never a hotbed of revolution, even though it did produce a few radical priests, like Pat Lavelle, Michael Flanagan, John McHale and, more recently, James McDyer and Des Wilson. For almost the first hundred years of its existence the students at Maynooth had to take an oath of allegiance to the queen or king of England! One can only imagine what these young men were thinking when they took this oath of allegiance. It must have caused some debate and soul-searching among the students before it was abolished. The Catholic bishops in Ireland and the college authorities were always determined to uphold the status quo. They were not unduly concerned about who was in power.

During my time in Maynooth some members of the staff and some senior students encouraged the use of the Irish language.

Some students were native Irish speakers from Donegal, Galway and Kerry. We were encouraged to speak the language by some of the teachers, including Tomás Ó Fiaich and Pádraig Ó Fiannachta, and by the student organisations, Cuallacht Bhríde and Cuallacht Cholm Cille.

One of my favourite pastimes in the college was playing music and singing. I was still learning to play the guitar and there were other students who were able to teach me. Two of my friends in the college were Tom O'Gara from Derry and Pádraig Standún, who was a student from County Mayo for the Tuam archdiocese. Tom O'Gara and I had struck up a musical partnership early on in Maynooth, as we both could play a bit on the guitar and we shared an interest in the same kind of folk songs. Tom was a marvellous singer with a very authentic folk voice. One of our favourites was 'Joe Hill'. We used to sing 'Cool Water' and 'Shenanndoah' together at variety shows in the college. Tom was great at reaching the high notes and was a good guitar picker. Pádraig Standún had not a musical note in his head but he was a genius at writing lyrics about real life, especially about broken or wounded people. Pádraig used to give me the words of ballads that he had written and suggested I try to put them to music. This is how I passed many an evening, when I should have been studying canon law.

Pádraig Standún gained a reputation in Maynooth for his outspoken and witty comments. Whenever he was appointed to practice preaching, he would have us all in fits of laughter. He would address us, including the dean and the college president, as 'fellow eunuchs for the sake of the kingdom' or in some other outrageous fashion and make fun of a lot of the church rules and regulations. He would have been in big trouble but for the fact that his bishop, Joseph Cunnane, was a close friend, having been a curate in his home parish. He had a great deal of respect for Pádraig's integrity, his obvious talent and his Behanesque sense of humour.

Tom O'Gara and Pádraig Standún represented a new breed

of student for the priesthood in the Catholic church – men who were not prepared to put up with the old puritanism and the authoritarianism that was so much part of the Irish church. These were modern, forward-thinking men bringing new insights and new energy to the church in the wake of the Second Vatican Council. They were rebels of a kind – and yet they were totally and utterly compassionate people – wonderful human beings who were offering their lives in the service of humanity as Catholic priests. I was always glad to have them as friends.

During my seven years in Maynooth the college changed from an enclosed seminary to an open university catering for men and women of all ages. In 1966, the college opened its doors to the laity. This was revolutionary in the context of the Irish Catholic church. The university has flourished since then while the number of students attending the seminary has declined steadily.

For seminarians, prayer and meditation were part of the daily routine. It was made very clear to us from the beginning that without a life of regular prayer the priestly life was impossible. We also had the regular retreats lasting a week or so during which time we listened to talks on the spiritual life and thought about our lives and our vocations in a more focused way. Spiritual reading was encouraged from books like *The Imitation of Christ*. From an early age I understood that the whole of life could be a prayer, and that has been my conviction ever since. I also believe in the need for solitude and meditation to quieten the mind from all its preoccupations and distractions – if we are to remain focused.

Many of my classmates gave up on the idea of becoming priests and left the college to pursue other careers. It was always a bit disconcerting when someone left, especially someone you knew well or someone you thought was better suited than yourself to the priesthood. For some, celibacy was the big issue; for others it was the discipline of the college. Whatever the reason, they left and they left me thinking even more about my reasons for staying.

While in Maynooth, I looked forward to the long summer holidays – the months of July and August. I spent some weeks in the Donegal Gaeltacht where I practised speaking Irish – always my favourite subject. One summer, my cousin, Séan McGrath and I went to work in Lourdes for a month. We hitch-hiked our way through France, which was a bit of an adventure since neither of us could speak much French and we did not have much to eat or drink with us. In Lourdes, we helped out at Cité Secours, a large hostel run by the French-based Caritas organisation. It was built to provide inexpensive accommodation for pilgrims who could not afford hotels. This was a good experience for me and I met up with other students from all over the world.

Maynooth college was no longer cut off from the outside world. We got the papers every day and had radios, and there was a television in a common room. Apart from football games the most watched programme at the time was *The Riordans,* an early Irish soap opera based on family life on a farm – actually filmed not too far from Maynooth. A group of us cycled out to see the filming on one occasion.

At the beginning of 1966, my second year in the college, the big news was the blowing up of Nelson's pillar – a familiar landmark in O'Connell Street, Dublin. This monument to the English Admiral Nelson was regarded by republicans in Ireland as another symbol of British imperialism and as such had no place in an Irish republic. I was not too sorry about Nelson's pillar being removed. The bombing was the chief topic of conversation in the college the next day. There were not too many complaining. Some group in Dublin recorded a song 'Up Went Nelson in Old Dublin', which was popular and was even played on Radio Éireann. Those were 'the good ole days'!

During the summer of 1966 we heard about the murder of some Catholics in Belfast. Things had been fairly quiet since 1964. There had been a fracas in Belfast in September 1964 involving the

Rev. Ian Paisley. During a Westminster election, the Tricolour was placed in the window of the republican candidate's office on Divis Street, off the Falls Road. Paisley threatened that, unless the RUC removed the flag within twenty-four hours, he would remove it himself. It was tough talk. The RUC removed the Tricolour by force. Mr Kilfedder, who won the election, thanked Paisley in his victory speech, saying that without his help the victory would not have been possible. Mr Paisley had earlier objected to the Union Jack on Belfast City Hall being flown at half-mast when Pope John XXIII died on 3 June 1963. This was the first time I ever heard the name of Ian Paisley, the man who went on to become famous for shouting 'No Surrender'.

Violence and tension returned to the streets of Belfast in 1966. On 27 May, a Catholic man, John Scullion, was shot and wounded. He died on 11 June. On 26 June, three Catholic barmen were shot as they left a pub on Malvern Street off the Shankill Road. One of them, Peter Ward, died. Three unionists were convicted – Gusty Spence, Robert Williamson and Hugh McLean. Spence had been associated with Paisley and Paisley had thanked the UVF for taking part in a protest march on 16 June.

While I had experienced some anti-Catholic bigotry in Fermanagh, it was not as widespread as in Belfast, where areas of the city were exclusively Catholic and others exclusively Protestant. There seemed to be an uneasy peace between these communities, which at times boiled over. Loyalists felt threatened by any talk of Irish unity. Little did I know that 1966 was to be a taste of more serious things to come.

Also that year, the Dublin government planned to hold commemorations to mark the 1916 Rising. I did not understand why the government had to make this into a big celebration of Irish freedom when part of Ireland had not achieved independence or any semblance of democracy. People in the north were being murdered around that time because they were Irish and the Dublin government did not seem to me to be unduly concerned. Since the country was partitioned, the southern government had done nothing about the blatant discrimination practised by a unionist government against Irish citizens in another part of the island. They stood idly by as the bigots in the Orange Order asserted their superiority and called for discrimination against Catholics every year on 12 July.

In Maynooth as part of the fiftieth anniversary celebrations of 1916 we had several talks, one by Seán Lemass who, as a young republican volunteer, had taken part in the 1916 Rising. I was pleased to meet him afterwards when a few of us were invited to Tomás Ó Fiaich's room for refreshments. I found Lemass to be very down to earth and a good talker. Of course, Tomás really enjoyed listening to him and asking him pertinent questions about his memories of 1916 and afterwards. Tomás Ó Fiaich (who was later to become the cardinal archbishop of Armagh) was born and reared in south Armagh. As well as being a first-rate historian, Tomás was committed to the Irish language and had a wide knowledge of European culture. He spoke a number of languages quite fluently. Looking back it is clear that he had an immense influence on me during these years. I admired the breadth of his knowledge of Irish history and his knowledge of European art and culture. He was a true European and knew each European country intimately. He often led historical pilgrimages to places in Europe that are connected to the early Irish missionaries. He had a special interest in St Columbanus – the first and greatest Irish missionary. He carried his learning well and was not in any way aloof or superior.

It became clear to me during those first few years in Maynooth that a sizeable gap had developed between the northern six counties and the twenty-six counties. The students and teachers from the twenty-six counties had no real understanding of what it was like living in the six counties. Many of them believed that we were better off economically and that we had a better education system and of course better roads! Some of them seemed to think that they would have been better off under British rule. Occasionally the subject of partition and discrimination in the north came up in conversation in the context of the 1966 commemorations – but mostly it was not talked about.

I got through the first three years in Maynooth and had not given too much thought to the future. I enjoyed the study, the sports, the music and the holidays. During my fourth and fifth years in the seminary I was forced to think a lot more about the strange life of the priest. I reflected on the reasons why I had come to Maynooth in the first place and asked myself many times if there was any good reason to quit. I never could find any but I still had doubts and worries about celibacy which I shared with the spiritual director. I accepted then that celibacy and priesthood went together in the Roman rite. I accepted that the priesthood was about commitment and commitment was about sacrifice. So the sacrifice I had to make to be a priest was marriage. I knew it was going to be difficult but I believed that it could be done. I was like everybody else, a sexual being, and the challenge was to integrate that sexuality into my life. It is, I have learned, a lifelong challenge. Without the love and support of good friends, it is hardly possible.

During these years in Maynooth, I was engaged in a process of discerning if this was the life for me. My suitability for the priesthood was also considered by the college authorities in conjunction with the bishop of my diocese. It was at the end of this process that I would go forward for ordination – if I decided to go forward and if the bishop and the college authorities approved. The college authorities would report to the bishop if they felt a candidate was not suitable.

I first considered the priesthood to minister to the people and serve them in the parish. I wanted to be there for the people, to celebrate the sacraments and especially the mass. Priests have done this for centuries, especially in the darkest days of Irish history, in the penal times. I have found that to be present with people at the most meaningful moments in their lives is, indeed, a privilege and a joy. The sacraments are about celebrating the key moments in life and the Eucharist is the greatest celebration of the Christian faith community.

In those early days, I did not see any political role for the priest. For me at that stage in life, the priesthood was about administering the sacraments and about living an honest and upright life dedicated to serving the people. There were no obvious political considerations – at least that's what I thought at the time. After a few years I was slowly but surely coming to see that the priest's role was indeed very political in the sense that it meant tackling injustice in society. The priest could not avoid being political – either in accepting the status quo or questioning it. There was no such thing as taking a neutral stance. He had a duty, according to the gospel, that he was ordained to preach, to oppose what was unjust in society – and I was well aware that there was plenty of injustice in Ireland, as there was in many countries in the Third World where Irish missionaries worked.

I was acutely aware of the injustices in the north and knew that there were people now prepared to confront those responsible like never before. On 24 August 1968 there was a huge civil rights march from Coalisland to Dungannon – the first ever in the north. I was not able to attend as I was playing football for Ederney in the Fermanagh final the next day. I was pleased to hear that a huge crowd took part and that it passed off peacefully. I was a bit worried when I heard the reports of how the marchers were being opposed and threatened by Rev. Ian Paisley and his mob. The RUC blocked the civil rights marchers from reaching the centre of Dungannon. However, the civil rights people achieved their aims of once again highlighting the injustices of the state.

After the success of this protest there were plans for another civil rights march – this time in Derry on 5 October 1968. Bill Craig, the minister for home affairs, banned the march because he claimed there was likely to be a clash with an Apprentice Boys of Derry parade planned for the same time. The civil rights people were determined to go ahead.

I was back in Maynooth on 5 October 1968 when the Derry march took place. We waited anxiously to hear how it went. That evening I watched the news on television, which showed scenes of the attacks on the civil rights marchers in Derry. I was horrified but not surprised to see the brutality of the RUC and B-Specials who attacked the marchers with truncheons and fists and boots. Because of the presence of television cameras the world could now see the kind of state that existed in the north-east of Ireland. I was impressed by the dignity and determination of the people who marched in Derry that day in the face of the most awful provocation from the RUC and the B-men.

Most of us in Maynooth who came from the north were interested in what was taking place in Derry and we were now anxious about the future. One of the students with me in Maynooth at the time was Hugh McAteer from Derry. His father, Eddie McAteer, the leader of the Nationalist Party, was at the front of the civil rights march when the RUC and B-men attacked it. (Hugh's uncle had been a leading IRA man in the 1930s and 1940s.) Hugh McAteer was in constant contact by telephone with his family in Derry and kept us informed about the situation. He was soon told by a family member about the local efforts in Derry to challenge his father politically and to undermine the old Nationalist Party. John Hume was one of a new breed of politicians to emerge with the civil rights movement. He had been a student in Maynooth only a few years before and left having obtained his BA degree to take up a teaching job in St Columb's in Derry. Hume had become involved in the credit union movement in the Bogside and was making a name for himself in the nationalist community in Derry. He had political ambitions and was being pushed by the clergy and, according to Paddy Devlin, by the Knights of Columbanus.*

It soon became clear that the Irish Catholic bishops were alarmed at the growing defiance of the Catholic population in Belfast and Derry. As Des Wilson comments:

> In Belfast, Catholic church officials moved to take control of the Citizens Defence Committees which had been set up in many areas to defend the residents from attack. The church authorities in Belfast directed clergy to take control of these committees and bring them all under one organisation, the Central Citizens Defence committee, whose chairman would be appointed by the local bishop ... church policy was to convince people they should rely upon government for protection rather than learn to protect themselves.†

During the Christmas and Easter holiday periods from Maynooth, I attended some civil rights meetings and protests in Enniskillen and Omagh to show support and solidarity with the people who were in the front-line of the protests. I did not see any priests present at any of these. I was excited about the new movement and I could sense a new spirit of determination in the nationalist/Catholic community. At last there was something the people could do to highlight the injustices in the six counties. They could march peacefully and be almost assured publicity – because there was certain to be a counter-demonstration by Paisley's supporters. The media were always interested if they thought there was going to be a disturbance.

In 1969 and 1970, Ian Paisley was hardly out of the news. Following his arrest and imprisonment, some of his followers set off explosive devices in Belfast and at a reservoir in County Down. The papers reported that the IRA was responsible. The man behind this bombing campaign was a member of Paisley's church

---

* Paddy Devlin, *Straight Left: An Autobiography* (Blackstaff Press, Belfast, 1993)..
† Des Wilson, *Democracy Denied* (Mercier Press, Cork, 1997), pp. 42–43.

and we might never have known this had he not blown himself up while setting a bomb at the ESB plant in Ballyshannon, County Donegal in October 1969. The aim of Paisley and the UVF was to topple the prime minister, Terence O'Neill. They wanted to make it appear that the IRA caused the explosions. They eventually succeeded in forcing O'Neill to resign on 28 April 1969. His cousin, Major James Chichester Clarke, succeeded him. However, the unionists were divided and unable to contain the situation. Their fifty years of misrule was coming back to haunt them.

At this time, Catholic church leaders were appealing for calm. Despite the fact that Catholic priests in Belfast had called on local republicans to defend church property when the unionist mobs attacked, the Catholic bishops still took a strong anti-republican line. In May 1970, Cardinal Conway of Armagh and several northern bishops issued a joint statement:

> In recent weeks many people have expressed anxiety about increasing violence in Northern Ireland. People are worried about the course events may take during the coming election campaign and throughout the summer. In these circumstances we feel it our duty to give expression to certain thoughts and moral principles, which we know, are already in the minds and hearts of our people as a whole.
>
> The overwhelming majority of our people do not want violence. They realise that it is morally wrong and that it is doubly so in Northern Ireland at the present time because of what it may lead to. It could lead to great suffering and death. It could lead to a repetition of the horrors we endured last autumn and even worse. And as always, the people who would suffer most are the innocent and the poor. The people who are mourning their dead of last August, the people who had to spend last winter in wooden shacks, know what violence leads to. The Catholic people as a whole abhor it.
>
> Since this is the case it would be a betrayal of the Catholic community – a stab in the back – for any individual or group to take it upon them to deliberately provoke violent incidents. So far as our people are concerned this would be quite a new turn of events but there is some evidence that it might have happened in recent days. If this is so then in the name of God and the whole Catholic community we condemn it.
>
> Such evil initiatives are contrary to the law of Christ and must bring harm to thousands of innocent people. Moreover, if such acts can be pointed to as the beginning of serious trouble, it is not the handful

of self-appointed activists who will be blamed but the whole Catholic community. Already people are not above suggesting that what has happened in recent days convicts the Catholic community for what happened last August (in Derry).

It is no justification for such conduct to say that there was provocation or to say, even with some justice, that much worse deeds have been done by others and have gone unpunished. Two wrongs do not make a right. Already the effects of recent incidents are being felt in the strain and illness and economic pressure, which innocent people are suffering. No one has the right to inflict a situation of this kind on the people.

We therefore ask our people to make their voices heard in repudiation of individuals or groups who may be interested in a continuation of violence. We ask them to co-operate with those groups who genuinely reflect the peaceful intentions of the people as a whole and who are working hard to restrain militant elements. We appeal in a particular way to the women – who are often the people who suffer most – and to parents. Your children could be maimed for life, psychologically and otherwise, by a continuation of these disturbances. There are many deep-seated wrongs to be undone in our society. Violence will only delay the day when they can be removed.

Significant changes have taken place with regard to the position of the minority in Northern Ireland during the past eighteen months. We regard it as essential that the programme of reform be adhered to without any deviation and pursued to its logical conclusion of fair treatment for all, in fact as well as in law. As these changes – and other vitally important changes, which have been promised – take effect there will be a genuine prospect of justice and peace and further progress by orderly means. To anyone who thinks rationally about the future of the people concerned and it is the people, human beings, that matter, not causes or ideologies – there can be no question of where the choice must lie between the violent way and the peaceful way. We warn those few individuals who would opt for the violent way that they have absolutely no mandate from the people.

The principles of our Christian faith, which must be our supreme guide, powerfully reinforce the message of reason and common sense. Next to the love of God the greatest commandment is love of neighbour. Our neighbour, as the catechism teaches us, is 'mankind of every description even those who injure us or who differ from us in religion'. Most of our neighbours here are our fellow Christians, united with us in the love and worship of the same Lord and Saviour, Jesus Christ.

There may be moments when this most difficult of all commandments calls for almost superhuman restraint. Even then we are bound by it. If we have recourse to God in prayer he will not deny us the grace to be faithful to this His great commandment.

As in all their subsequent statements, they failed to place the people's movement for justice and basic human rights in its historical and political context. They failed to confront the violence of the British and the unionists which was far greater than the violence of those in the nationalist community who turned to rioting. The reforms granted by the British government were always 'too little and too late'. The government at Westminster was not prepared to concede nationalists' demands for their rights and entitlements.

The weak response of the church leaders, in my opinion, allowed the British to harass and intimidate the Catholic people in the Falls area of Belfast and throughout the six counties. In July 1970, the British army commander-in-chief, Ian Freeland, declared a curfew on the nationalist Falls Road area of Belfast. British soldiers carried out house-to-house searches. Six people were killed during rioting which followed. A week earlier, the Provisional IRA had been in action for the first time in the Short Strand when the people there came under attack from pro-British unionists. This marked the beginning of the long war.

As the violence worsened in 1969 and 1970 the Catholic middle-class and the senior clergy began to panic, especially when they saw that the people were turning to the IRA. It was looking like the church and the new Catholic middle-class were losing their influence in the nationalist community. The Social Democratic and Labour Party (SDLP) was formed in August 1970 by some of those who were prominent in the civil rights protests. Gerry Fitt, an elected politician in Belfast, became leader, with John Hume, a teacher from Derry, as deputy leader. The more republican-minded people shunned the SDLP. The vast majority of the priests and all of the bishops supported and promoted the SDLP from then onwards.

I had to get used to the indifference of the vast majority of the students in Maynooth to what was happening on the streets of Belfast and Derry. None of the theology teachers were from the north and few of them had any knowledge of the place or any interest in what was happening. They were more concerned with moral issues relating to contraception and the safe method! There were two groups of theology professors – the ultra-conservative and the liberals. The senior professor of moral theology, Frankie Cremin, was very conservative, while the younger men like Enda McDonagh, Donal Flanagan and Paul Surlis were liberal and less dogmatic. They followed a similar line to the English theologian, Charles Davis – emphasising the primacy of conscience in the Christian spiritual life rather than the primacy of the magisterium of the church. Some teachers of theology at that time like Davis came up against church authority because they questioned the church's teaching or emphasised the church's teaching on individual conscience as defined in the Second Vatican Council.

The Second Vatican Council, which began in 1961, was the most important event in the recent history of the Catholic church. Bishops and priests were called to preach the gospel of justice and peace with renewed vigour. The council reminded us that priests were called to follow the prophetic rather than the clerical model of the church. The prophets stand up for the people and become the voice of the people. They bring good news to the poor – not the well-off.

The subject of ecumenism was rarely mentioned during my time, but in the final year a Jesuit priest, Michael Hurley, was appointed to give a series of talks on the subject, which was highlighted in the Second Vatican Council. On one occasion, the students from the church of Ireland hostel in Rathgar were invited to Maynooth to meet with us and we were invited to their place. The visit to Rathgar was arranged on the day of the FA cup final. I went along to Rathgar out of curiosity. I must say that a few of us from both traditions preferred to watch the football than take part in the theology discussion. It's no wonder that ecumenism has not prospered in Ireland.

During my final years in Maynooth there was only one teacher who showed any enthusiasm for the subject of theology and made it interesting and relevant. His name was Paul Surlis, a priest from the west of Ireland, who spoke to us about the social dimension of the gospel. He showed me that this way of interpreting the gospel was something significant for him and that it had serious political implications for the church and for all of us who wanted to be priests. I should say that Dr Enda McDonagh was on sabbatical during these years so that we did not have the opportunity of hearing his lectures.

Paul Surlis was the only teacher I remember who emphasised the teaching of the church about social justice. He was not kept on in Maynooth – surprise, surprise! He went to the US where he got a job lecturing in St John's University in New York. Most of the other professors of theology and scripture were conservative and out of touch with the new theology and the real world. They did not encourage much debate or soul searching and certainly they had nothing very interesting or relevant to say about the conflict in the north.

In October 1970, when she was making headlines throughout the world, I thought it would be a good idea to invite Bernadette Devlin to speak to the students in Maynooth about the developing situation in the north. After all, there were all kinds of speakers invited to talk about issues that were not as important. I thought the younger people in the college would identify with her analysis of the situation. I went to the president, Dr Jeremiah Newman (later the bishop of Limerick), to seek his permission to invite Bernadette to speak to the students. It was a rule of the college that all societies had to have the president's permission when inviting outside speakers. The history society to which I belonged had hosted Tom Barry and many other famous republicans from the past without any problem. I thought it would be a mere formality to host Bernadette. However, as soon as I mentioned

Bernadette Devlin's name, Newman's face became flushed, and in an angry and loud voice he declared that under no circumstances would he allow 'a communist like Bernadette Devlin' into Maynooth. I suppose I should have known better but I was on a learning curve about the official church and Irish radicals.

I turned on my heels and went back to tell the others on the committee that our proposal was shot down. I did not think that Newman would have known that much about Bernadette's politics or that he would have shown such hostility to someone who had become so popular throughout Ireland – indeed throughout the world. However, he had obviously sussed her and her political leanings out. Later, I was to learn about how Maynooth students and professors were in the past expelled and humiliated for having any association with radicals or 'left wingers' of any description.

I did not protest too strongly on that occasion, for I knew that Newman was a tough character and would not change his mind and I thought I might even get into trouble with my bishop. I also knew that if I went ahead and asked Bernadette and she agreed to come to give a talk, I would be out on my ear – a few months before ordination!

In the early months of 1971 I was preparing for ordination, which was fixed for April in St Joseph's, Ederney, my home parish. During the final year, students had to practise giving sermons, first to the other students in the college and then in the churches near Maynooth. I gave my first ever sermon in the church in Batterstown, County Meath. I was nervous before such a large audience. I felt sorry for the poor congregation which had to put up with many of us practising our preaching skills – but they did not complain. They knew we were learners. This was the final preparation for the real thing. I was almost twenty-five years of age and I had spent much of my life in college, though I had quite a variety of experiences of manual work, either on the farm or on the building sites or even washing and drying dishes in Lourdes! I was glad to be moving on to yet another part of the journey. I had prepared the best I could, I thought, so it was out into the real world now.

In my final year in Maynooth I also gained some experience of the kind of pastoral work a priest might be doing in a parish when I worked with a Legion of Mary group in Dublin. This experience brought me into contact with real people living lonely lives, many on the poverty line. They reminded me of my own upbringing – except that we never had loneliness. The Legion of Mary was founded by a Dublin man, Frank Duff, as a way of promoting Christian service and Marian devotion involving the laity in the church. It involved visiting older people in their homes, visiting hospitals and the homeless in places like the North Star hostel. I went to the North Star a number of times and saw there the results of alcohol abuse and neglect of people who had been deprived in some way or other.

At this time I also made my first prison visit. At the request of some concerned people at home, I went to see two young men from County Fermanagh who were serving a sentence in Mountjoy jail, having been arrested in Clones, County Monaghan, for some minor offence. I found two very frightened and traumatised boys about eighteen years of age. I think it was then I realised, for the first time, the terrible effect of imprisonment on young people. These young men needed counselling instead of imprisonment.

In the summer of 1969, I went to work on a building site in London. The growing conflict at home was on the news every day. The day after the RUC invasion of the Bogside in Derry, I took part in a sit-down protest near Downing Street, in which many of the Irish emigrants took part. In London in 1969 and 1970, I discovered how difficult it was for some Irish to live away from home. Loneliness often led to over-indulgence in alcohol. Those with a strong family network were able to survive and many, like the McGee brothers from Longford, became very successful in business.

This trip to London was my first real taste of 'the bright city lights' and the first real test of my vocation. There was nobody there to supervise us. I became friends with a young woman I met on the boat. We talked and saw each other a few times afterwards but our friendship fizzled out. I was confident about the choice I had made and was determined at this stage to see it through. I think she was sent as a final test of my vocation! I still wanted to be a priest and that meant a commitment to a particular way of life – a very difficult way of life. It was meant to be a life-long commitment to serving God's people. I agree with Thomas Merton who wrote about celibacy:

> Celibacy is not first of all a thing of the flesh but of the spirit. It is the choice to commit myself to God, Christ, to be the love of my life – all other loves being within that love and empowered by it. Celibacy is first of all giving as person. It doesn't preclude other loves, relationships, experiences of such love, even appropriate physical expressions.*

* M. Basil Pennington, *Engaging the World with Merton* (Paraclete Press, Massachusetts, 1988, 2005), p. 37.

5

# Ordination and Baptism of Fire

Ordination was fixed for the Sunday after Easter 1971. I was to be ordained along with my cousin, Seán McGrath, who was going to the missions. He had joined St Patrick's Missionaries, Kiltegan, who were involved in great work with the poor in Africa and South America. The bishop of Clogher at the time, Dr Patrick Mulligan, agreed to ordain us together in St Joseph's church, Ederney, in our home parish. The day of ordination was a big day for me, for my family and for the local community. I don't think there was ever an ordination in the parish – not in living memory. Seán and I prepared for the day by going on a retreat to the Graan monastery outside Enniskillen. The church in Ederney was packed for the ceremony. Some of the students in Maynooth had come along to lend a hand with the singing or just to give me moral support. Many of the priests in the diocese turned up, as was the custom on such occasions. We had rehearsed the evening before and so the ceremony went smoothly.

After the first mass the following evening we had a party in the parish hall. Many people from the parish of Cúl Máine (Irish name for my native parish) joined in the fun and the dancing. The well-known singer, Pat McGeegan, father of the boxer, Barry McGuigan, played that night at the dance. One of the musicians in his band had been in Maynooth with me. Another recently ordained young priest who liked to dance discovered soon after-

wards that the parish priest reported him to the bishop for caus-
ing public scandal – dancing with a nun! Luckily for him the
bishop did not take the complaint too seriously. It did not seem
to hinder that priest in his progress in the church for he is now a
much-revered monsignor in the diocese.

After the seven years in Maynooth college I was now anxious
to get involved in the real world. I was asked by the bishop to go
to work in the parish of Enniskillen for the summer months, to
cover for a priest who worked each summer at the Lough Derg
pilgrimage centre in County Donegal.

The other two curates in the house we shared made me very
welcome. I was 'the new kid on the block' – one of two new priests
ordained for the diocese of Clogher. I had already felt a strong
sense of fraternity and friendship among the ordinary priests in
the diocese. Many of them came to my ordination ceremony in
Ederney and wished me well. I was grateful to them for their
support and generosity. Now I was one of them!

The curate's house where I was living was situated in Darling
Street – next door to St Michael's church and across the street
from the parish priest's house and the Church of Ireland (Anglican) cathedral. It seemed odd that all the priests were based in this
one street in this large parish. Each of us living in the large curate's
house had our own living quarters but we dined in a common
dining-room. The food was good – a lot better than in Maynooth.
One of us was always on call for the Erne hospital or for callers
at the door who were often looking to get mass cards signed or
for confessions. Two housekeepers cooked and tidied the house.
Each day was very structured and everybody knew what he was
supposed to be doing. One of the three priests was always on duty.
There was mass to be said either in the church or in the Convent
of Mercy every day and a number of masses to be said on Sunday.
There were confessions at set times every week, home visitation,
the Legion of Mary meetings, etc.

The parish priest was an aloof man from County Monaghan. He had been teaching Latin and Greek in St Macartan's college in Monaghan all his priestly life until he was appointed parish priest of Enniskillen. He had little or no previous pastoral experience. He found it difficult to relate to the ordinary people – but easy enough to relate to the teachers and professional people. One day we got to talking about the political situation then unfolding. He gave me a history lesson and told me that the 1916 rebellion was a huge mistake and had brought nothing but trouble. I did not argue with him. I was too inexperienced to take on the parish priest in my first parish! However, I felt there was a huge difference in outlook between us and I wondered if he was representative of many of the senior clergy in the diocese.

One of the other priests was a native of Belfast and spent much time training and managing the camogie team. I knew that in our county the boys had always been catered for in the GAA but the girls were neglected for many years. Now a few people, including Fr Peter, were trying to get a camogie league going. There were only three or four teams in the whole county. This was not his only interest, for I soon learned that he was concerned about the travelling people who spent part of the year in Enniskillen. Already, I could see the priest's ministry was varied and challenging.

The other curate in the house was quiet, reserved, and interested in church music. He was an accomplished organist and was responsible for the wonderful choir in the parish. He was from County Monaghan and was keenly interested in the unfolding political situation. I gathered that he was strongly in favour of the civil rights movement. He did not say much but when he did I knew that he was very critical of the unionist regime.

Enniskillen is an old market town situated on an island – the island of Ceithleann – and joined by a number of bridges to the mainland. It attracts many tourists each year. The town has expanded over the years all around the shore of Lough Erne surrounding the island of Ceithleann. Enniskillen has a worldwide reputation for its famous boys' grammar school, Portora, opened in 1777. Oscar Wilde and Samuel Beckett were among the many distinguished past pupils of Portora. St Michael's does not have anyone quite so distinguished – yet!

For many years, nationalists in Enniskillen suffered the worst effects of discrimination by the unionist government in jobs and housing and unemployment – just like in Derry, Newry and in other nationalist towns in the six counties. It was a garrison town where the British army always maintained a base and it was the place where the RUC training depot was situated – just down the street from St Michael's church. There were always a few Catholics in the RUC; they made up about 5 per cent of the force. Few ever moved up the ranks, however.

I knew quite a number people in Enniskillen from my school days there. Many from around my home village of Ederney had moved to Enniskillen to find employment in the new factories. (Unemployment in the six counties generally was 15.5 per cent; in Fermanagh, it was 33 per cent for nationalists.) I quickly settled into the new parish and enjoyed the social side of it all. There was plenty of pastoral work, such as visiting the patients in the local hospitals, going to the youth club, the senior citizens functions and visiting the sick in their homes. Never a dull moment!

On 12 July 1971 I watched as the Orangemen assembled for their annual parade in the town. It was amazing to see these country-men wearing their sashes and bowler hats arriving for their big day out. I thought it was strange how they could take over the whole town for the day. During the parade, I received a 'sick call' to the other side of town. I had great difficulty in getting there – but managed to make it before the man died. The family were very grateful to me and I felt I had done something worthwhile that was very much appreciated by a family at this difficult time for them.

Feelings were running high during these summer months in

1971 after two young Catholics were killed in Derry by the British army. There was rioting in some nationalist areas of the six counties. The SDLP felt obliged to withdraw from the local parliament at Stormont when the British government refused to hold an 'impartial inquiry'. Feelings were running deep about this incident throughout the whole nationalist/Catholic community in the six counties.

In late summer 1971, the IRA exploded bombs in Belfast and in different parts of the north. There was some talk during July that the British were going to introduce internment without trial, a tactic that they used in nearly every decade previously. Unionists demanded that it be reintroduced as the only way of dealing with 'the insurrection'.

At the breakfast table on the morning of 9 August 1971 'the quiet priest' announced that he had heard that internment without trial had been introduced early that morning, and that a large number of Catholics/nationalists from all over the six counties had been taken away. Under the Special Powers Act passed by a unionist government in 1922, anyone they considered a threat to the 'stability of the state' could be arrested and held without trial for as long as the unionists deemed it necessary.

We learned later that day that several of those detained were from Enniskillen. In fact, the housekeeper's brother-in-law was one of those lifted. I called to see some of the families of those arrested and they were obviously distressed and angry about what had happened. Some of those lifted had taken part in the early civil rights marches. The British army, which carried out the operation, was working on information supplied by the RUC.

The headlines in the *Fermanagh Herald* of the week of 14 August 1971 read: 'Twelve Men Seized in Dawn Raids – Shock and Anger in County as Internment Without Trial is Announced'. That about summed it up – 'shock and anger' was what the nationalists felt. The nationalist senator, P. J. O'Hare, who was editor of the *Herald* at the time, had his finger on the pulse of nationalist Fermanagh.

Around lunchtime that day I received a phone call to say that one of those arrested was my young cousin, Maurice McGrath, who was eighteen years of age. Later I went the fifteen miles to Ederney and called at Maurice's home. We learned that he had been brought to Omagh barracks and from there to Magilligan near Derry. Later that week he was taken by helicopter to a prison ship, the *Maidstone*, anchored in Belfast Lough. After some months, he and most of the others were transferred to Long Kesh prison camp, situated beside a British army base near the staunchly loyalist town of Lisburn in County Antrim. The camp consisted of what were called compounds with four nissen huts in each compound. Some of the huts contained bunk beds.

There were altogether 342 men (all from the Catholic community) arrested between 5 a.m. and 6 a.m. on the morning of 9 August 1971. Many in the nationalist community across the north were angered by this decision of the British government to appease the unionists. There was an immediate and angry response. Some took to rioting in the streets of Belfast, others to marching and protesting. The worst trouble took place in west Belfast. Two British soldiers and ten civilians were killed. One of those killed was a Catholic priest, Fr Hugh Murphy, who was shot while giving the last rites to an injured person in Ballymurphy. Some 240 houses in Ardoyne were attacked and burned by loyalists. Many Catholic families fled to the twenty-six counties for safety.

Like many others, I was deeply upset and angry that the British government had authorised and carried out the imprisonment of people without trial – and then allowed the unionist gangs to run riot in Belfast. We learned later that some of those lifted that day were tortured. At the time, I felt that all I could do was show support to the families of those who had been taken away. These people were once again on the receiving end of the British government's mistaken policy in Ireland. It was a time that called for leadership within the nationalist/Catholic community.

A protest demonstration was arranged for the Diamond in the centre of Enniskillen on the night that internment was introduced. Men went around the county with loud-hailers to inform people about the protest. That night about 2,000 people came along to the Diamond; it had been many years since such a crowd had gathered in the centre of the town. Local civil rights activist, Frank McManus, recently released from prison for taking part in a civil rights protest, spoke to the gathering, as did some other activists. During one of the speeches a stone was thrown and a large plate glass window was smashed. A Free Presbyterian minister from Lisbellaw, Ivan Foster, was leading a counter demonstration. The stone that started the trouble and caused the RUC to move in against the nationalist protesters came from the Free Presbyterians. It is a well-known trick to provoke a reaction from the police.

In the days that followed, British troops who had been moved to RUC stations in border areas were attacked by IRA gunfire in the villages of Belleek and Belcoo. Nobody I knew was too surprised at this reaction. These usually quiet villages along the border were constantly in the news for the next twenty-five years.

Another anti-internment rally was planned for the following Friday night, again in the Diamond in Enniskillen. I walked down the few hundred yards from the priest's house to the Diamond and saw a large contingent of RUC in their land rovers. Once again a crowd of about 2,000 had gathered. A lorry was used as a platform for the speakers. Jim Donnelly, a nationalist councillor, chaired the proceedings and Frank McManus was again one of the main speakers. Like before, Ivan Foster held a counter demonstration, with his crowd waving Union Jacks. In the middle of the speech, tear gas was fired at the platform by the RUC. A riot ensued and seventeen men were arrested and taken to the local

RUC barracks. One of those arrested was Fr Seán McManus, the Redemptorist priest who was once in my class. They were later charged with disorderly behaviour and released to await trial.

Internment without trial affected many in the nationalist community throughout the six counties. Many families had somebody belonging to them or knew somebody who had been arrested and held without trial. The people in jail were, as far as I was concerned, political hostages. They had a great deal of popular support in nationalist Ireland. A song by Barleycorn called 'The Men Behind the Wire' was a best seller and was at the top of the charts in Ireland for most of the year. RTÉ, the 'national broadcaster', refused to play it.

When it became known that several of the internees had been severely tortured in British army custody some people in the nationalist community were incensed. A few were convinced that it was time for armed action against the state. Fifty years of one-party unionist rule, special laws and RUC intimidation led to a lot of frustration and deep anger in the working-class nationalist communities. Social and economic conditions in these areas were deplorable due to neglect and a deliberate policy of discrimination. Now the British were going to face the wrath of the ordinary nationalist people throughout the six counties. There would be no going back this time. For some it was time for armed resistance. For many, like myself, it was time for determined passive resistance. I saw that the effect of the civil rights movement and the passive resistance was to destabilise the shaky Unionist government. I believed then that to pursue this strategy would bring down the corrupt system of government in the six counties. I was not sure what would happen after that. I suppose I hoped that the British would hand over to Dublin what really belonged to the Irish people according to the Irish constitution. I would have to say that, at the time, I had no idea how things would pan out or how the unionists were going to react as events unfolded. A growing number of unionists were now more inclined to look to the Rev. Ian Paisley for leadership. He was vehemently opposed to any form of unity or even contact with the twenty-six counties. His slogan was 'Never! Never! Never!' and on this slogan he built the Democratic Unionist Party.

As the anger in the nationalist community increased, the Catholic bishops, during the week of 21 August, called for prayers for peace at all masses the following Sunday. The nationalist political leaders, including those of the newly formed SDLP, called for a rent and rates strike.

Some who felt the time was right for armed action against the British joined the IRA, sometimes called the 'Provisionals' since they named themselves the Provisional Army of the Irish Republic to distinguish them from the 'Officials'. Their main objective at this time was to protect the besieged nationalist people. After years of indifference, the southern political establishment had drifted away from the north.

In the midst of all that was going on since internment was introduced, I had to get on with the usual parish work and attend to the sick at home and in hospital. One of my earliest and lasting memories is a visit to the Erne hospital to attend to a man who was seriously ill having suffered a heart attack. He had not been 'practising' for many years and was anxious to make his confession and receive communion. I gave him the sacrament of the sick, heard his confession, gave him holy communion and he was very happy when I was leaving. Later that day I heard that he had died. I felt, having heard about that man's death, that being a priest was indeed a fulfilling vocation. It was a real blessing to be able to help people to be at ease with themselves and help them realise that they were always close to God and that God loves them – no matter what. I have had many similar experiences over the years.

Hearing confessions was a whole new experience for me. This

was something you could not rehearse in college; you learned a little from your own experience as a penitent. Many people came along with their usual sins which they had repeated since childhood. Some poured their hearts out and others came to talk about a crisis in their lives – difficulties in a marriage relationship or a family dispute. All human life was there. The number of people going to confession among the faithful has declined considerably in the last ten to fifteen years, except in places like Lough Derg and Knock and around liturgical holy days during the year. Very few come to confession nowadays compared to 1971. Today confession is heard most often in a bright room or at the altar rails – and takes the form of a celebration of the outpouring of God's love and forgiveness rather than an ordeal to be gone through.

The three months in Enniskillen passed by very quickly. That short stint certainly introduced me to the real life of a diocesan/secular priest in an Irish parish. It was busy but I wondered if the Second Vatican Council had made any difference in the way the church was organised at parish level. As far as I could see, the structures were the same as ever and there was no involvement of the laity in the life of the parish – except in a peripheral way in groups like the St Vincent de Paul and the Legion of Mary. I had not had trouble with any of the priests. There was a good spirit in the house – but I think it was the hierarchical and seniority system that annoyed me most. Even at the table we sat in seniority! I was to learn a lot more about seniority in the years to follow. It was on seniority that parish priests were appointed, which meant that you would be almost sixty years of age when your turn came around. It also meant in those days that a man who had spent all his life as a teacher was taken out of a school and made a parish priest with little or no experience of parish work.

IN SUMMER 1971 I was asked by the bishop to teach religion in a vocational school in Monaghan and to engage with the youth of the town. The chaplain who had been there before me, Eugene McCabe, was killed in a car crash earlier that year. I looked forward to this new challenge; I was responsible for the religious formation of a large number of young people. For many it would be the only contact they would have with a priest.

In September I moved my belongings to the Beechhill nursing home in Monaghan town, where I was to live for the next year or so. As well as teaching religion in the vocational school, I was to be chaplain at Beechhill convent and nursing home. It was also a maternity hospital run by a religious order of nuns. I had to say mass there most mornings during the week.

I enjoyed teaching religion and celebrating the liturgy with the students on special occasions. However, I did not like the idea of the rigid and structured timetable of school. I had that all my life in schools and colleges and I wanted to get away from it. The vocational school in Monaghan was mixed religion and so were the staff. I thought it was great to see pupils of different religious traditions mixing and getting on so well. It was a new experience for me coming from a situation where there was tension between Catholics and Protestants – even when they attended the same school as they did in Enniskillen Technical College.

If religious education is about anything it is about tolerance and respect for others, people of different faiths and traditions, nations and groups. It is about learning to celebrate diversity and I am glad to say that was the way it was in the vocational school in Monaghan during my time there. In religious education class we discussed issues like world poverty, the sacraments and other religions, and we explored our own Catholic beliefs. It was quite a change from the way religion was taught when I was at school. I felt that a good deal of what went for religious education was a form of indoctrination. There was no discussion and no reference to other faiths. I wanted to adopt a more open approach to religious education, encouraging the young people to ask questions.

I believed that if they did, their faith would be healthier and more solidly based.

I heard a teacher say that you cannot teach people what to believe but you can teach understanding. Education is about understanding and respect. Otherwise, it becomes indoctrination. It has sometimes been said that Catholic education is a form of indoctrination. I would hate to think that children were being indoctrinated in any of our schools. Equally, I would not like to think that children did not have the opportunity to explore all these great issues at school and have an opportunity to discover how wonderful they are as human beings. A teacher I once knew used to say that education was about teaching young people how to think, not what to think.

Sometimes someone in the religion class asked a question about the conflict in the north and we would talk about it but otherwise we steered clear of the subject. I tried to teach the young people about the Christian values of respect and tolerance. I was acutely aware that this was something the unionist government in Belfast failed to show towards Catholics in the six counties. I was also conscious of the injustice of internment without trial as my neighbours were still locked up in Long Kesh. Some of them went on hunger strike to establish that they were political prisoners and not criminals. That distinction has always been at the heart of the republican struggle in Ireland.

On 4 December 1971 a loyalist gang placed a bomb in McGurk's bar in North Queen Street, Belfast. Fifteen people were killed and many were injured. A group calling itself 'The Empire Loyalists', a cover name for the UVF, claimed it. This was the worst atrocity so far in the conflict. The owner of the pub, who lost his wife and young daughter in the explosion, said that he forgave those who planted the bomb.

ON CHRISTMAS EVE 1971 I arranged with the prison chaplain to go to Long Kesh to say midnight mass. It was only a few months after Brian Faulkner had introduced internment without trial and the Catholic community was still in shock. Long Kesh reminded me of what I had read about the Nazi concentration camps, where prisoners were locked up not knowing what was going to happen to them. There was plenty of barbed wire and bright lights, Alsatian dogs with armed guards. There were lookout posts all over the place. I thought there was no hope of anyone ever escaping from here. I have since discovered that prisoners can be very inventive and courageous. That is how there have been some spectacular escapes from what was described as 'the most secure prison in Europe'.

Many of the prisoners that I met in Long Kesh were anxious about their families and loved ones. Some had been through internment before, in the 1940s and 1950s, and were better able to cope. The older men helped to sustain the morale of the younger people for whom this was a very new experience. I learned that there were some other people interned whom I knew, one who had been a student in Maynooth with me.

At midnight mass I saw that the morale of the prisoners was very high – in spite of the uncertainty and the grim conditions in which they were held. During the mass I read from the prison letters of Dietrich Bonhoeffer, a Methodist minister and theology teacher who at thirty-seven years of age was put in jail by the Nazis in 1943 and executed in 1945 for plotting to assassinate Hitler. Bonhoeffer's contacts through the Abwehr had alerted him and his co-conspirators to the military's dissatisfaction with Hitler and had reassured the plotters that Hitler's death would split the military from the Nazi Party, effectively ending the war. Bonhoeffer's own role in the plot was to use his ecumenical contacts in the United States and Britain to gain assurances that the allies would not exploit Hitler's death to mount a devastating attack, to ensure that the coup would lead to peace. I read from his letter to his parents dated 17 December 1943:

> There's probably nothing for it but write you a Christmas letter now to meet all eventualities. Although it passes my comprehension that they may possibly still keep me here over Christmas, I've learnt in the past eight and a half months that the unexpected often happens and that what can't be changed must be accepted with a 'sacrificium intellectus' ... Above all you mustn't think that I'm going to let myself be depressed by this lonely Christmas; it will always take its special place among the other unusual Christmases that I've kept in Spain, America and England and I want in later years to look back on the time here, not with shame but with a certain pride. That's the only thing no one can take from me.

That night in Long Kesh, we sang Christmas carols and other Christmas songs. It was an emotional experience for all of us. I drove to Fermanagh that night and arrived in the early hours of the morning. My head was full of thoughts about what had just taken place in the jail and about what was happening in our country. I knew that something very serious would happen if the government kept these young men locked up indefinitely.

I knew from that night onwards that it was now a very challenging situation for me as a priest who could see what was happening and as someone who saw a grave injustice being done to one section of the population. I could not remain silent about that blatant injustice. I felt angry about it and about the poor response of the church leaders. Where were they? What had they to say about this? Were they in agreement with the government?

The next day I wrote a letter to the papers about my experience in Long Kesh that night. It was the first letter I ever wrote to the papers. The *Irish News* published the letter the following week. I described the moving experience of saying midnight mass in Long Kesh. I compared the prison to a Nazi concentration camp – with the barbed wire and the guards and the dogs everywhere. I contrasted the high morale of the prisoners with the hostile attitude of the prison warders and the hostile environment in which they were being held. I concluded that Long Kesh was a microcosm of 'Northern Ireland', for in this statelet we were all prisoners.

After the experience in Long Kesh on that Christmas evening in 1971, I was determined to support the prisoners and their families as best I could. I went to Long Kesh prison on many Sundays to say mass with the prisoners and found it a demanding but rewarding ministry. I wanted to keep in touch with the prisoners from County Fermanagh, who often felt isolated in that depressing place. Their families made huge sacrifices to visit them and bring them food parcels.

There were four or five other priests going to Long Kesh every Sunday. These were priests who happened to be free from parish duties and were available to the full-time chaplain. We usually said two masses in two different compounds. There were ten or twelve compounds, with over a hundred prisoners in each – forty in each of the nissen huts. There were twenty beds on each side of the hut. The internees appointed one of their men 'to look after' the priest. Mass was always well attended and the men were fully involved saying the words of the Eucharistic Prayer along with the celebrant – something I never experienced anywhere else. After the second mass, there was time for tea and a chat. The prisoners shared their home-made bread which they had received in food parcels brought by visitors the day before. I sometimes was asked to bring in cigarettes.

A week or so after that Christmas experience in 1971 I went to a conference in Maynooth about peace and justice. Des Wilson was there as an invited speaker. Garret Fitzgerald from Fine Gael, who was to become taoiseach, was also one of the speakers and I remember being very angry at his arrogant tone. I tried to express my annoyance but it did not come out right. This was all new to me – debating our conflict with Irish politicians who thought they knew it all and who refused to place the responsibility for the situation with the British and the unionist ascendancy. Fitzgerald has often been presented as some kind of an intellectual who has a better understanding of the northern situation than most. The arrogance of these people – especially in Fine Gael – is very annoying.

The week after the conference in Maynooth I attended another meeting – this time of northern priests in Dungannon. This was an altogether more positive experience in that the priests in attendance were talking about the realities of repression and harassment of the Catholic people and they were seeking ways of showing opposition to what the British and unionist governments were doing. There had been several meetings of priests from around the north. They had written many letters to Cardinal Conway urging him and the Irish bishops to issue an unequivocal condemnation of torture and internment without trial. Of course, they did not issue such a condemnation. If they had it might have helped to give people hope that their religious and moral leaders were speaking out for them. It might also have persuaded the Dublin government to take a firmer line with the British.

After the introduction of internment and the violent reaction, many nationalists came south of the border for safety. The influx of northern people began to have an impact on the towns and communities all along the border from Derry to Newry. Quite a few northerners had come to live in Monaghan, which is only about twenty miles from Armagh city. Some had been threatened by the RUC or unionist death squads, others were 'on the run' from the RUC and British army or the unionist death squads. They found a few sympathetic people in Monaghan and in other towns like Clones, Dundalk and Castleblaney who provided accommodation and work. I came to know many of these displaced people at that time.

The unionists, organised in paramilitary groups, had already begun targeting places in the twenty-six counties along the border. It was suspected that there were a number of loyalist/unionist

sympathisers living in the south, especially in counties Monaghan, Cavan and Donegal. In those early years of the conflict,
Monaghan was to become known as the 'county of intrigue' because of all the British undercover activity going on there.

Around that time, the gardaí in Monaghan began to take a
special interest in anyone they thought was associated with republicanism, especially the young fellas who lived in the town and
in particular in the Tully estate. From that time on the greatest
'crime' in the twenty-six counties was to be a republican or even
to show sympathy for republicans. I thought for a while that the
gardaí were obeying orders from the Dublin government, first
Fianna Fáil led by Jack Lynch and then Fine Gael led by Liam
Cosgrave. Imagine my shock when I discovered some of them
were also obeying orders from MI5 – the British secret service!

A young teenager called Jim Lynagh used to tell me about the
harassment and beatings he and others received from the gardaí.
His parents, who were strong and active Catholics, also expressed
their concerns to me about this situation. The young people were
angry and I was not sure how it would end.

It was clear to me coming from the north that when internment without trial was introduced many young republicans had
made up their minds that armed resistance was the only adequate
response to this act of war on the Irish people of the six counties.
There was nothing that I could have done to stop this happening. Others in the nationalist community and some human rights
activists, while understanding the reasons for armed action, felt it
was necessary to use peaceful means to protest against the injustice of internment without trial.

On Sunday, 30 January 1972 some courageous people decided
to hold a peaceful public march against internment in Derry. As
usual the march was banned by the Stormont regime. The previous day I was in Dublin for my cousin's wedding. I had thought
about going to Derry but it was not possible to get there from

Dublin after the wedding. I came back to Monaghan on Sunday afternoon, the day of the anti-internment march, and heard on the evening news that there was serious violence in Derry and that some people had been shot by British soldiers. When I heard the next morning that thirteen men had been shot dead by British paratroopers on the streets I was very angry. I felt outraged in a way that I do not think I had ever felt before. Seventeen others were seriously injured that day, one of whom, John Johnston, died the following June.

I knew that this massacre of the innocents would affect all the nationalist people in Derry and throughout Ireland in a way that nothing had before. For me it was confirmation that the British army was not neutral and could not bring about an end to 'the troubles'. I believed that its presence would only further exacerbate the situation.

The next day I went to school but I was not in the mood for talking the usual small talk, I felt so upset. Only one or two of the teachers talked about what had happened in Derry. One, who did not hide his republican beliefs, was in an angry mood. He decided on the spur of the moment to take his class to the centre of Monaghan town to protest outside the courthouse about what had happened in Derry. I admired him for his concern – but it was to be the end of the road for that teacher in the school.

I went to the funerals in Derry of the thirteen victims of Bloody Sunday. I felt I had to be there to show my solidarity with the people and with the organisers of the anti-internment march. There was a huge crowd both at the church, St Mary's, and in the city cemetery overlooking the river Foyle. The scene in St Mary's was the most emotional I had ever seen with thirteen coffins in front of the main altar. As well as sadness, I was still feeling angry deep down. I met up with Fr Tom O'Gara, who had been a witness to the horrific killings and had tended to some of the dying. He was clearly still in shock at what he had seen. We were all growing up very fast.

Walking away from the city cemetery that day I knew that all had changed utterly for me and more especially for my country.

# 6

# Bloody Sunday – Solidarity with the People

It was almost twelve months since I was ordained and I could hardly take in all that had happened in that time. Nothing had prepared me for this kind of terrifying war situation and nothing could have prepared me for what was to come. I began to see my role as a priest in a new light. It was to show solidarity with the people who were being attacked and abused by the state and the forces of the state. I felt compelled to support the prisoners and the families of those locked up in prison without trial.

I was still feeling the pain and the shock of Bloody Sunday and felt it was important to do something to show solidarity with the people of the Bogside. So a few of us organised a holiday for children from the district in March 1972 – just before St Patrick's day. I asked some people in the Monaghan youth club to help. The response was wonderful. I had been in contact with my friend, Tom O'Gara, in Derry and he got a few people there to organise the children they thought most in need of a break. The young people in Monaghan were enthusiastic about the whole idea and the adults showed great generosity and made the Derry people very welcome in their homes. It was a short respite for them but it showed that people outside of Derry and especially people in the twenty-six counties really cared about what was happening in the north. (Tragically, one of the young girls from

Derry, Kathleen Feeney, was shot dead the following year when she was caught in crossfire.)

The evening that the Derry children left Monaghan – whether by coincidence or design I do not know – there was a confrontation in Monaghan between gardaí and local youths. This was the beginning of a period of hostile relations between some young people in Monaghan and a section of the gardaí. Many young people in Monaghan were incensed about what happened in Derry on Bloody Sunday. It had touched a raw nerve. Occasionally, some young fella would shout anti-British and pro-republican slogans when the gardaí came around. The young people were then arrested and taken to the garda station. I realised at this time after Bloody Sunday that the conflict in the north was going to have an effect in border areas within the twenty-six counties. There were strong ties of family with people in the north; there was an emotional bond with nationalists/Catholics in the six counties that you would not find to the same extent further south.

In Monaghan town I used to meet some republicans who were based there in one of the hotels. We discussed various political ideas and options that might produce a settlement and an end to the violent conflict. After all, many of them were 'on the run' and it was in their interest to have an early settlement – but they always said it had to be an honourable settlement. The war had caused great disruption in their lives, resulted in the deaths and imprisonment of many of their comrades. Some of them were floating the idea of a federal Ireland as a way of persuading the unionists that their best interests lay in a united Ireland with devolved government in each of the provinces. A federal system, these republicans argued, would give the unionists a real stake in the country and real power. I found it interesting that some people in the republican movement were thinking and talking in such terms about a political solution in 1972. However, nobody was listening to them. They were not in communication with the leaders of Irish nationalism in Dublin. In fact, the authorities in Dublin were doing all in their power to have them all locked up. We were often told in the media that the republicans had no political ideas and had nothing to offer. It seemed to me even then that they were the only people putting forward ideas that might move the situation forward and bring an end to the violence. It took a very long time for that fact to get through to the politicians in Dublin. They, along with the British, were pursuing their own political agenda.

After Bloody Sunday in Derry in 1972, some of the worst state violence against the nationalist community took place in north and west Belfast and in towns and villages along the border. On 9 July 1972 a Catholic priest, Fr Noel Fitzpatrick, and two others – sixteen-year-old John Dougal and thirty-year-old Patrick Butler – were shot dead in Ballymurphy in west Belfast as they went to the aid of Margaret Gargan, a thirteen-year-old schoolgirl who had been shot by the British army. Following on Bloody Sunday in Derry, the British prime minister, Ted Heath, who came under pressure from around the world and especially from Irish-America, closed down the Stormont government in March 1972 and replaced it with direct rule from Westminster. Several British ministers were appointed to run the six counties – or 'the province' as they called it. Unionist/loyalist death squads continued to kill Catholics simply because of their religion. All Catholics were considered 'treacherous' or 'traitorous'.

In July 1972, a notorious unionist death squad known as 'the Shankill Butchers' claimed their first victim, a thirty-four-year-old Catholic, Francis Arthurs. He was captured, stabbed and left to die. Many more Catholics were to suffer a similar fate at the hands of this notorious gang.

It was clear that British undercover agents were very active during these months carrying out Kitson-style counter-insurgency attacks. Up until 1972, most of the killings had been in Belfast and

Derry. The British army had in recent months been posted in large numbers all along the border – with the approval of the Dublin government.

The IRA re-organised in the border counties and the action shifted to border towns and villages such as Newry, Roslea, Newtownbutler, Clones, Derrylin, and Belleek. In June 1972 two British soldiers were killed near Roslea; in August two more soldiers were killed near Lisnaskea and two UDR men were killed in Enniskillen. As I saw it at the time, the British had provoked a violent reaction by all their violent actions since 1969 and especially by their premeditated attack on unarmed civilians in Derry on Bloody Sunday.

I felt a sense of deep regret when the IRA killed local people. I did not think they should be singled out in this way and thought it could only provoke more bloodshed as well as greater bitterness in the community. In September 1972 Thomas Bullock, a member of the Ulster Defence Regiment (UDR), and his wife Emily were killed near the border at Aghalane, Derrylin. On 22 October a UDR man, John Bell, was killed by the IRA near Newtownbutler. After these killings, I was dreading the retaliation and, sure enough, it came swiftly from the British army.

Two days later, on 24 October, members of the Argyll and Sutherland regiment killed two farmers on a farm near Newtownbutler by stabbing them – making it look like it was a loyalist reprisal. The two Fermanagh farmers, James Naan, aged thirty-five, and twenty-five-year-old Andrew Murray, were found stabbed to death at a farmhouse near Newtownbutler the day after they were killed. At first, it was thought that loyalists were responsible. A local author, Eugene McCabe, based a story on this hypothesis, which was subsequently made into a television documentary.

Throughout 1972 it was clear that there was now a concerted and well-organised assault on members of the nationalist community. The Dublin government sat on its hands while Catholics were being attacked. In December of that year, in the village of Killeter, County Tyrone, not far from my own home village of Ederney, a young woman, Kathleen Dolan, was killed as she walked across the street when a loyalist car bomb exploded outside the post office. She was on her way to post her wedding invitations.

A few days later on 15 December 1972 a young man from Donagh near Lisnaskea, Louis Leonard, was shot dead in his butcher shop in Derrylin and his body placed in the fridge. It was only when he had not returned home from work that his wife, Betty, became anxious and raised the alarm. His brother found the body in the fridge the following day. In the months leading up to his death Louis had been harassed by British soldiers and a week before he was killed a British army captain threatened him. Nobody was ever brought to justice for this killing.

These killings by the British and their agents instilled great fear in the Catholic community, which, of course, was the intention. There was also a growing sense of anger that the British and their agents could get away with killing Catholics at random. Of course, the British propaganda machine was busy emphasising that the IRA was responsible for all the deaths. The Dublin Fianna Fáil government led by Jack Lynch was weak. They were not willing to create an international situation to show northern nationalists that they were concerned about their plight. Had they acted at that time they might have stopped the escalation of the war in the north.

I was still teaching in the vocational school in Monaghan and organising the youth club in the town. To reduce the boredom of teaching I used to play records (vinyl in those days) in the class and then talk about their meaning. Occasionally I brought in the guitar and sang a few songs. I also began singing at concerts in and around Monaghan town with a friend on the teaching staff, Teddy Taylor. Teddy was a wonderful guitar player. I had written a few songs and we made a record together in a very basic recording studio one evening before Christmas. We thought it would sell better at Christmas. Unfortunately, it did not make it into the charts! (Sadly, Teddy passed away some years ago. What a loss to his family and friends and the music world. He was rated one of the best jazz guitarists in Ireland.)

It was in the youth club that I met a new breed of young people, such as Jim Lynagh, who were being affected by what was happening a few miles up the road in Armagh, Tyrone and Fermanagh. They were now clearly in sympathy with the IRA approach of attacking British soldiers and RUC. The local gardaí were aware of this. In the youth club we organised games, music classes and drama. It brought together young people from all the different schools and social backgrounds. It was an uphill struggle to keep it going and to keep everybody happy. It did not really have the support and resources needed to facilitate the number of young people in the town. Monaghan was a fairly prosperous market town and did not suffer economically as much as Clones and other border towns because of the conflict in the north.

I continued to travel to Long Kesh on Sundays to celebrate mass with the internees. A year after internment was introduced there were about 1,000 men interned without trial and after two years the number had risen to 2,000. About twenty women were interned in Armagh. The Catholic bishops of Ireland remained silent about this immoral situation. I believed that they were now clearly on the wrong side and they had shown this by their silence.

On 28 December 1972, as this terrible year came to a close, I received a message that my cousin's house and pub near Pettigo had been blown up by a bomb. Miraculously, even though the roof was blown off the house by the force of the explosion, none of the nine children or their parents was physically injured. The British undercover were really busy that year and were using agents in the UVF to carry out their dirty work. That same night, a UVF bomb went off on Main Street, Belturbet, killing two people, and another went off in Clones, injuring some more. It was one of many bombs planted by the UVF in Clones around that time which first led to suspicions that some local people in the Clones area were sympathetic to the UVF and were making it easy for them to carry out their activities south of the border.

I went to visit my cousins in Pettigo the day after the bombing. They had already moved into the old house where they used to live. The parents were just thankful that none of the children was killed or injured. It was miraculous, considering the state of the house that had been bombed. Most of the children were too young to understand the full import of it all.

(Altogether in 1972, 467 people were killed. There were 10,628 shootings and 1,853 bombs. For the first time the RUC began firing lethal plastic bullets and an eleven-year-old boy, Francis Rowntree, was killed by one of these. He was the first of many to be killed by these deadly bullets fired indiscriminately by the RUC.)

When the ceasefire broke down in 1972 the IRA resumed bombing of commercial property. On 21 July the organisation exploded a number of bombs in Belfast. Eleven people were killed and more than a hundred injured. Before the end of July the IRA exploded three car bombs in the small village of Claudy in County Derry resulting in the deaths of nine people. In Newry, nine more people were killed in an IRA bomb at the customs post.

In the first three weeks of August the IRA planted over 100 bombs. We were clearly in a war situation. The world seemed not to care. The United Nations offered no help. British propaganda presented the armed insurrection as a terrorist threat to democracy.

I had to cross the border frequently to get to my home in Fermanagh. I think that I must hold some kind of record for the number of times I was stopped and the time I spent at British army checkpoints!

# 7

# Remembering my Cousin, Michael Leonard

On 18 May 1973 I returned from the youth club to St Macartan's college, where I was now living. One of the priests was waiting to talk to me, which I thought was a bit odd since it was quite late. He sat me down and told me that he had received 'bad news', a phone call to tell me that my cousin, Michael Leonard, had been shot by the police in County Fermanagh and seriously injured. He then told me he had in fact died. It took me a while to take in what he was saying. I was numb for a while. I phoned home and discovered that it was true but there were no more details.

The next day I went to Ederney and heard some further details of how he was shot by the RUC and waited so long for medical attention that he bled to death. I was angry when I heard that he had been shot in the back while he drove his car towards Pettigo. I went that day to the chief inspector of the RUC in Kesh to vent my disgust. I accused him and his officers of murder. He protested that it was 'an accident' by a young police officer. He said that his gun slipped as the Land Rover was pursuing Michael and the bullets had hit him in the back. I did not believe him.

Michael Leonard was twenty-three years old and lived with his father and mother on a farm in the townland of Tievemore near Pettigo. A well-known cattle dealer in Donegal and Fermanagh, Michael was one of six children. His father, Maurice, was my mother's older brother. I had grown up with his family and used to spend summer holidays in his house when I was young. He was a lively young fellow – a few years younger than me – and great fun to be with. I remember that he could never sit still; he was always walking about when he came into his own house or any house. He had spent some years at St Macartan's college in Monaghan and was known to most of the teaching staff where I was now living. Engaged to a woman from Ederney whom he had planned to marry the following year, all his dreams and plans were cut short that May afternoon on the road from Letter to Pettigo. After he was shot, he was eventually taken to the Erne hospital, Enniskillen where he was pronounced dead and where a post mortem was held.

The funeral cortege from the hospital in Enniskillen to his home in County Donegal was one of the biggest ever seen in Fermanagh. Large numbers attended the wake during the next few days. Michael's father, Maurice, was well known all over the north-west in cattle-dealing circles. People also knew him as a great storyteller and singer. There was never a dull moment in his company but now he was in deep shock and sorrow. Maureen, Michael's mother, was in a similar state. It could be said that until she died many years later she never fully recovered from the shock of her son's killing, or 'murder' as she called it.

The funeral mass, which took place in the small church in Lettercran near his home was attended by a huge crowd. The bishop had instructed that the parish priest of Belleek/Pettigo, Fr Dan Ward, was to be the main celebrant and that my cousin, Seán McGrath, and I were to be con-celebrants. The words spoken by the parish priest were carefully chosen and typically measured as not to cause too much offence to the authorities.

There were all kinds of rumours and stories about the shooting – that Michael had driven through a checkpoint after he came out of Rowe's shop. There was no evidence for any of this. Another cousin had just been released from Long Kesh where he had been interned. I now believe that the killing of Michael Leonard was a well-timed operation and not the 'chance' or accidental killing that the RUC claimed at the time.

After the killing I was convinced more than ever that the RUC was a very dangerous and ruthless outfit, not just among some individuals on the ground but at the very top – and it was politically controlled. I was determined after that to do whatever I could to reveal the truth about this organisation. I knew too well that this was going to be difficult since it might give the impression that I supported the armed campaign against them. At the time of Michael's funeral, I made it clear in the press that his killing should not be used as an excuse for retaliation.

An inquest about a year afterwards concluded that a policeman shot Michael Leonard 'accidentally' when his automatic gun slipped as the Land Rover hit a bump on the road. I was sceptical even then about this explanation. In view of all that has been revealed since I do not believe this story. I often wondered why the police would go to such lengths to stop somebody in relation to previous motoring offences. Surely, they could have stopped Michael Leonard any day of the week as he was often in Fermanagh to see his girlfriend as well as on business.

It is clear to me that the British government was engaged in a two-pronged approach to the insurgency – a political/propaganda approach and a military approach as defined by Frank Kitson, the counter-insurgency 'expert'. The political approach was to make proposals for power-sharing and curry favour with the Catholic church and the Catholic middle-class and have them denounce the IRA and anybody else seeking radical change as 'wreckers of the peace' and supporters of terrorism!

The military approach was to target 'suspects', especially young people around the border areas, and keep the pressure on them to frighten them and deter them from joining the IRA. It seems clear to me now that when my cousin was killed by the RUC there was another agenda and that it was in the context of a shoot-to-kill policy as advocated by Kitson. The RUC and British army were on red alert for IRA members and were to shoot suspects on sight. There were other civilians killed at that time to teach 'the rebellious Irish' a lesson. The purpose from their point of view was to create a climate of fear and convince the world it was the IRA that was ultimately responsible for all the killings. They hoped that by pursuing this policy the grassroots would turn against the IRA. The Catholic bishops and middle-class Catholics who supported the SDLP played along with this duplicitous British policy.

After Michael Leonard's funeral, I returned to the vocational school in Monaghan but was finding it difficult to concentrate on my work, with all that was going on in my life and in the country. Five British soldiers were killed by the IRA in a bomb at Knock na Moe hotel in Omagh on the day Michael Leonard died. Two weeks later, a young RUC man was killed on patrol in Enniskillen. A few weeks after that in Belfast a unionist death squad brutally murdered SDLP man Paddy Wilson and his secretary, Irene Andrews. This was a dark and dangerous time and it was to continue for many more years – because nobody was prepared to deal with the root causes. There were plenty of condemnations of the IRA but no analysis of why the IRA was once again involved in a military campaign.

Few of the teachers in the school were prepared to talk about the conflict in the north, except to remark how dreadful it all was. One of the teachers, Eddie O'Donnell, used to give out to me and say the Catholic bishops were not doing enough to help those under attack and that their statements were not helping the situation. I eventually got annoyed with him one day and told him that he should go and complain to the bishop himself and not to me. He said that he would be prepared to go to the bishop and he asked me to arrange a meeting. The bishop agreed to meet Eddie and a number of other republicans, including Kevin Mallon, who was living in Monaghan at the time. I believed it was an earnest effort on their part to find a way forward.

I went with the delegation to the bishop's house and left having made the introductions. In hindsight, I should have insisted on staying for the meeting but the bishop had chosen another priest to sit in. I was hoping there might be some kind of useful discussion but the meeting did not last long and was not productive. I met Eddie and the rest of the republican delegation in the Oriel hotel later than evening. They told me that the meeting broke down after about five or ten minutes. The bishop simply repeated the official position of the Irish bishops towards republican violence.

The republicans were well aware by then of the official attitude and the hostility of the Irish bishops down the years. Kevin Mallon, a veteran republican, left the bishop in no doubt about the republican position and republican intentions. If nobody else took on the British, they would carry on the fight, he told him, until they got their rights. I spoke to the bishop some time afterwards – and he confirmed what I had been told – he felt there was no further point in talking to these men. I thought this was a wrong attitude to adopt in the situation. It would only further alienate the republicans and convince them that nobody in a position of power or influence was willing to listen sympathetically to their arguments and their analysis of the situation.

It was my belief then that, in the critical situation that had emerged, something more than ritualistic condemnations of violence was required from the Irish bishops and the Dublin government. Unfortunately, nothing more creative or more imaginative ever occurred – except on those occasions when a few Protestant clergy initiated meetings with republican leaders. All through the years the bishops, and especially their spokesman on the north, Cahal Daly, continued to issue condemnations of the IRA and refused to meet with Sinn Féin leaders when asked to do so.

The weakness of the Irish bishops' response to the British

government-sanctioned torture of prisoners and internment without trial was plain for all to see. They were not willing to speak out, which was wrong and could not be tolerated. They engaged in 'behind the scenes moves', which were never effective and only encouraged the British. The official church behaved in a similar way in South Africa – until a few church leaders like Archbishop Hurley of Durban began to speak out.

There was not a single bishop in Ireland at that time prepared to go out on a limb and unequivocally condemn the British. After 1987, Cardinal Ó Fiaich came close but felt too vulnerable because of the stance of some of the other bishops to challenge the traditional role of the Irish hierarchy. I spoke to him and he did not want to cause any trouble within the Bishops' Conference or at the Vatican, so he had to be circumspect in what he said in public. He was aware that the British were keeping a close eye on him and that his statements were being reported to Rome.

The armed resistance of the re-grouped IRA continued for more than twenty years. This was a period that none of us who lived close to it will forget. The trouble with war is that, once it starts, it is very difficult to stop unless one side surrenders. The late Helder Camara, bishop of Recife in Brazil, talked a lot about the 'spiral of violence'. There was a long history in Ireland of armed resistance to British occupation and repression from 1798 onwards. In every country seeking freedom from British colonial rule, armed struggle was often considered to be the only solution. The civil rights movement tried a different approach – to bring about justice and equality through peaceful means. Many republicans were convinced that it was not possible to bring about equality within a unionist-dominated six counties. The unionists were too entrenched and the British government too arrogant to bring about any effective reforms. Republicans knew that after Bloody Sunday, anyone who thought about organising a peaceful protest had to consider the risk of people being beaten or shot down on the streets.

Those who believed in militant republicanism held to the principle that as a last resort they had the right to take up arms to end British tyranny in Ireland. Some of them saw it in the context of the old Catholic moral principle of the lesser of two evils. Republicans believed that those who governed in Westminster and those involved in the British military were just as ruthless as during the period of the Black and Tans (1918–21). The British were experts at propaganda.

In January 1973 about twenty women were interned without trial in Armagh jail. That summer a number of schoolboys aged fifteen years were also interned. There was no public outcry in the twenty-six counties, in the international community, or from Catholic church leaders.

On 20 January 1973 a car bomb planted in Dublin by British agents exploded, killing one person and injuring thirteen. The Fine Gael/Labour government under Cosgrave came to power the following month and went on an all-out offensive against the republican movement. They refused to confront the British government, which was behind the bomb in Dublin.

After two years' teaching in Monaghan vocational school, I was fairly sure that teaching was not what I wanted to do with my life. I spoke to the bishop, Dr Mulligan, and told him that I would prefer to work in a parish. He had received a request from the bishop of Down and Connor for priests to help there and he asked if I'd be interested in working in a parish in Belfast for a few years. I told him that I was willing to go but it turned out they wanted me to teach in a secondary school – so we both turned that down. My bishop had already filled my old job in Monaghan and now he had no parish available for me. In September 1973 he asked me to help out in the parish of Lisnaskea and to teach religion in the local secondary school, St Comhgalls. I was happy enough to be going back to my native county and I accepted the new placement enthusiastically.

Even though I had made many good friends in Monaghan, I felt it was time to move on. Most of the people there did not really understand the anger and frustration of nationalists in the six counties. In general, they were misinformed in the Irish media. Of course, many good people in Monaghan were understanding and sympathetic; they also understood our history of British oppression. One man in particular stands out in my memory and that was Paddy Turley, editor of the local newspaper, *The Northern Standard*.

# 8

# Frank, Charlie and Fr Tom

In the dark times there will also be singing. There will also be singing in the dark times.

– Bertholt Brecht

Soon after I arrived in Lisnaskea in September 1973 I renewed my friendship with two great characters I had met some years earlier: Frank Maguire (who was later to be elected MP for Fermanagh/South Tyrone) and Charlie McNally, a well-known actor and entertainer in the area. They were at this time both involved in a second-hand car sales business. Since my own car was the worse for wear, I was persuaded by Frank Maguire to buy a 'new' second hand car from them. There was no guarantee with these cars, which were imported from England, but Charlie's recommendation that the body was sound and Frank's boast that the engine was 'clean' was as good as any guarantee. The first car I bought from them was very sore on petrol and I soon changed it. The second gave me some bother – a lot of bother and caused me to be late for school on a few occasions – so I had to change again, this time for a new car in another garage.

Charlie McNally was then a well-established entertainer and in big demand all over the northern part of the country. He knew that I was fond of singing and entertaining so he asked me to join his troupe. I travelled with him and his group to concerts,

Me, with sisters Pauline and Teresa, at Moneyvriece primary school, 1955

St Micheal's College, 1956–57 [I am in the second row at the far right]

Blessing my mother and father on ordination day

My uncle's wedding in 1942.
From left to right; front row: Joe
Moss, Maurice Leonard, Monty
Valentine and Hugh McGrath.
Middle row: Cissie Valentine,
Annie McGuiness, Annie McGar-
rity, William and Winne (uncle &
aunt), Fr McCormack and Maire
Leonard (my mother).
At the back: Jack Gilligan, Anna
Moss, Alice Gilligan and Bridget
McGarity

Fr Joe, the folk singer

Seán MacBride, Bernadette (McAliskey,) and myself

With Daniel Berrigan, outside Armagh Gaol

With Rev. Brian Smeaton

Des Wilson

At hunger strike memorial in Glasnevin Cemetery

Opening the roads, near Garrison, 1991

The RUC at Kevin Barry O'Donnell's funeral in Coalisland

Kathleen O'Hagan, with Damien (in arms) and Patrick

Rosemary Nelson, Breandán MacCionnaith and Frances McHugh at a meeting in Lisnaskea

or 'shows' as he called them, all over Fermanagh, Tyrone and Donegal. It was great fun. There were characters like Peter Clifford, Frank McManus (known as 'Fiddler' since he belonged to a musical family) and Eileen Mulligan who travelled with Charlie entertaining people during a very bleak time in our history.

One weekend in 1973 Charlie and I went to England to perform at a Fermanagh Association function in London's Irish Centre and at a concert the following night in the town hall in Luton. The London function was a gathering of the great and the good, which I did not enjoy. There was a lot of tension in England at this time following a number of IRA bombs. The proceeds of the Irish concert in Luton were in aid of the prisoners' families. The hall was packed. Frank Maguire was there to say a few words about the prisoners. Before that, I was on stage singing a popular song at the time, 'The Men Behind the Wire'. While I was singing, Charlie, who was the compère, came up behind me on the stage and whispered to finish up and to get off the stage. I thought to myself, I could not be that bad! Then he said in a solemn tone that there was a bomb scare. I stopped singing in the middle of the song and handed the microphone to Charlie to explain what was happening. I made for the nearest 'exit' sign as quickly as I could. Charlie was a nervous man at the best of times and he did not take long in telling the people what was happening before making for the exit door himself. Frank Maguire was standing just inside the door at the back of the hall, very calm, joking away and making sure everyone else was keeping calm. He showed me a large crucifix in his hand and told me that 'everything would be all right'. He brought this crucifix with him in his pocket everywhere he went. He believed it would keep him safe because he was living in extreme danger at that time. He received frequent death threats – but he was undeterred.

Everyone left the hall calmly and orderly and about an hour later Frank came back to the house in Luton where we were staying. He was laughing about the whole thing. He told us the police had searched the building with sniffer dogs and declared it a hoax, which he suspected from the beginning. We concluded that it was probably concocted by the local police and was aimed at the function in the town hall because Frank was billed to attend – and not because I was singing 'The Men Behind the Wire'. I did not sleep well that night. Charlie and I had to get up very early the next morning to fly to Dublin; I had to be in school in Lisnaskea at 9.15 a.m. I was an hour late and told the headmaster that I had a puncture on the way to school. I had to tell a small lie because I could not say that I was just coming from a benefit concert in England.

We had many a laugh about our trip to London and Luton. A day or two later we were performing at a concert in County Monaghan and Charlie called me on stage 'Please welcome Fr Joe, straight from the West End of London.' The audience did not know what he was talking about! I continued to take part in shows with Charlie and Eileen Mulligan for a number of years. It was one way to deal with the tension of the time. We travelled one night as far as Shannon town in County Clare for a concert in the GAA centre. We came straight back that night, arriving home about eight the next morning and did not think anything of it.

I was not long in Lisnaskea when a brother of one of my pupils was killed in an explosion on the border at Anaghgore near Newtownbutler. On 12 October 1973 Raymond McAdam died when a bomb was thrown into a shop where he worked along the border road from Clones to Newtownbutler. I went to the wake and spent time with his family.

Towards the end of 1973 I received word from Derry that one of the children who had been in Monaghan with the Derry group a year earlier – Kathleen Feeney – had been shot dead as she walked along the street on an errand to the shop. A stray bullet hit her during a gun battle between the British army and the IRA.

I was deeply saddened to hear about her untimely death in such tragic circumstances.

I continued to travel to Long Kesh on most Sundays during 1973–74. When priests arrived they were taken in a minibus to the various compounds. The driver of the van was known as 'Snake'. He never stopped talking and complaining. I sensed that the prisoners were not too fond of him. Among those on the minibus I remember Fr Denis Faul, Fr Cunningham, a Dominican priest, Fr Murphy and Fr Tom Toner, the chaplain. I remember going to say mass the Sunday after Long Kesh was burned to the ground on 16 October 1974. That action was provoked by constant harassment and beatings of the prisoners by the British army and the prison warders. The prisoners apologised for the state of the place. Then they gave me detailed descriptions of how the burning happened and how the British reacted brutally. Many of the prisoners were bruised and sore but they were upbeat because they believed that they had gained a lot of publicity for their cause.

AFTER THE YEAR in Lisnaskea my bishop transferred me in 1974 to the parish of Inis Muighe Saimh (Belleek/Garrison), which is situated in north-west Fermanagh on the Fermanagh/Leitrim/Donegal border. It is between Lough Melvin and Lough Erne, surrounded by the Dartry mountains – a beautiful place. It was a new experience for me to be working full-time in a parish. I was sent there because the parish priest was eighty years of age and was, according to the bishop, getting frail and needed help. I was not too long in the parish when I came up against the British army at road checkpoints. These were always scary, especially at night, when I was on my own.

Shortly after I arrived in the place I received a phone call quite late one night to attend to a very ill man at his home. The other priest was on holidays so I went with the local doctor. A British army checkpoint was in place, stopping all vehicles on the main

Garrison–Belcoo road. It was raining. They stopped the doctor, who was in front of me, and they made him get out of the car, take out his medicine case and open it on the road in the rain. He was a quiet man, co-operated and said nothing. They asked me for identification and looked in my boot. I was feeling very angry that we could not go to attend a very ill person without being stopped and searched by these foreigners. I kept my cool on that occasion anyway. I went on then and gave the sacraments to the ill man. He died later that night. For years afterwards his sister reminded me that I had attended to her brother before he died. She was always very grateful – Irish people are like that.

I still kept in contact with my friend, Tom O'Gara, who was a curate in a parish in Derry city. Tom was a pleasant man, always smiling and always ready with a humorous quip. As he walked his whole body moved. He was athletic and was a great soccer player in his day. He was a bright spark and took a science degree in Maynooth. He was only slightly interested in theology – preferring instead to discuss issues of the day with whoever was willing to discuss them. He was a great priest – identifying closely with the people. He was on the streets of the Bogside on Bloody Sunday to comfort the wounded and dying of that fateful day. A photograph of him with his hand to his head looking down at a dead body is part of history. Sometime during the year after Bloody Sunday, Tom was transferred to the Pennyburn parish on the Buncrana road side of Derry city. He became known locally as 'Bomber' after he took over a bus that had been hi-jacked and a bomb placed on it by republicans. Tom drove the bus away from a built-up area to a relatively safe spot where it was made safe.

A short time after that the newly appointed bishop, Edward Daly, told Tom to 'take time out'. Tom arrived up that night to my house in Garrison and spent a few days relaxing and assessing the situation. We went fishing in a boat on Lough Melvin trying to catch some of the famous Gilaroo trout – the fish with a gizzard. We talked about his situation and concluded that for him, after all he had been through in the past few years, a spell in Maynooth might not be such a bad idea. He went back to Maynooth for the year and then returned to the Derry diocese, to the parish of Moville across the border in County Donegal. He became very popular with the people there because of his easy manner and outgoing personality. He was down to earth and a bit unconventional, which endeared him to the people even more. He had his own way of preaching and priesting. His sermons were kind of short stories which left people thinking and wondering. He would tell them about the day he buried a dead dog and he wondered did dogs have souls and if they did what happened after they died. He only ever spoke for a few minutes but people did not forget what he said.

I used to spend as much time as I could with him in Moville, talking and walking along the seashore around that beautiful coastline. He was a really interesting and provocative person, and a great man to spend time with. He liked to sing and he liked conversation. He always liked to be a wee bit controversial – just for the heck of it! We talked a bit about the situation then unfolding in the six counties. I felt obliged in those early days to take a stand, to stand for justice and fair play, alongside the people who were denied their rights. I thought that, as an ordained minister, I could find ways to act in solidarity with people and groups to resist and overcome their oppression. Whenever I could, I tried to help those of a different political persuasion and reached out wherever possible to others of other faiths and stood with them in their concerns and demands for justice.

During my stay in Garrison, 1974–75, I devoted my time to local community development issues – trying to involve the people in the parish and build up a parish community focused on economic and cultural well being. I was becoming familiar with the notion of empowerment. One priest who had made a huge impact in his remote parish of Glencolmcille in County Donegal was Fr James McDyer. I thought if any man could help us he could, so I invited James McDyer to talk at a public meeting in Garrison. I also invited Paddy Doherty from the Bogside in Derry, who was then attempting to set up a centre for alternative learning for young people in the city, and Brian Smeaton, a Church of Ireland priest from Belfast to share their ideas about community development with the local people. It was a good meeting and the people began thinking about what they could do to bring new life to their local community. They were up against it because they were being increasingly isolated as the British government, at the behest of the local unionists, closed all the border roads. There was no strong voice against this policy of closing border roads. It was a difficult time to organise anything because of the constant presence of British soldiers in the area and the destruction of the local infrastructure.

During these years in the Garrison/Belleek parish I came to know some wonderful musicians. This area is steeped in Irish traditional music, as the late Paddy Tunney has recorded. Music sessions made life a little more tolerable during these dark days along the border. I also had contacts in the showband scene and persuaded people like Seán McGrade, who managed a number of good bands, to organise some concerts to bring a bit of excitement and hope into the lives of the young people. We arranged concerts that were open to students from all the schools. The concerts in the schools were a small effort to raise morale at a dark and difficult time. The music kept the spirits up but I knew it was not going to solve the political problem. I was even becoming more despondent as there was no end in sight to the terrible conflict, which was claiming lives almost daily. Some time after this, the women's peace movement led by Mairéad Corrigan and Betty Williams emerged in Belfast in protest against the violence. The main focus was on republican violence – which was only one side of the story.

# 9

# Confronting Church and State

After the experience of four years as a priest I had many questions about the role of the priest in this war situation. I soon realised there were no easy answers. This had always been a controversial issue in Irish history. My instinct was for a pacifist approach to achieving justice in Ireland but I realised, through discussions with republicans, that there was no point in talking pacifism to the IRA while ignoring what the British were doing to the people and especially to Irish republicans. I came to understand that my role, as a priest, was to stand with the people against the reign of terror being inflicted on them by the British government and their agents – the RUC, UDR and their own British soldiers – more than 20,000 of them at this stage.

Taking on the church establishment and speaking out against the traditional alliance of church and state was probably the most difficult of all. However, there was no other way that I could be a priest and witness to the gospel as I understood it. In our situation, Catholics were being discriminated against and unjustly treated by the state. They were being assassinated by pro-British/loyalist murder gangs – aided and abetted by agencies of the British government like MI5.

In September 1975 I decided to take a one-year course in Adult Education at the Mount Oliver Institute in Ravensdale near Dundalk, in one of the most historically interesting and picturesque places in Ireland or anywhere else for that matter.

Dundalk was only a few miles south of the border and had the name of being 'a republican town'. Many northern republicans had come for safety and security when it was not safe to stay in their homes in the six counties. There were a number of students from Australia and New Zealand and some who worked on the missions in Africa and South America and seemed to have a greater understanding of the conflict than the students or teachers from the south. I found a good deal of cynicism among some from Ireland, and not much compassion.

In Dundalk I had time to think, to read and write. I decided to put my thoughts on the conflict in the north on paper for discussion. I published a pamphlet entitled 'Thoughts on Liberation in Ireland' in which I confronted the Catholic hierarchy's support for the status quo. I decided to launch this pamphlet at a press conference in Liberty Hall in Dublin – a place with a lot of significance for Irish republicans and socialists. I invited all the people I had come to know as friends of liberation and justice to come along and we had a bit of a celebration. It was not often that people of a like mind from a religious and political perspective came together. There was good support from people involved with the Student Christian Movement (SCM) in Dublin. Our launch received some publicity in the national press. I felt that I was now able to contribute to the debate about the conflict and our future. I discovered the power of the pen to provoke debate and hopefully to change attitudes.

In December 1976 I attended the first ever conference on the theology of liberation at Townley Hall, Drogheda. It was organised by the SCM – people like Mary Condren, Peadar Kirby and other students. The speakers at the 1976 conference were Tim Hamilton, SJ, Peter McVerry, SJ, John Maguire, a Christian Marxist who lectured in UCD, and Rosemary Radford Reuther from the US. I was most impressed with Rosemary Reuther, who spoke about the development and the growth of feminist theology. I had been brought up in a very male-dominated church and society. The patri-archal system was in place and the patriarchal way of thinking was the dominant one. The feminist liberation theology challenged this entire patriarchal world-view. I was glad to have a chance to meet Rosemary and talk to her about my concerns. I found her very en-couraging in my exploration of a new theology for Ireland.

I had by now become disillusioned with the Irish Catholic hierarchy because of the one-sided attitude to the violence in the north. I was also annoyed by their refusal to implement the teaching of the Second Vatican Council in Ireland. Some were preaching out of the Council of Trent. Their agenda was con-trol. I was so incensed about a report in the *Irish Independent* of a sermon about limbo given by the bishop of Cork, Dr Lucey at a confirmation ceremony, that I wrote a critical letter to the paper. After this, I began sending letters to the national papers and this brought both praise and criticism from predictable quar-ters. There were, as always, some staunch Catholics to defend the bishop no matter what he said:

Sir – With your kind permission, I wish to offer his Lordship, Dr Lucey, Bishop of Cork and Ross, my sincere apologies on the arrogant attack on him in his role as pastor of his flock in the Irish Independent (19/5/'77). Realising the inadequacy of this attempt at reparation, I would ask the people of Cork and Ross to rally to the support of so good a pastor. I will leave Fr McVeigh to others who will be better able to deal with his most unseemly remark. However, when Our Lord sent forth his Apostles to preach the gospel, He said to them, 'He who heareth you heareth Me.' Maybe, Fr McVeigh might reflect on this in the context of his remark. This might also be an opportune time to have an airing publicly of the catechisms produced by the Institute of Religious Education, Mount Oliver, Dundalk (the address given by Fr McVeigh). Vatican II was a pastoral council not a dogmatic one, so in matters of dogma we must refer to the Council of Trent which is still binding. The teaching of the Holy Catholic Church has been that 'nothing defiled can enter Heaven' and as we are all born with this inherited sin called Original Sin, Bap-tism is essential. As you will see from this further quotation of Our Lord himself when he said to Nicodemus, 'Unless you are born again of water and the Holy Ghost you shall not enter the Kingdom of heaven.' Christ is King and the Church is triumphalist and if we try to pretend the

Church is not, what have we in our mind when we say in the Our Father, 'Thy Kingdom Come'. We have assuring us that the church is Triumphalistic, a quotation from Our Lord, 'I have overcome the World' and Our Lady of the Rosary of Fatima concurred when she said, 'My Immaculate heart will Triumph in the end.'

T. Jones, Portmarnock, County Dublin

Another letter went as follows:

Sir – Some of us would like to know who Fr McVeigh imagines himself to be. Quite obviously he has little respect for authority and that lessens his stature as a priest. Perhaps he has read too much of Barth and Kung and too little of St Thomas Aquinas. To sow the seeds of dissension among the faithful is always a serious matter but for a priest to do so is, indeed, reprehensible.

F. J. Murtagh, PC Fairview, Dublin

Sir – I admit Fr Joe McVeigh is a fine singer and an accomplished guitarist. It would seem however, from his derogatory remark in your paper concerning Bishop Lucey of Cork that Fr McVeigh never read the Dogmatic Constitution 'On the church' of the Second Vatican Council. In the Constitution, Chapter 3, Fr McVeigh will read: Among the foremost function of bishops is the preaching of the Gospel. Bishops are heralds of the faith – they bring new disciples to Christ. They are authentic teachers, teachers authorised by Christ – they preach the faith to the people entrusted to them for their belief and for application to morals … Bishops keep their flock from error by watchful attention.

Fr Cyprian Conefrey, OFM, Ennis, County Clare.

It was nice to get the compliment about my singing and guitar-playing! It was a pity he did not think so highly of my prowess as a theologian, but when it came to the subject of limbo, I was no dud. When I read these letters, I could only laugh at the absurdity of it all. I wonder what these gentlemen would have to say today about bishops 'keeping their flocks from error'. It seems to me it might be the other way, the flocks keeping the bishops from error.

I also got into a bit of trouble with the authorities in Mount Oliver for using the Mount Oliver address. They were afraid of the repercussions if it was thought that I in any way represented the views of the college or was speaking from the college. They felt that I was not entitled to use that address since I was only a student in the place. I had then to write another letter to the paper explaining this and stating that my views did not represent the views of Mount Oliver. I also took the opportunity to make a few general points. I stated that I was not against authority but that I was against any person, no matter what his status in the church, taking it upon himself to say who does and who does not get to heaven. I stated that this was a perversion of the gospel of love and nobody but God could judge.

One day I received correspondence from a senior priest in my own diocese of Clogher, now long deceased, in response to a letter I had published in one of the papers. I quote from it:

> Dear Joe,
> First as to Des Wilson for whom you have an obvious sympathy, I think he reacted with too much anger and intemperance. I would go so far as to describe it as arrogance. For that reason his plea can only be regarded as counter-productive as far as the Church is concerned ... About preaching the Gospel of Jesus, it is not primarily a gospel of freedom and justice. It is a gospel of love and selflessness and brotherhood with personal sin looming large and menacing in the background. There is freedom and there is justice in the gospel but they are presuppositions, however, important and even necessary. But the priorities must be observed.
> Yours etc.

Here, in concise language, was the traditional Catholic fundamentalist, pro-establishment interpretation of the gospel, which I was doing my best to challenge. At least this man had the courage to write his views. Others just talked behind my back – a common pastime in Ireland. This man was typical of most of the clergy at the time. They felt it their duty to support the status quo at all costs. The people who professed this kind of theology had close affinities with certain parties not renowned for their forward thinking or radical politics. They supported one or other of the two main parties in the twenty-six counties – Fianna Fáil or

Fine Gael. These were good on rhetoric at times but were bank-rupt when it came to policies to confront injustice – especially the injustice of partition and British occupation and the inequality in Irish society. If you spoke about inequality, they would think you were raving: 'What inequality, for God's sake?'

After the time in Mount Oliver I was more convinced than ever that my role as a priest was to support the struggle for human rights, by taking up the cause of justice and by reaching out to those who considered themselves our 'enemies' in the loyalist working-class community. The ecumenists were reaching out to the middle-class Protestants. I thought it was more important to reach out to the working-class in both communities and engage in dialogue with them. They were the people most alienated from the churches and from society. It is at the edges that the truth is to be found.

It is easy enough to talk about non-violence in the abstract or in an academic setting. It is different when you are trying to put it into practice in the midst of a war. I will always admire the people who worked tirelessly using non-violence for justice and human rights throughout all these years.

I always felt that I was called to work in solidarity with the people working for justice. This sense of solidarity has given me the strength to keep going for many years. One of the great joys of being a priest is being able to connect with all the people who give their lives in the service of the poor and oppressed in many different ways and in many different places. I also find it a joy to be associated with so many wonderful and compassionate people, who are answering the call to work with the poorest of the poor and to be the 'voice of the voiceless'. I admire all those courageous activists for justice throughout the world. I admire all who take the side of the oppressed. Those who resist war and injustice are my soul brothers and soul sisters. Those men and women have inspired me through these difficult years.

Throughout history there had been constant condemnations

by Catholic bishops and clergy of the Irish revolutionaries who fought the British. There are those who saw no other way to defend themselves than to take up arms. They were not prepared to be brutalised and humiliated any longer. Later, there was retrospective approval for the men and women who took up arms. This is a constant theme of our history. Clerics had too often interfered in politics in Ireland as elsewhere, on the side of the powerful against the oppressed, solely in the material interests of the church institution. Apart from being immoral, it was based on an entirely flawed theology that had always supported the status quo as the right thing to do.

Most clergy avoided speaking about social justice issues. One priest from a southern diocese was honest enough to admit the problem: 'In a very real sense Northern Ireland is another country. Priests in the republic are no different from their people, in the level of their ignorance and their apathy. And the further south you go the more likely you are to find a man who knows more about Costa Brava and the Appian Way than he does about the Bogside or the Falls Road."* He was merely expressing the truth about the attitude of most Irish priests to the conflict in the north.

When I was a student in Maynooth I was encouraged and inspired by the leadership shown in various communities throughout Ireland by people like Bishop Peter Birch in Kilkenny, James McDyer in Glencolmcille and Des Wilson in Belfast – all of whom took the side of the people – the poor and oppressed.

However, the official statements of the Irish bishops were predictable and not too sympathetic to the plight of their people in working-class areas of Belfast and Derry. It was the usual condemnation of 'the men of violence' and an entreaty to pray for peace. There was no talk about respect for human rights. Commentators in the Catholic religious press had nothing helpful to say. It was the same old story, as we read in the pro-British press

* Ray Brady, *Intercom Magazine*, April 1992.

about the two warring tribes, the Catholics and the Protestants, who could not live together. There were the usual ritualistic condemnations of 'the men of violence'.

After the year in Dundalk I was asked by my bishop to work in the parish of Monaghan in September 1976. Since I had been there last the town was bombed in 1974, on the same day as Dublin, by a well-organised loyalist/unionist group. It had left a deep scar on the people of Monaghan. Nobody said anything but I sensed the anger and the hurt.

By this time a number of young men from Monaghan town, including Jim Lynagh, had been put in jail accused of membership of the IRA. Monaghan, like Dundalk, was well known as a republican town where many from the six counties had come for refuge. Late one night, not long after I arrived there, a man from Fermanagh arrived at the door of the parochial house. He was on the run and had nowhere to stay. I secured a place for him to stay and put him on a bus for Dublin the next day.

In the parish I tried to introduce some of the ideas I had learned in Mount Oliver, about building community and improving the celebration of the Sunday liturgy. We formed a parish liturgy group and a folk music group for mass. Some of the priests approved and some were not very enthusiastic. For the first time I came up against a number of priests who did not want any innovation. It was a difficult environment to work in. I adjusted the best I could and tried to accept that the older priests were used to doing things their way.

As well as being involved in the parish life, which was my main focus, I maintained contacts with people in the Student Christian Movement and with Brian Smeaton and Des Wilson in Belfast, and others, who were anxious to create a debate about the conflict and offer some alternative thinking to that presented in the media and in the Catholic journals.

In the parish throughout 1977 I heard about the growing hostility between the gardaí and some local republicans and people who were suspected of being republicans. I was kept informed about the harassment of some young people in the parish by gardaí, and heard about the brutality suffered by people while in garda custody. I must say I was a bit shocked at first to hear about the number of beatings and their viciousness because, in my naivety, I never thought that the gardaí would indulge in this kind of behaviour. I was very much aware that it was carried out by the RUC but I did not believe that the gardaí would act in such a manner or be allowed to carry on doing so. I was soon to realise that I was misguided in these beliefs.

On 25 June 1978 I preached at mass in St Macartan's cathedral in Monaghan. In the homily, I made two appeals. The first was for the return of the body of RUC constable, William Turbitt, from County Armagh, if, as it was believed, he had been shot by the IRA. William Turbitt was abducted some weeks before near Monaghan and was presumed dead. I appealed for the return of his body to his family, if republicans knew his whereabouts. Secondly, I appealed to public representatives in Monaghan to speak out against the ill-treatment of people in garda custody.

It was a defining moment in my life as a priest. The consequences were far-reaching and unforeseen. My appeal was made as a result of the public concern about the actions of some gardaí in Monaghan. The previous week a young man I knew was so badly beaten that he had to spend three weeks in hospital. I also appealed for an end to the torture of prisoners in the H-Blocks and called on public representatives to speak out about this issue.

My appeal for the return of the body of Constable Turbitt was made on humanitarian grounds and I felt that since I was showing concern for what was happening to republicans at the time I might be able to influence them to return the policeman's body. I was only slightly aware at the time that some bodies of those killed by republicans had not been returned to their families. I did not know why – I presumed they would all be returned when it was safe for them to do so. Sadly, for a number of families that has not happened.

There was a huge reaction to my sermon in the cathedral, more than I ever could have imagined. I should say that the body of Constable Turbitt was returned a short time later. A leading republican, since deceased, came to me after mass and said that he was touched by my sermon and would do what he could to have the body returned. A short time later, the same republican told me that the body was to be exhumed and returned to the family.

The response to the appeal for the gardaí to stop beating those in custody was unbelievable. I suppose I could say what I liked about the north and about the RUC, but I soon discovered that criticism of the gardaí was not tolerated in this close-knit community in the twenty-six counties. A large number of gardaí lived in Monaghan and many were married into Monaghan families. After mass I was verbally attacked by one woman who told me I was a disgrace for bringing such matters into the pulpit.

In an immediate response to my sermon, the local gardaí 'downed tools' and refused to direct traffic in Monaghan town after masses. They had been doing this for years to maintain traffic flow on the main Derry–Dublin road. The gardaí (Catholic) also refused to pay at church collections. This was their way of putting pressure on the church authorities to do something about me.

A short time after this there was a protest march in Monaghan about the conditions in the H-Blocks. It was organised by a local H-Block committee and there were mainly republicans on the march through the town. There was a strong garda presence. I was standing looking out of the window of the parochial house, as they walked along Park Street. Just then I saw two gardaí grab a woman protester by the hair and throw her into the back of the squad car. I heard later that they had taken another man out of the march and brought him to the garda station. They had beaten him very severely in the barracks, so badly in fact that the priest in charge in Monaghan was called to the barracks to see him. The priest told me later that day that the man had received a severe beating and was barely conscious. He was moved to the hospital. I went to see him the following day and he looked to be in great pain. He remained in hospital for several weeks.

After this, I decided I was not going to remain silent any longer. I wrote to garda headquarters in Dublin; the letter was also signed by Fr Raymond Murray from Armagh and a local teacher. The teacher was visited by the gardaí and threatened with the loss of his job. I made a public statement to the press calling for an inquiry into the activities of the garda 'heavy gang' in Monaghan. This story made the front page of the *Irish Times*.

Garda headquarters decided to hold their own private investigation. They sent a senior garda, Inspector Fanning, and then a deputy commissioner, Joe McGovern, who was originally from Belcoo in County Fermanagh and whom I had met before. He interviewed me at length about the situation. I told him everything I knew and I showed him photos of one young man who had been beaten black and blue while in garda custody. He assured me something would be done about it. He stayed in Monaghan town for about a month but I never heard much about any changes in personnel. The culprits remained in place. The garda special branch and some of the rank and file had been well and truly politicised at this stage – and clearly they had the backing of the government for an all-out assault on republicans in the border areas. There was going to be no serious change of policy while Des O'Malley was justice minister.

The gardaí had a free rein to abuse republicans since the early 1970s. Because of the number of complaints, a Garda Complaints Board was established in 1987. However, it made no difference.

It has been alleged that there were British moles working in the garda síochána. In Richard Deacon's book, *C*, a biography of the head of British intelligence, Michael Oldfield, we read: 'But MI6's main success was in establishing agents inside the Garda, the Irish Army and government departments.' One of the most important informants was a senior garda officer who up to 1981 (at least) was still in the force. He not only provided information on the IRA but on the activities of the former taoiseach, Mr Haughey, and other prominent political figures. The man they called 'the Badger' from Monaghan was an MI6 agent since the early 1970s and when interviewed said that he was sanctioned by senior garda officers. Nothing was ever done about him. Fred Holroyd, who I met later, once worked for British intelligence, was running 'the Badger' and many other gardaí.

'The Badger' was important to the British. Two files on him, one from the office of Tory MP, Teddy Taylor, went missing, according to *New Statesman* (May 1986), even though the office was locked. The other file disappeared from 10 Downing Street.

During these years the Dublin government launched an all-out assault on republicans. Between 1972 and 1976, 2,724 suspected republicans were arrested under Section 30. Between 1980 and 1984, 11,035 were arrested. Of the 21,000 people arrested between 1972 and 1986 only 17 per cent were charged with an offence. The Offences Against the State Act was used for interrogation, collecting information and intimidation.

An unusual number of people died while in garda custody: two between 1970 and 1974, twenty between 1975 and 1979 and fifteen in the years 1980 to 1983. Of these thirty-five deaths, twenty-three died in garda stations and twelve in prisons.

Judge Barra Ó Briain's report in 1989 revealed that 80 per cent of convictions in the special criminal court were secured by forced confessions. The gardaí were also accused of bugging of solicitors' phones, fabricating fingerprint evidence, conspiring to commit perjury and altering evidence.

In this situation, I had no choice but to take a public stance against the state and the police in the twenty-six counties. It was not a popular decision, but I had heard too many stories and seen too many people suffering to remain silent.

# 10

# Talking to Loyalists

A regular visitor to Monaghan during those years was a Church of Ireland clergyman based in Belfast, Rev. Brian Smeaton. We had become good friends. I first came to know him through Des Wilson's 'Holy Show' concerts in west Belfast. (During some of the worst times in Belfast Des had the novel idea of bringing a group of people, mostly clergy, together for what he called 'A Holy Show'. Brian Smeaton, who had struck up a friendship with Des, liked to entertain people – and so was invited to take part in the Holy Shows.) Brian and myself spent a lot of time discussing the political situation. I was trying to get a better understanding of the loyalist attitudes, as Brian understood them. In February 1978 Brian told me that Andy Tyrie, the leader of the UDA, was willing to meet people 'from the other side' to talk about Irish culture, history and his idea of an independent Ulster. Tyrie had become interested in the theories of a local Belfast writer, Ian Adamson, concerning the Cruithin, whom he claimed were the first settlers in Ireland long before the Celts. Tyrie regarded these people, the Cruithin, as his ancestors and the true ancestors of all who lived in the north of Ireland. This was his reason for taking up the cause of 'an independent Ulster'. I was not impressed with the Cruithin theory, but I still thought it would be worthwhile to meet him, if it could help in any way, to end the random killing of Catholics and bring some better understanding to the situation. Brian had been telling him about the folk club we had formed in Monaghan in 1978. Tyrie said he was interested in finding out more about the folk music tradition in Ulster and wanted to organise something like that for 'his community' in east Belfast.

I told Brian that I would be willing to meet Tyrie and so a meeting was arranged in the UDA headquarters, somewhere in east Belfast. I stayed with Brian the night before in the Shankill Road area and went to meet Andy Tyrie very early next morning, wearing a pink shirt that Brian had loaned me, which was clearly too tight for me and most uncomfortable. After a few minutes I settled down, though there were men coming in and out of the office and giving me strange looks. That made me feel a bit uneasy. I am sure they were wondering who I was and what I was doing there at that time of the morning. However, I knew that when I was with Brian Smeaton, I was safe enough.

Tyrie talked a bit about the tribe known as 'the Cruithin' and how, if the theory put forward by Ian Adamson was true, it made nonsense of the theory that the Gaels were the first inhabitants of Ireland – and that Ireland was a Gaelic country. I heard him out but said I was not convinced about the Cruithin story. We then talked mostly about the folk music scene and he showed a strong interest in local folk music. He knew of Len Graham, the great Ulster traditional singer. He was interested to hear more about others who were involved with folk music, people like Paul Brady and Tommy Sands who were regular visitors to our folk club in Monaghan. He said he would like to organise a workshop about the Ulster folk music tradition somewhere in east Belfast and might need the help of some singers and musicians, and that if I could help in getting them, it would be appreciated. I listened most of the time because I was anxious to show that we had more in common than what divided us. We parted company on the understanding that I would enquire about the possibility of getting some well-known singers to take part in a music workshop. I spoke to a few people about the whole idea and they sounded positive. Then the La Mon House hotel bomb on 17 February 1978 happened and that ended that project. Twelve people (all Protestants) were killed and many more were injured. I did not pursue the matter any further, as I knew that, in the prevailing climate, it was now a non-starter.

I continued to talk to Brian Smeaton about the situation and the possibility of persuading the UDA to stop killing Catholics. Some months after that, Brian Smeaton suggested I should meet another UDA leader in north Belfast called Davy Payne, who was willing to talk to me. So, I went, with Brian, to meet Davy Payne at his house, somewhere off the Shankill/Crumlin Road. Davy Payne was a former paratrooper in the British army and now a brigadier in the UDA. I trusted Brian and felt I would be safe enough in this part of Belfast. I noticed many loyalist paraphernalia on the walls in Payne's sitting-room. Davy and his wife made me welcome and served us tea and scones. It was clear that he had a good deal of respect for Brian. He spoke about the need for a political solution that would end the war – but he felt that the onus was on the IRA. I said that I could not speak for the IRA but I was hoping that our meeting could contribute to an end to the killing of Catholics. I said that I thought there had to be some kind of political resolution involving all the protagonists. I do not know what my meetings achieved – or if I was wise to engage at all with people who would continue killing Catholics. I thought that if I could do anything to bring an end to the sectarian killing of Catholics then it was worth the risk.

However, as events afterwards showed, there was not going to be an early end to the killing of Catholics and nationalists. I think Brian Smeaton was trying to create some kind of new thinking within loyalism that would force them to break their links with the British secret services. I am only guessing that was his agenda, from remarks he made to me.

I was only becoming aware at this time that the UDA was infiltrated by British intelligence – MI5 and the Force Reconnaissance Unit and that they were operating to a British agenda. That agenda was the elimination of well-known republicans, the instilling of fear in the nationalist community and the threat to the people of the twenty-six counties that they would pay dearly for showing any support for republicans. The story of this infiltration became clearer with the revelations about a former British soldier, Brian Nelson, who became an MI5 agent within the UDA in the early 1970s.

The next time I heard about Davy Payne was in January 1988, when he was arrested outside Portadown. His car contained a consignment of weapons – sixty assault rifles, rockets and handguns, a portion of the South African arms shipment assigned to the UDA. I am sure they were not for duck shooting. The UDA disowned him. Davy Payne has since died. Another portion of the South African weapons were assigned to Paisley's friend in Ulster Resistance, Noel Little, whose phone number was discovered written on Davy Payne's hand.

I never could have imagined, when I first became involved in the political situation in the six counties, that I would one day be sitting in the home of a leading loyalist drinking tea and eating home-made scones. I was prepared to do it if it would in any way contribute to a better understanding between our communities. I believed, as did Brian Smeaton, that the working-class unionists were being used both by the unionist ascendancy and the British. They too needed liberation and most of all they needed leadership.

Some years later I had a brief chance encounter with another leading loyalist and member of the 'Shankill Butchers' gang. (The 'Shankill Butchers' were responsible for killing at least nineteen Catholics by cutting their throats. Their leader was a man called Lenny Murphy, who was killed by the IRA in November 1982.)

One day in June 1997 a human rights activist from Dublin, Sr Majella McCarron, a native of Fermanagh, arrived in Belfast with a human rights worker from the Philippines and asked me to drive them to a meeting with some loyalists on the Shankill Road. The Philippino woman was on a fact-finding mission to Belfast. I hesitated but did not like to refuse, so I said I would drop them off at the office on the Shankill and come back whenever they were finished. They said they would not be any more than half an hour. I returned after thirty minutes and kept the car engine running, thinking they would be coming out any time now. Having waited fifteen minutes, there was no sign of them. I did not know what to do. I was becoming increasingly uneasy in case someone came along and recognised me. I drove up and down the Shankill a few times and returned after another ten or fifteen minutes. It was a busy time of the afternoon. There was still no sign of them. I wondered what had happened or could there be something wrong. I did not want to think too much because my mind tends to go wild in situations like this.

Then the door of the office opened, and out stepped 'Basher' Bates whom I recognised, almost immediately, from photographs I had seen of him in the press. He had a big reputation as a member of the 'Shankill Butchers'. On this occasion, 'Basher' was carrying a bundle of papers. I called to him from the car and asked him if the two women visitors were still in the office. He said, 'Aye, they are. They'll be out in a minute. I have to photocopy some stuff for them. Sorry about that, mate.' He then went into the building next door, obviously to use the photocopier. I was very relieved to hear this and when the two women came out some time later I felt more relaxed. They apologised for keeping me waiting, but I don't think they realised how much I had perspired in that time. Within a week, 'Basher' Bates was dead. He was shot dead on 11 June 1997 at the exact same place where I was talking to him. It later emerged that he was killed by an enemy within his own ranks.

# 11

## Mother's Death and a Letter
## from the Bishop

One of the most devastating things to happen in my life was the sudden death of my mother in July 1978. She had taken ill at home. I suppose we were used to her being ill over many years and did not think it was that serious. After a few days in bed at home, her doctor advised that we take her to the hospital in Omagh. She was very weak but I still did not think it was very serious. Having entered hospital, her condition became more complicated and she suffered kidney failure. She died unexpectedly a week later.

I was devastated when I heard the news. I had been with her in the hospital and left about an hour before she died. I regretted afterwards that I had not stayed but I did not think there was any immediate danger. All of us were shattered because we depended so much on her. My sister was working as a nurse in New York at the time and I had to phone her to tell her to come home as soon as possible. I met her at the airport and it was heart-breaking having to tell her that mam had died. Even though she had suffered from high blood pressure for years, we always thought she would live on for many years more with the help of medication.

I found it very difficult celebrating the funeral mass. It was the most emotional experience I ever had to endure, listening to the local parish priest talking about my mother, whom I would not see again, while I tried to hold back the tears as I sat near the altar.

I was numb for a long time after her death. I could not even think about her without feeling sad and desperately lonely. I often visited the little graveyard outside Ederney where she is buried to find comfort and peace. I had lost a part of me and a part of me died too. It is only in recent years that I can talk freely about her and remember her. I see her smiling and laughing at the most innocent things. She had the great gifts of innocence, wisdom, love and courage. She had not much of the modern conveniences and her work must have been drudgery but she never complained. She carried on in spite of bad health and weakness. It is true to say that I loved her more than anybody else.

My mother was a much more dominant personality than my father. She had a different life experience, with the death of her father when she was young and the death of her mother when she was about twenty years of age. She was a woman of great wisdom and unshakeable faith, always pleasant and gentle. She spent her whole life working for her children, making sure that we had the best opportunities available. She enjoyed life and enjoyed people's company. She had many friends in the local community and her death was a cause of much sadness not just to us but also to many in the community who knew her.

After the funeral I went back to Monaghan and carried on with the parish work as well as I could. Looking back, I was still in a kind of a daze. I found comfort in visiting people and talking to people. I needed company. I was lucky to have a few good friends in the Monaghan area. It was the lowest time of my life. I was hardly able to concentrate on anything.

In time I came to realise that we are all here on earth for a short while and then we must move on. It is still a big mystery to me. However, we all must grieve the loss of those we love and some time, hopefully, come to terms with the loss – as we hope to meet up again in some new form of life.

I carried on with parish work and called home to visit my father and my mother's grave as often as I could. One of the most difficult things I had to do in the parish in Monaghan, soon after my mother's death, was go to a house where a man had hanged himself from a wooden beam in the attic. It was very hard to look at this and then try to console his distraught wife and family. I have had to do the same a number of times since then and it is never easy. It is very distressing but it is amazing how you get the strength to do it at the time.

I had the feeling over some time that the other priests in the house were not happy with me. I was not sure what their problem was because they never talked. I know I was hardly ever in the house. One job I did not like on Mondays was counting the Sunday collection. The dining-room table was cleared and the money was poured out. The four priests would assemble round the table and engage in conversation while counting the money. I was supposed to be present for this exercise, which took up most of Monday afternoon. I felt it was a job that some of the parishioners could be doing. There was no need for all the priests to be there! Sometimes I missed it and that did not go down well with some of the others.

However, I felt that I was doing everything else that I was asked to do and I was also making an impact in the parish with the younger people. I worked to improve the celebration of the liturgy on Sundays. I assembled a folk group for a mass in the cathedral and many people of all ages liked that. I felt I was doing my bit, particularly in relation to the younger people.

In June 1979, at the annual retreat in St Macartan's college, Monaghan, a letter in a small brown envelope was hand delivered to me by another priest – a close confidante of the bishop. The letter, from my bishop, Dr Patrick Mulligan, stated that I was

being transferred to another parish. I was flabbergasted! I asked
to meet the bishop during the retreat and told him that I would
have to think about the whole situation as the change seemed
very precipitative. There had been no prior discussion or consul-
tation. I had heard through the grapevine (from a reliable source)
that I was going to be transferred as a result of the sermon and
the anger expressed by the gardaí.

After a short consideration I wrote to the bishop informing
him that I could not accept the way I was being treated and I
was resigning from the diocese. He called me in to talk about the
situation. He also invited the parish priest of Monaghan, the man
who drove me to Maynooth all those years ago. They both asked
me to rethink my decision to resign. I told them I believed I was
being moved at the request of certain high-ranking officers in the
local gardaí and that I was not accepting their right to interfere in
my life as a priest or in where I should be ministering. I had good
information about the garda request.

After further discussion and having considered all they had to
say, I said that I would take back the letter of resignation, but I
was taking a leave of absence from the diocese. I wanted to go to
the US as a priest 'in good standing' and that was one of the reasons I withdrew the letter of resignation. During this crisis in my
life, I kept in touch with Fr Des Wilson. I knew he was the only
one who would understand my situation and who would advise
me about the best course of action.

I then went to see my former history teacher, who was now
Cardinal Ó Fiaich, in Armagh. I told him about my row with
the bishop and about my decision to take time out. I knew he
could not or would not interfere in the affairs of another diocese.
I asked him if he could help me find a place to study or to work
in the US. He suggested a course in Peace Studies, which was
being organised by an acquaintance of his in Manhattan college,
New York. I applied immediately and was informed that it was

too late for that year but that I would be accepted for the course the following September (1980).

At least now I had a purpose in going to the US and something definite to do when I got there. I thought it was also important that my family and friends should feel I was not just going to get away from the country and out of the priesthood. The next year was a difficult time in my life. I helped out in the parish of Threemilehouse and Corcaghan outside Monaghan town. But my heart was not in it. Unknown to the people, I was hurting and I was biding my time until I went to America.

Looking back, I think I was emotionally drained after the previous few years – the death of my mother, the reaction of the gardaí, the row with my bishop – they all took their toll on my emotional and physical health. It was going to take a while to recover.

In September 1979, in the midst of my personal troubles, Pope John Paul II visited Ireland. It was an important event – the first pope ever to visit the 'island of saints and scholars'. For many it was a memorable occasion, but for me and for many others it was a great disappointment. I thought he missed an opportunity to take a broader view of the conflict and to state clearly the British government's responsibility for the conflict in Ireland. I wanted him to announce unequivocally that justice was the basis for lasting peace in the six counties and the sooner the British accepted this the sooner the conflict would be resolved. I was also disappointed because Pope John Paul II avoided the main issue that concerned many people at the time – the plight of the protesting prisoners in Long Kesh.

The pope did not visit the six counties for, as it was stated, 'security reasons'. It was said that the assassination of Lord Mountbatten by the IRA a few weeks previously in August 1979 and the IRA bomb near Warrenpoint, which killed eighteen British soldiers, ruled out a visit by the pope to the north for safety reasons.

The pope's visit was clearly stage-managed and Cahal B. Daly, who was then bishop of Ardagh and Clonmacnoise, scripted some of his speeches. Cahal Daly was a rabid anti-republican who had already written extensively about the situation. His analysis was flawed, as far as I was concerned, because even though he spoke and wrote a lot about violence he did not address the root causes of the violence in Ireland. At least Cardinal Ó Fiaich tried on a number of occasions to deal with this as honestly as he could – but he clearly did not have any major input into the pope's speech in Drogheda.

I went to see Pope John Paul II in Drogheda on 30 September 1979. That was the nearest the pope came to Armagh or Belfast. Drogheda is in the archdiocese of Armagh and is still remembered as the place where, in 1649, Oliver Cromwell slaughtered thousands of Irish Catholics who would not conform to English rule. The cathedral in Drogheda, north of the Boyne, contains the relics of St Oliver Plunkett, the bishop executed by the British in the Tower of London in 1681.

As expected, the pope spoke at length about the conflict in the north. 'To the men of violence, on my bended knees, I beg you …' This is all that anyone remembered of his speech in Drogheda. He did actually appeal to those responsible in government to institute justice and respect for human rights – but that received no attention in the media afterwards. I was asked to take part in a television documentary about the pope's visit and I made the point that most commentators and the media failed to refer to that part of the pope's Drogheda speech where he appealed to those in government:

> True peace must be founded on justice, upon a sense of the untouchable dignity of man upon the recognition of the indelible and happy equality between men, upon the basic principle of human brotherhood, that is of the respect and love due to each man because he is man.

The Irish and British media and the anti-republican politicians and clergy only heard one sentence that the pope uttered. I was disappointed because his advisers must have been aware that this would be how his speech would be reported in the pro-British press. And of course the speech was made for the media, because the leaders of the IRA were hardly present in Drogheda that day – well not at the pope's speech anyway. I could only conclude that this emphasis on the IRA was deliberate.

John Paul II's speech, as reported, contained nothing that would challenge the British or Dublin governments or, indeed, the Catholic hierarchy in Ireland to change their approach. During the week-long visit he would not be visiting Long Kesh or the H-Blocks where the protesting prisoners were being held in terrible conditions. He did not see the heavily armed British army patrols on the country roads or on the city streets, stopping and harassing young nationalists/Catholics.

Instead of being touched, moved and inspired by the pope's visit, I was despondent. I was growing increasingly disillusioned with the church leaders in Ireland and with the attitude in the Vatican, not just to the political situation but also to issues of inequality and injustice in the church itself. Some commentators have maintained that the pope's visit in 1979 marked the end of an era for Irish Catholicism. It was, they say, the 'last hurrah' for the old triumphalist church. They have a point. Something did change after that and it may have been connected with his visit. However, there was so much else to be revealed, about a leading Irish bishop and then the sex abuse scandals in the coming years, that the Catholic church in Ireland was to be rocked to its foundations. Its power and influence were to be seriously undermined during the decades following the pope's visit.

# 12

# Talking to the IRA and the Free Presbyterians

The IRA rejected the pope's plea in 1979 – as I expected they would. The organisation was not going to do anything that looked like capitulation. The prisoners in the H-Blocks were continuing their struggle for the right to be treated as political prisoners, not as criminals. The Dublin government led by Garret Fitzgerald, who had little sympathy for the republican or the nationalist cause, refused to intervene on behalf of the prisoners. The war continued in the streets with killings by the British army, the pro-British loyalist death squads and the IRA.

One day after the pope's visit a young man came to talk to me in Threemilehouse about the situation in the H-Blocks – Séamus McIlwaine from Knockatallon, not to far away and also in County Monaghan. (Séamus was one of the thirty-nine prisoners who escaped from Long Kesh in the 'great escape' in September 1983. He was killed by the SAS near the border in County Fermanagh in 1986.) I supported the demands of the protesting prisoners and the campaign of the H-Block committee. I was becoming more and more concerned about the effects of the IRA campaign on the thinking of the general public. It was clear to me that they were not winning much public support in the twenty-six counties for the cause of the prisoners. I thought that it might be a good idea for the IRA to call a ceasefire to win public support for the prisoners in Long Kesh.

Throughout my time in Monaghan town I had built up a good relationship with some senior republicans. Many republicans living in Monaghan were from counties Tyrone, Derry and Armagh. They regarded me as someone who was genuinely concerned about the welfare of the republican prisoners. I had made several public protests and public statements about the situation in Long Kesh and went to visit Jim Lynagh when he was in prison.

I felt that I could appeal to the IRA leadership from a position of understanding within the broad republican family. They knew that I was not representing the hierarchy or the SDLP so I wrote to the IRA leadership on 27 May 1980, asking them to consider a ceasefire in order to focus maximum attention on the plight of the prisoners in the H-Blocks. The republican prisoners were engaged in a no-wash protest and were being held in the most awful conditions. Cardinal Ó Fiaich had visited them and compared it to the 'sewers in Calcutta'. I felt that while the IRA campaign was continuing apace it would be difficult to get maximum support for the prisoners from the Irish church or from the Dublin government, or indeed from the general population throughout Ireland. I was conscious of the hostility and the fear I had encountered on my trip around Ireland with Brian Smeaton in 1978. I thought that if the IRA declared a ceasefire we might have a better chance of getting popular support for the prisoners' struggle and also of putting more pressure on the Dublin government and the Catholic hierarchy.

On 24 May 1980 a meeting was held in the Four Seasons hotel, Monaghan about the situation in the H-Block, chaired by Fr Piaras Ó Dúill, a Capuchin priest from Dublin. Once again, I stated my support for the protesting prisoners. I also stated my reservations about the ongoing IRA campaign. I argued the need for a ceasefire, if only for tactical reasons, because I thought the IRA leadership might be prepared to consider it from a tactical viewpoint since they had already made clear many times where they stood on the principle of armed struggle.

Many years later, I discovered that another priest, James Mc-Dyer from Glencolmcille, who was known and highly respected all over Ireland, was also making similar private overtures to the IRA leadership at that time. In his autobiography he writes about making contact with Daithí Ó Conaill, one of the main republican leaders in 1980. He also made several proposals about the benefits of having an IRA ceasefire. He writes that he was given a sympathetic hearing but was told later that Ó Conaill 'could not convince the north'.

Cardinal Ó Fiaich was interested in my initiative and wanted to know if I was making any progress. I told him that it was certainly being taken seriously and that J. B. O'Hagan, a leading figure in the republican movement, was to report back to me. The answer I received was that there would not be a ceasefire – 'not at this time'. The 'not at this time' I thought was interesting and alerted me to the fact that the IRA would, when they felt the time was right, consider a ceasefire – but that would take a lot of negotiating before it happened.

In hindsight, it may have been naive on my part to expect an IRA ceasefire and to think that the middle-classes throughout Ireland and the official church would have swung round in support of the republican prisoners in the H-Blocks. The Catholic middle-class in the south had shown over the years that they were not much interested in the plight of nationalists in the north and they were certainly not sympathetic to republican prisoners. Few of them had any experience of discrimination and harassment at the hands of the British army or RUC. It is doubtful that they would have supported the republican prisoners in Long Kesh even if the IRA had called a ceasefire.

The tension within the parish of Monaghan and the conflict with the bishop during the last few years had an adverse effect on my health. I had stomach trouble and I had to spend some time in hospital in Drogheda. The main cause of my illness was stress. As far as I was concerned the main cause of the stress was the situation I was living in. I thought that a break from Ireland would do me some good and reduce the stress level. I explained to my father and the family that I was going on a course to New York. I don't think they were too happy about it as they suspected there was more to it, that I was not telling them everything. In a sense that was true because I had not told them anything about my 'run in' with the bishop.

One of the abiding memories of my sojourn in Monaghan was the day we held a meeting with a group of Free Presbyterians in the Hillgrove hotel in Monaghan. I had written to invite Rev. Willie McCrea, but he wrote to say he could not be there and hoped that I would 'see the light' and be saved 'from eternal damnation in the fires of hell'. Anyway, a group of about thirty Free Presbyterians from Monaghan and Fermanagh turned up for the meeting. I chaired the proceedings and made a few introductory remarks. I had invited theologian, Mary Condren and a few others in the Student Christian Movement to sit in with me on the discussion. I knew that Mary Condren had an excellent knowledge of the scriptures and that was going to be needed in this discussion. It was quiet at the beginning. I knew Mary would be provocative. She asked the Free Presbyterians to explain how they, claiming to follow Christ, could hate those who espoused Roman Catholicism and show such grave disrespect to the Roman Catholic faith.

The Free Presbyterians had their bibles with them and were quoting from them at great length about 'the anti-Christ' – referring to the pope. Mary Condren did not need a bible because she knew the text. She kept on challenging their fundamentalist beliefs and their anti-Catholicism and how that squared with Christ's command to love your neighbour. Somebody in our group went out, and came back with a pint of Guinness. All hell broke loose! They turned on him for disobeying God's word in the bible. Mary objected by saying that Jesus turned the water into wine. One of the Free Presbyterians got to his feet and, waving an umbrella at her, shouted that 'the Lord' had changed the water into non-alcoholic wine, some kind of non-alcoholic grape juice!

There was a good bit of shouting back and forth, which went on for more than half an hour. I saw we were not going to make any progress in understanding, so I brought the meeting to a close, thanked everybody for coming and wished the Free Presbyterians well. I did not see the light that day – but I felt the heat.

# 13

## The Hunger Strikes

I left for America in July 1980. I had mixed feelings but I suppose the predominant one was anxiety about the future. I was anxious about my own situation as a priest, my health and the political situation. I knew that things in the H-Blocks at Long Kesh were very grave a there was already talk that some of the prisoners might die if something was not done soon. In New York I stayed first with cousins until I got my bearings. I had to find some parish work to get some accommodation and some pocket money. I had little enough money and was not being supported by my diocese any longer. It was to be a precarious existence for the next three years. But I did not go hungry. I liked pizza – which was available on every street corner and was not very expensive!

One thing I noticed right away about New York was that you could travel anywhere without being stopped and harassed by the police or the military. I could not believe it. Here was a city of fifteen million people and everybody could travel wherever they liked without being stopped. That was a big change from home where I was used to being stopped and questioned every time I went down the road. After a few weeks, I was beginning to relax.

Having made some enquiries, I discovered that there was a parish in Madison, New Jersey looking for a priest for the summer months. The priest in charge was a Cavan man, Finbarr Corr, a decent guy who did his best to make me feel at home. He was a bit too progressive for the conservative bishop in New Jersey and soon after left the priesthood and married. He wrote his story in a book titled *A Kid from Leganinney*, his native townland in Cavan.

One evening shortly after I arrived in Madison, out of curiosity I went into a local pub beside the Catholic church and ordered a beer. I was standing at the counter and after a while this lean-looking man with dark hair and a familiar face came over and stared at me: 'In under God, Joe McVeigh, what are you doing here?' he asked in a tone of astonishment and in a strong south Derry accent. It took me a minute to get over the shock that someone in this out of the way place recognised me. Who was it but a man I knew well in Maynooth, Finbarr O'Kane from Glenullan in south County Derry. He was a student for the priesthood in Maynooth for six years and left for personal reasons. He was active in the civil rights movement in Derry and was on the platform on Bloody Sunday. He was so traumatised by the terrible events of that day that he left for the US shortly afterwards. It was a big coincidence that I should bump into him in this small town in New Jersey where very few Irish lived.

I told him jokingly that I had come to seek my fortune in America, the land of 'the free and the brave'. I asked what he was doing in the US and he told me he was studying for a doctorate in philosophy at Drew University in Madison. It was his third year there and he was nearly finished his doctorate. I had lost touch with him after Maynooth, so we quickly renewed our friendship and it was not long before the war situation in the six counties became the chief topic of conversation. I had the impression that Finbarr was enjoying his time in New Jersey but that he was missing home dreadfully. (Sadly, as I was writing an early draft of this chapter I learned that Finbarr O'Kane had died in a hospice in Derry and was buried in his native Glenullan. I have since knelt and prayed at his grave.)

Finbarr was passionate about the situation back home in Ireland. I don't think I ever met anyone as passionate about it. I thought I was getting away from it all and here in the middle of New Jersey I was right back into it again! However, Finbarr was also very humorous and had great stories about Maynooth and some of the strange professors. He was always asking questions – more of himself than of me. I began to feel at home, knowing he was living near me in Madison and I could call and talk to someone who had similar interests and concerns. I enjoyed his company in those first few months in that somewhat foreign land. Finbarr had hardly ever been home since Bloody Sunday almost ten years before that – except for his mother's funeral. He used to talk a lot about his mother and the things she would say. 'As my mother always said …' was a favourite saying of his and he emphasised 'my' and 'mother' in that wonderful south Derry accent. He was anxious to know more about the situation in Long Kesh so I brought him up to speed as best I could.

I was in America about a month when I received a phone call to say that my own father had suffered a heart attack and was quite ill in hospital. I was advised to come home as quickly as possible so I took the first flight home. After a few anxious days, he began to show a steady improvement and it was clear he was out of danger. I stayed at home for about three weeks, until I was certain he was making a good recovery. The doctor assured me that he was doing well and with medication he should live to a ripe old age. My father retired after that and has gone on to live a full and enjoyable life playing cards and bingo most nights of the week.

I went back to the parish in Madison, New Jersey and met up again with Finbarr O'Kane at Drew University where he had a room. I saw a car advertised and called the number. When they heard I was an Irish priest staying in Madison – and just 'off the boat', as they say – they said that I could have the car for nothing! It was quite old and battered but it was all right for short journeys. I then had to get a driving licence and insurance. It was like starting out all over again. Soon afterwards I signed on for the Peace Studies course in Manhattan college, which in spite of its name is situated in the Bronx. I went to live at the St Philip Neri church rectory on the Grand Concourse in the Bronx. The pastor there, Fr Shannon, was a decent man who arranged for me to stay at the presbytery and to help in the parish at weekends. The associate pastor, Seán from Cork, was also very helpful. I kept in touch with Finbarr O'Kane and went to see him occasionally.

Before the end of the first month at the college I was feeling disappointed and frustrated with the course in Peace Studies. It was not what I had expected. While there was some good information about the amount of money the US was spending on the military and on armaments I felt that it did not apply directly to our situation, which was what I was most concerned about at the time. I spoke to the head of the faculty and told him about my disappointment with the course. Following our conversation, he asked me to give a talk to staff, students and members of the public about the conflict in Ireland. The professor was not too happy with my presentation, which he thought to be too sympathetic to the republican side. I was definitely not happy at Manhattan college after this. The other first-year students, average age nineteen to twenty, were all from middle-class American homes. They had no clue about Ireland or what the US government (their government) was doing in the world, and seemed to care less. They wanted an easy degree. 'Peace Studies' was supposed to be an easy subject to pass. I found the whole experience frustrating, so I left the college in November, having handed in a letter explaining my reasons for quitting and regretting that it did not work out.

Meanwhile, I had met up with a well-known Jesuit priest and peace campaigner, Daniel Berrigan. Daniel was a sprightly man of about sixty with a wicked sense of humour. He had no time for the US Catholic hierarchy because of their support for the US military. He sympathised with my plight and advised me to apply to New York Theological Seminary – an ecumenical place where I could at least do some serious scripture study. A friend of his worked there and Dan gave me his phone number. When I called him and told him that Dan Berrigan had given me his number I was accepted for the course straight away. So it's who you know in New York as well!

I went to the New York Theological Seminary while still staying at the St Philip Neri church in the Bronx and saying weekend masses. There were a number of excellent lecturers in this college, including Norman Gottwald, a well respected biblical scholar in the US and author of *The Tribes of Israel*, a classic commentary on the Old Testament. I found this course much more stimulating and interesting than the Peace Studies course I had left. However, it came to an abrupt end for me when the first hunger strike in Long Kesh started. From that time onwards, I concentrated on raising awareness about the plight of the prisoners in Long Kesh and Armagh.

I had heard reports that the prisoners in Long Kesh were about to embark on a hunger strike. After four and half years of almost solitary confinement and being refused permission to go to the toilet unless they put on the prison uniform, a small number of republican prisoners embarked on a hunger strike to further their claims to be treated as political prisoners, as they had before. The national H-Block/Armagh Committee led by Fr Piaras Ó Dúill and Bernadette McAliskey organised protests and meetings. They outlined the basic demands of the prisoners which, if granted, would resolve the crisis. Cardinal Ó Fiaich was deeply involved in trying to find a resolution to the crisis in the H-Blocks. So too was the Sinn Féin leader in Belfast, Gerry Adams. The first hunger strike began in the H-Blocks of Long Kesh on 27 October 1980. Seven prisoners, led by Brendan Hughes, began the fast. The IRA leadership tried to persuade them from taking on such a serious action.

I had no time to feel sorry for myself any more. Things were now too serious and I had a duty to do something to help those prisoners. I thought about the sufferings of the hunger strikers and their families. I felt I could not stand idly by. This was a big challenge for me to do something to highlight their plight.

I spoke to a few friends including Finbarr O'Kane and we decided to hold a three-day vigil and fast outside the United Nations building in New York City. Finbarr left his studies in the university to be with me at the UN. I was very grateful to him for the support and to the many others who came along – people from Fermanagh and Tyrone and from all over Ireland living in New York and New Jersey. One young man from Pomeroy in County Tyrone, Seán Quinn, volunteered to be tied to a large wooden cross to symbolise the suffering of the prisoners. We made it on to Channel 5 News. I was interviewed by Bob O'Brien, which was quite an achievement since I had no contacts in the media. Some people in other Irish groups were a bit annoyed at us getting so much publicity, that was a problem within the Irish solidarity groups in New York at that time. There was great competition for publicity and great rivalry instead of creative unity. I discovered that there are egotists there as everywhere. I also discovered that the FBI and the CIA were never too far away from protests and solidarity meetings.

At one stage during the protest, I caused some consternation among a group of Irish and Irish-Americans gathered in a building beside the UN to discuss community relations in 'Northern Ireland'. A professor from Queen's University Belfast was over giving a talk on community relations. The great and the good were gathered there and listening attentively. During the talk, I walked into the room with a blanket wrapped around me. I said, 'Excuse me, Mr Chairman. I am a priest from the north of Ireland and I would like to say something to you about the hunger strike in Long Kesh.' The chairman rose to his feet, visibly angry, and said that I most definitely could not speak since I was not invited and had merely interrupted their meeting. I did not argue any further as I could feel the anger mounting in the room. I could see the looks of hostility. It was a fairly small meeting, about thirty people. The Irish consul representing the Dublin government was there in the front seat. I left the room happy that I had made a few people think about the reality of life in Long Kesh – and the urgency of the situation there.

I was not invited to any official Irish functions after that. I had been invited to one or two before and actually met Brian Lenihan, who was then minister for foreign affairs in the Dublin government, at one of these meetings. I knew I had made a few enemies but I did not really care. I just wanted to stir consciences.

Through the protest action outside the United Nations I made a lot of contacts outside the Irish solidarity groups. Many people, of all nationalities, identified with the hunger strikers. The British embassy, however, and those Irish-Americans who always support the British and detest Irish republicans were not too happy with me. It was during the action at the UN I realised for the first time the power and influence of British propaganda in all the media outlets in the United States. All the main newspapers and television networks seemed unashamedly pro-British and anti the IRA. The American public were completely misinformed about the situation in Ireland and in particular about the reasons for the hunger strike in Long Kesh. The usual line was that the prisoners were a bunch of IRA no-good terrorists who had no support in the community. It was of course the same line in RTÉ.

Some of us set up an ad hoc solidarity group to counter the propaganda. I took part in television and radio interviews. We held pickets and protests. What amazed me at the beginning was the ease with which the television stations could always find an Irish person to take the British side. In hindsight I should not have been too surprised. I also discovered while in the US that the Dublin government had done nothing to highlight the discrimination against nationalists, the British shoot-to-kill policy, and their use of plastic bullets in the six counties. They had done nothing to promote the nationalist cause in the media. In fact, it seemed to me that they also were doing their best to prevent the truth about the conflict being told. They were very subservient to the British and pursued the British propaganda line that the IRA was the problem. It made me very angry – and very determined to do something about it.

The first hunger strike was called off in December 1980 when the protesting prisoners were led to believe that they had achieved most of their aims. When it emerged that the British government did not intend making any concessions the protesting prisoners announced a second hunger strike.

Hunger striking has a long history in Ireland. In fact, it can be traced back to when the Brehon laws existed from the fifth century. It was also used in the period of the Black and Tan war in Ireland. Indeed, Irish republican and mayor of Cork, Terence MacSwiney, died on hunger strike in London's Brixton jail in 1920.

Back home in Fermanagh at Christmas 1980, I went to see Bernadette McAliskey. She told me the future did not look good. We were up against an intransigent British prime minister, Margaret Thatcher, and we had a weak government in Dublin. A few weeks after returning to New York in January 1981 we heard that Bernadette and her husband, Michael McAliskey, had been shot and seriously wounded in front of their three children by members of the UDA from Lisburn. We were all deeply concerned. Many people gathered in St Malachy's church for a special mass to pray for their recovery. Thankfully, they survived, though it took a long time for them to recover from their horrific injuries.

A second hunger strike began on 1 March 1981 when Bobby Sands, who had been leader of the republican prisoners in the H-

Blocks, refused to take food. Brendan 'Bik' McFarlane took over as leader of the prisoners. While on the blanket, Bobby Sands had shown himself to be bright, intelligent and with leadership qualities. His passions were music and poetry. He was a young man with everything to live for, but he had deeply-held beliefs and was determined that the British government would not criminalise him or the Irish struggle. It is clear from his writings that he had an exceptionally strong sense of history and of the continuity of the Irish struggle for freedom. 'I am a political prisoner,' he wrote in a diary he kept when he went on hunger strike on 1 March 1981: 'I am a political prisoner, because I am a casualty of a perennial war that is being fought between the oppressed Irish people and an alien, oppressive, unwanted regime that refuses to withdraw from our land.' He went on, 'I believe that I am but another of those wretched Irishmen born of a rising generation with a deeply rooted and unquenchable desire for freedom.'

Shortly after Bobby Sands had begun a second hunger strike, I read in the *New York Times* about the sudden death of Frank Maguire, MP for Fermanagh/South Tyrone, which came as a great shock to me. I had seen Frank when I was home at Christmas. He was in bed with the flu. At least that's what he told me but he must have been more seriously ill. I was deeply shocked and could not help thinking about all our exploits when I was in Lisnaskea and afterwards in Garrison. I was most disappointed that I could not go home for the funeral. I was still doing the course in the New York Seminary and I also had to think about Immigration since at this time I had only a visitor's visa. I had applied for a student visa.

Not too long after Frank's funeral, I heard a report that there was a move to enter Bobby Sands in the by-election in Fermanagh/South Tyrone against the unionist candidate, Harry West. I thought this was a great idea. There were other nationalist candidates going forward but I knew that for Bobby to have a chance there had to be a straight fight with Harry West. All that was required was for the SDLP not to field a candidate and for Noel Maguire, Frank's brother, to withdraw and support the Sands' campaign. When I received confirmation that Bobby Sands was allowing his name to go forward in the election I phoned Noel Maguire and said I thought he should consider making way. Noel waited until the very last minute and then withdrew from the contest. The SDLP man Austin Currie did not have time to present his papers. That left a straight fight between Bobby Sands and the unionist candidate, Harry West.

I was aware that there was a solid republican vote in this constituency. I was hopeful that if the nationalists could be persuaded to vote for Bobby Sands against West then he could win the election and that this would bring world attention to the plight of the prisoners. I was hoping, that if he won the election and became an MP, a deal would be done with the British, the hunger strike would end and lives would be saved.

I decided to go home for the election fixed for 7 April. I could not bear to be in New York knowing that I might be able to do some good at home in the election campaign. I did not know what was ahead of us, but it was going to be difficult and dangerous. I thought if I could persuade a few more people to vote for Bobby Sands, then my presence there would be worthwhile. There were some nationalist politicians like Austin Currie calling on people not to vote for Bobby Sands and asking them to spoil their votes. I thought this was disgraceful. I knew how the nationalist grassroots in Fermanagh felt about Harry West and the unionists and, that when the time came, the people would vote for Bobby Sands.

I attended a public press conference in Enniskillen organised by Owen Carron, Bobby Sands' election agent. It showed a broad united nationalist front – except for the SDLP. Dissident SDLP councillor, Tommy Murray, was on the platform, as were Sinn Féin's Danny Morrison and Jim Gibney, who stayed in the con-

stituency for the rest of the campaign. Bernadette Devlin McAliskey was there, even though she was still on crutches and recover-
ing from the attempted assassination some months before. The
parents, sister and brother of Bobby Sands were also present.

I made a statement for the press at that conference, which I
had drafted with the help of Finbarr O'Kane over the phone:

> As a Catholic priest I feel there is a moral issue in this election. I re-
> sent the implication in the statements of some politicians that anyone
> who votes for Bobby Sands is a supporter of violence. I do not support
> violence. The people of Fermanagh/South Tyrone have now a chance to
> protest in a non-violent and peaceful way. A vote for Bobby Sands in
> this election is a vote for justice and a vote against violence. Without
> justice there cannot be peace. I believe that, as a priest, I have a respon-
> sibility to support and care for prisoners as Pope John Paul II asked us
> to do during his recent visit to Ireland.

In this statement I was trying to counter the argument put forward by some SDLP leaders and some church leaders, that 'a vote
for Bobby Sands was a vote for violence'. I stated quite clearly
that you could be a pacifist and work with people of all political
persuasions for justice and human rights – in fact you had no
choice. I was sick and tired of the rhetoric about 'violence' from
people who had never condemned the primary violence in our
country.

On the Sunday before the election I was asked to speak at
masses outside Belleek Catholic church, which I did. Most people
walked by without looking at me as I spoke through a loud hailer
urging them to vote for Bobby Sands. One or two came to talk
to me afterwards. The tension was high at that time. The Sands
family were staying in Fermanagh during this time and I was very
impressed by their dignity and strong loyalty to their son and
brother. You could see that they were proud of him and amazed
at the support he was getting – even though they were anxious
about his worsening condition.

We had several motor cavalcades travelling through the cons-

tituency, from Coalisland to Dungannon through the Clogher
Valley and the hostile territory of Fivemiletown, through Lisnaskea, Maguiresbridge and on to Enniskillen. There were cavalcades in the north of the constituency on another day. The RUC
made life as difficult as possible for those campaigning for Bobby
Sands. They had roadblocks and surveillance everywhere.

The result of the election was announced in the Fermanagh college on 9 April 1981. Bobby Sands won the election and succeeded
Frank Maguire as MP for Fermanagh/South Tyrone. There was
great joy in the republican community. The unionists, and those few
nationalists who opposed him, were sulking. After this momentous
election victory there was waiting and hoping and praying that this
would be enough to change Thatcher's mind and persuade her to
meet the demands of the prisoners. In the immediate aftermath
of the election, I was part of several delegations from Fermanagh
to urge those in high places to put pressure on the British government. We went to see Cardinal Ó Fiaich, the papal nuncio in Dublin, and then some British officials in the Northern Ireland Office
in Stormont. Members of the Sands family and Owen Carron,
Bobby Sands' election agent, went to see the taoiseach, Charles
Haughey.

Our meeting with Cardinal Ó Fiaich on Holy Saturday, 18
April 1981 was interrupted by his secretary. I thought for a moment
that there might have been news of a breakthrough in the hunger
strike but the cardinal was called out to be told that Pope John
Paul II had been shot and seriously wounded in St Peter's Square
in the Vatican. The cardinal was visibly shaken when he came back
into the room. He was clearly deeply concerned about the situation in the H-Blocks and was worried that if Bobby Sands died
there would be further bloodshed. He assured us that he would do
whatever he could to bring about a resolution.

The election victory was a great boost to the prisoners' morale
but was not in itself going to deflect them from their strategy. They

were determined to force the British to meet their demands, which would in effect recognise that they were political prisoners. Only when that happened would they give up their hunger strike.

It is clear from reading his diary that Bobby Sands understood the full consequences of his decision to go on hunger strike. He wrote: 'I am standing on the threshold of another trembling world. May God have mercy on my soul … My heart is very sore because I know that I have broken my poor mother's heart and my home is struck with unbearable anxiety. But I have considered all the arguments and tried every means to avoid what has become the unavoidable: it has been forced upon me by four and a half years of stark inhumanity.'

In the early hours of 5 May 1981 I was lying awake at home in Ederney, listening to the radio. There was a news flash to say that Bobby Sands had died: 'After sixty-six days on hunger strike, Bobby Sands died in Long Kesh prison hospital.' It was one of those moments in time that I will always remember. I knew that something of huge historic and political significance had happened. I did not sleep well that night.

In the days that followed I felt angry with British and Irish government leaders for letting our elected MP die like this. I was sorry for Bobby's parents, sisters, Marcella and Bernadette, and brother, Seán. I saw the anguish they were suffering. They were very dignified throughout this heartbreaking time. They supported one another and received support from within the community.

I went to the wake for Bobby Sands in his parents' home in Twinbrook, on the outskirts of Belfast, along with Michael Doyle, an Irish priest working in Camden, New Jersey. We sat quietly in the room along with a few others, including Gerry Adams, his wife Colette and his young son. Nobody spoke. There was nothing to say. I left after a while, but Michael stayed all night in the house comforting Bobby's parents, John and Rosaleen, and the grieving family members. Michael was the right man in the right place. He had a great empathy with people in distress and was well known in America for his work with the marginalised in Camden, New Jersey.

Michael Doyle and I went to see the parish priest in Twinbrook. We asked him if we could concelebrate the funeral mass with him, since Bobby Sands was my MP and I had come to know his family quite well and as Michael wanted to show solidarity with the family. The parish priest said that the bishop had made a ruling that there were to be no concelebrants at the mass. I thought this was odd, since the previous deceased MP for Fermanagh/South Tyrone, Frank Maguire, had a cardinal, several bishops and a large number of priests concelebrating his funeral mass. Frank Maguire had once been OC (Officer Commanding) of the IRA prisoners in Crumlin Road jail. There was not much we could do about the refusal. The parish priest was carrying out orders. The Catholic clergy behave like soldiers sometimes. I was very angry.

The death of Bobby Sands was a defining moment in modern Irish history. In a way it was also a defining moment in my life. Nothing could ever be the same again. I attended the first four funerals of the hunger strikers – Bobby, Francis Hughes, Raymond McCreesh and Patsy O'Hara. After the death of Ray McCreesh, Cardinal Ó Fiaich made the following statement: 'The death of Raymond McCreesh exemplifies the cruel dilemma in which Northern Catholics are caught. I would have no doubt that he would never have seen the inside of a jail but for the abnormal political situation.' This statement showed that the cardinal had a broader understanding of the conflict than most of his colleagues in the hierarchy. He was lambasted in the British press. The *Daily Express* described him as 'the Cardinal who is like a recruiting officer of the IRA'. Another British editor called him 'the chaplain of the IRA'. The English cartoonists also mocked him in a disgraceful manner.

Soon after the funeral of Patsy O'Hara, at the end of May 1981,

I returned to the US, emotionally drained and certainly in need of a rest and a break. In New York the situation in Ireland was a constant topic of conversation among the Irish, Irish-Americans and those who had no connection with Ireland but who were concerned about justice and peace. The conflict in the north of Ireland was in the news in a way that it had never been before – and people throughout the world were now aware of it.

Some Irish groups in New York were busy organising meetings and protesting outside the British consulate. One group, called The American Irish Unity Committee, held a conference about the situation in Long Kesh in the Biltmore hotel, New York on 22 July 1981. I was invited to speak, along with Seán MacBride and Paul O'Dwyer, former president of New York City Council. Seán MacBride was a founder member of Amnesty International. He won the Nobel Peace Prize in 1974, the Lenin Peace Prize in 1977 and many other awards for his human rights work. He had also been chief of staff of the IRA at one time. This meeting received a lot of attention in Irish media circles and the Dublin government would certainly have noted it. They were well aware that feelings were running high in the United States about the hunger strike.

I was now staying at Holy Name parish house on the Upper West Side of Manhattan with Fr Bob, who was a friend of justice campaigner Dan Berrigan. I helped with weekend masses, for the dwindling English-speaking community. It was once an all-Irish parish but now it was predominantly Haitian and Latino. There was a French-speaking Haitian priest living in the same house, who served the large Catholic Haitian community in the area. I met some native Irish there and they were glad to see a priest 'from the old sod'. The house seemed to be an open house for priests and bishops coming to New York from all parts of the world. One of the leading liberation theologians and ecumenists in South America, Sergio Torres, came to stay with us for a week.

The author of a number of books about liberation theology, he was particularly interested in the ecumenical dimension. I spent as much time as I could in conversation with him, learning how liberation theology had come about in South America. I wanted to know about the similarities and differences between Ireland and Latin America.

The protests in support of the prisoners in Long Kesh continued in New York. In August a group of us, including Fr Dan Berrigan, occupied the British consulate on Third Avenue. Although there was a picket every day outside the consulate, the British government refused to budge.

In August 1981, as the hunger strike continued, Sinn Féin's Owen Carron was elected MP for Fermanagh/South Tyrone, vacant since the death of Bobby Sands. Two other hunger strikers, Paddy Agnew and Kieran Doherty, were elected TDs in the twenty-six counties and held the balance of power there. These electoral successes and the massive crowds at the funerals showed that the republican movement was now a force to be reckoned with in Ireland and that it had a great deal of international support.

Nine other republican prisoners died in quick succession after Bobby Sands – Francis Hughes, Raymond McCreesh, Patsy O'Hara, Martin Hurson, Kevin Lynch, Joe McDonell, Kieran Doherty, Tom McElwee and Mickey Devine. I became acquainted with a few of their families who came on speaking tours to New York. When Michael Devine died there were still a number of others on hunger strike, but their parents intervened and the protest was eventually called off on 3 October 1981. The role played by Fr Denis Faul in putting pressure on the families is controversial to this day. Soon after the hunger strike ended the British government announced that the prisoners could wear their own clothes. During the period of the hunger strike, eighty people died on the streets – many as a result of attacks by the British army and RUC.

# 14

# After the Hunger Strike

The electoral successes during the 1981 hunger strike convinced some within Sinn Féin that this was the way forward. Gerry Adams, Danny Morrison and others like Jim Gibney and Tom Hartley were in the forefront of the new political thinking and strategy in Sinn Féin. Others in the party, including Ruairí Ó Brádaigh and Daithí Ó Conaill, disagreed with this policy of taking seats in the Dáil/Leinster House, and following the 1986 árd fheis they left Sinn Féin and formed Republican Sinn Féin. At this árd fheis 429 out of 628 delegates voted in favour of the electoral strategy and for Sinn Féin to take seats in Leinster House, if elected. The re-emergence of Sinn Féin throughout the island of Ireland can be traced to this time and especially to the election of Bobby Sands as MP for Fermanagh/South Tyrone. Other republican prisoners were successful in the elections in the south. It could never be claimed again that republicans had no popular support.

On returning to the United States in July 1981 I was invited by Monsignor Jack Egan from Chicago to speak in Notre Dame university about the conflict in Ireland, especially the reasons for the hunger strike. I gave my address to the students and the meeting was good humoured until a man at the back of the hall started to heckle me. 'What do you say about the IRA murders?' he shouted, while I was speaking. I had not noticed him in the audience before. Then I recognised him as a Cork priest who was a student at Maynooth with me and was now studying in Notre Dame. He was shouting very loudly and then left the hall in protest at my presence. I doubt if he would have protested as loudly had a Brit been there to speak.

My purpose in going to Notre Dame was to try to explain why Irish republican prisoners were prepared to sacrifice their lives for the cause of Irish freedom. Because of the hunger strike, there was a keen interest among ordinary Americans in the situation in Ireland. There were enough bishops and priests going out there to do the condemnation bit and to give the British/Dublin government slant. Few were ever attempting to help people in the US to understand why there was a war going on and why young men were prepared to die for their beliefs. I wanted to analyse the role that the British were playing in Ireland in fomenting violence. I felt it was important to give the students the other side of the story, one which they did not usually hear.

I discovered that the main Christian churches in the US did not pay much attention to the conflict in Ireland. They had a highly organised network of Justice and Peace offices in New York and throughout the United States but they devoted most of their time, energy and resources to the situation in Central and South America. Some were also concerned with South Africa. The National Council of Churches (NCC) had their head office beside where I was staying in New York. The main reason they were not engaged with Ireland was because none of the Irish Catholic leaders had invited them to become involved.

I got to know two people who worked there. Sister Marjorie Tuite, a Catholic nun, and a Presbyterian clergyman, Bill Wipfler, who specialised in human rights issues in Chile and Argentina. They were clearly concerned about Ireland. Sr Marjorie was very well known in the United States for her work on human rights. She was a larger than life person, a real bundle of energy and determination. Sadly, she died suddenly in 1982.

Bill Wipfler was an experienced human rights activist – a slight man who had suffered a heart attack and was supposed to be recuperating. He outlined how they did their work in Chile and he showed me files and files of statements from victims of police and military torture in Chile and Argentina. These people at the National Council of Churches (NCC) headquarters were most helpful in advising me how to go about the work of documentation. This was their big message – document all cases of discrimination, torture and harassment. Document everything. I tried to do that when I went home and published some of it. The people at the NCC told me that they did not want to hear stories second or third hand. They wanted authentic documentation and detailed authenticated statements from the victims of injustice.

Another nun who worked with Sr Marjorie, Regina Murphy, worked on the issue of corporate responsibility. She went after companies who invested in the north and called on them to make the implementation of human rights and equality a condition for their continued investment there. She also did much to promote the MacBride Principles in the United States. The MacBride Principles (called after Seán MacBride, one of the people who devised them) were a way of campaigning for fair employment in the public and private sector in the north. They were modelled on the Sullivan Principles, which attacked racial discrimination in South Africa.

Through the US peace movement I became acquainted with Brendan Walsh and his wife, Willa, who lived at the Baltimore Catholic Worker house in a poor and run down part of Baltimore. The Catholic Worker movement was founded by Dorothy Day, a New York journalist who converted to Catholicism, and Peter Maurin, a French street philosopher, on May day 1933. They started with a newspaper, *The Catholic Worker*, and a desire to help the homeless and poor on the streets of New York. Soon after, they established a soup kitchen and a hospitality house.

Later still they organised draft resistance and anti-nuclear protests. There are now Catholic Worker communities in many
countries around the world.

I used to stay at the Catholic Worker house in Baltimore and
sometimes in New York. The house in Baltimore was in a part
of town that was ignored by the city and federal authorities. The
Walsh family and friends ran a soup kitchen for hundreds of
homeless people who came for food once a week. What a terrible situation, in a country where there is so much wealth, money
spent on weapons of mass destruction and all kinds of military
projects. It became very evident that it is mostly African–Americans and Latinos who are at the bottom of the heap in the United
States. (That became more evident when Hurricane Katrina hit
New Orleans and the gulf coast in 2005.) The Catholic Worker
houses in Baltimore and New York provided a platform to those
who wanted to give the real story of what was happening in Ireland.

I met with Carolyn Forché in New York City, where she was
living. Carolyn was then one of the most talked-about poets in
the United States. She had spent a few years in El Salvador working alongside Archbishop Oscar Romero. She introduced me to
people from El Salvador and Nicaragua – people who had built
up strong solidarity groups in New York and Washington. I became acquainted with members of the Nicaraguan support group
who were in close contact with the Sandinistas. I was meeting
people from all over the world, almost daily. What a change from
Monaghan! I found it really exciting and energising to meet so
many interesting people, all concerned about human rights and
justice. Since arriving in New York in 1980 the world had become, for me, a small place.

I met many people involved in Irish support groups, mostly
Irish-Americans but some with no Irish background at all. They
were always looking for more information. We used to hold our

meetings in the basement of Washington Square Methodist church and I took part in some religious services when invited and enjoyed the concerts and plays staged there.

I spent almost three years in New York city. It was a formative period in my life, a time of discovery about myself and about the world. Ireland was a small place, New York was huge and the world was so vast. Apart from my involvement with the Irish situation, I learned a lot about life in that wonderful and crazy city and in the US in general, the politics of the US government and the cynicism of some of their political leaders.

I saw for the first time in my life real poverty – people living on the streets, without food, without shelter. When I was protesting outside the UN in 1980 an older man used to come to his 'home' or resting place for the night – a round iron cover over hot pipes which was warm and where he could sleep quite comfortably with an old coat over him. I came to know people who lived on the streets and in the subways – 'bag ladies' who did not talk to anybody, drunks and down and outs, drug addicts and Vietnam veterans.

One evening while driving through the Bowery in downtown Manhattan, my very old car (at least fifteen years) broke down. As soon as I stopped and opened the bonnet (or hood), I had about ten men around me looking into the car engine. They all offered a different explanation for the breakdown and some even offered to take the engine apart to fix it. It was getting late and I had to go to the Bronx. I decided it was time to get out of there so I locked the car and went home on the subway. I was not expecting to see the car ever again. But it was still there the next day, the down and outs on the Bowery had looked after it for me. They offered to give it a push and sure enough the engine started. These were all great people, so funny, so humorous in spite of their miserable existence. They had nothing and they could joke about it. One guy said to me, 'Mister, could you spare me a hundred dollars?

... twenty dollars? ... ten dollars? and then he smiled broadly: 'How's about a dime?' I looked at him exasperated and he burst out laughing at my startled reaction.

A black man sitting beside me on the subway asked me one day, 'Mister, have you got a gun?'

I asked him why he wanted to know.

'I wanna give you one piece of advice 'cos I know you're a stranger here – and you look nervous. You're better to be caught with one than without one 'round here.'

I could understand where he was coming from, but I never took his advice. These were rough and violent years in New York city and throughout the United States. There were numerous muggings and shootings – mainly because of drugs. These were the Reagan years, and as in the Thatcher era in England there was not much thought given to the poor and the homeless. The poor depended on the churches, the soup kitchens and the Catholic Worker houses of hospitality. It was shocking to see such poverty alongside such wealth in the richest cities of America. I understand from my friends still working with the homeless in New York, Baltimore and Washington that the situation has not improved. Homeless people have no votes.

In America I met up with two African-American preachers and singers, Brother Kirkpatrick and Brother Jones, who were concerned about justice issues and about the prisoners in Ireland. They used to sing at some of the Irish functions. They knew all the civil rights songs and the gospel songs. I sang along with Brother Kirkpatrick at a concert in New York university in aid of the Kurdish people. We sang one song together, called 'O Freedom'. Sadly, Brother Kirkpatrick passed away some years ago. Also on stage that night was the legendary folk singer, Pete Seeger. I had the pleasure of meeting him afterwards. He was a most engaging and down-to-earth man.

In November 1982 I visited my old friend, Fr Michael Doyle

at Sacred Heart church in Camden, New Jersey. The poverty in Camden shocked me. I had never seen anything like it before except in pictures of the Third World. Each day between seventy and a hundred people came to the priest's house for food parcels for their families. Camden was once a prosperous American city; now it is famous for drugs and prostitution. There were prostitutes everywhere along the streets. Most of the 'customers' were lorry drivers and workers in Philadelphia – across the river Delaware.

I went from there to Charlottesville, Virginia to talk with Carolyn Forché about the situation in Ireland and the possibility of a liberation theology for Ireland, a theology that would offer an alternative to the dominant one in the country. Listening to Carolyn I was beginning to learn to communicate the situation to those who knew little or nothing about it. I had to put flesh on the injustice and poverty. We kept going back to the subject of political violence. It became clear that if I were going to explain the situation in Ireland from an Irish viewpoint, I would have to distinguish between the primary and secondary violence. Carolyn coached me for an interview on National Public Radio in Washington about the way to deal with questions about the IRA. She advised me to show how the IRA came about and how they garnered support in Catholic communities, that there was a larger, more serious violence – institutional violence. She emphasised the need to avoid rhetoric and ideological language. Before I left for New York and Ireland Carolyn encouraged me to continue my work in solidarity with the people. A priest, she told me, had standing and authority and could command a platform. That time spent with Carolyn Forché was very important to me and gave me a new sense of what I had to do and some ideas about how to do it. I intended to pursue human rights work in whatever context I found myself. This, for me, was the priority. I had many friends and contacts who were all, in different ways, engaged in human rights work.

After the sorrow and pain of the hunger-strike I saw it as my

duty to tell the truth about the systematic intimidation and harassment of Irish nationalists and to highlight the root causes of violence in the north-east of Ireland. I also saw it as my duty to defend
the republican prisoners and those in custody.

I wanted to see an end to all violence but I knew there was not
going to be any form of surrender by Irish republicans. I was also
aware that selective condemnations by bishops or priests of the
IRA were ineffective and would only be used by the British for
further propaganda. As far as I was concerned, I needed to take
a principled stand about the causes of violence and the different
kinds of violence in our situation. This is where I differed with Fr
Denis Faul. I had come to know Denis well during my time visiting Long Kesh and I admired the work he had done along with
Frs Brian Brady and Ray Murray in highlighting human rights
abuses by the state. But when he began to attack republicans
more vehemently than the British I had to take a different stance.
Priests and religious in other countries such as South Africa and
South and Central America were facing the same kinds of difficult moral issues and taking a more progressive approach without
being compromised.

Some writers in Latin America had developed a new approach
to politics and theology and a new understanding of the meaning
of violence. Church activists there and in South America made
it their business to befriend writers and human rights activists in
the US. They strongly believed that there is power in 'the word' to
create change and to bring about justice.

After the 1981 hunger strike I was convinced of the need for
radical political and social change in Ireland and I saw the power
people had in bringing about that change – the power of human
rights campaigns and international pressure. People's decisions,
including their choice at election time, must be respected.

My time in America was significant. I experienced freedom
and insecurity, and had to take total responsibility for my life

for the first time. In many ways I had to grow up. I discovered things about myself – my insecurity and my lack of discipline, for example – that I might never have discovered had I not gone there.

Just before returning home in 1982 I was arrested in New York for an anti-nuclear protest organised by Fr Dan Berrigan and about thirty other peace activists. I should say I got myself arrested since it was a deliberate strategy planned beforehand by the leaders of the protest. On the way to the police station (or precinct as they call it) I was handcuffed to a cop who asked me where I came from. When I said the north of Ireland he replied, 'Why did you not tell us before we put you in the car?' His parents were from County Armagh and County Roscommon. I said I wanted to be arrested in solidarity with the others, but he did not understand. We were all charged with 'trespassing on United States government property', a nuclear research building in Manhattan. It was my first taste of being on the wrong side of the law. I went to court in Lower Manhattan with all the others the next day. The case was adjourned. We did not have to say anything in the court, except whether we pleaded guilty or not guilty. We all pleaded guilty. The hearings dragged on for several months and I was back home in Ireland before they reached a verdict in August 1982. Eventually I received a letter from the lawyer stating that 'the charges against you were adjourned in contemplation of dismissal. This is a formal disposition which means that if you do not have any further problems for six months from the date of the disposition, the charges will be regarded as dismissed.' Some others who had been in court many times before were sentenced to various terms of imprisonment.

Looking back, my life has taken some strange twists and turns. At times, it was stressful. Other times, it was exhilarating. I realised that a priest can only survive – especially in times of stress – if he has reliable friends in his life. You need to have a friend with whom you can share your thoughts and ideas and express your fears and anxieties. I was lucky to have made several good friends in the United States and I knew I had a few good ones in Ireland.

# 15

# Back Home in Ireland

I returned to Ireland for good in June 1982. I had been feeling homesick for a year or more and there was so much more I felt I could do at home, especially after the hunger strike. I had spoken to the new bishop, Joseph Duffy, about an appointment in the diocese and he told me that I would be appointed in September. I would have time to rest and recover during the summer months. I appreciated the bishop's positive response.

I could hardly believe it, when after a few weeks at home I heard the sad news that my friend, Fr Tom O'Gara, had died after a short illness in hospital in Derry. He was only thirty-five years of age. Just before leaving New York, I had received a letter from him with money for my fare home. I never got to thank him. I went to the wake in his parents' house outside Muff in County Donegal and then to the funeral mass in Moville. It was truly a sad and emotional occasion. I felt annoyed that I had not seen Tom since my return. He was always a friend I could rely on – even if we disagreed on some things.

The whole parish was at the funeral, as were most of the priests from the Derry diocese and many of our classmates. During the mass, Pádraig Standún, his friend from Maynooth, paid Tom this wonderful tribute:

> Are you there, Lord … ?
> Are you out of town … ?

Or are you your own worst enemy ... ?

How else can we explain your letting one of the finest people you had going for you die at thirty-five?

O'Gara, the light of many of our lives, is gone,

The warmth, the sparkle, the caring but apparently carefree spirit, that gave so much joy, so much comfort, so much love –

How can we face the greying years without him?

Lord, but you're the hard task master.

I find it hard to even like you, these days.

And yet, those who have been touched by his life, know that we have been uniquely privileged ... The greatness of this self-effacing man, the success of the priesthood, the unconventional priesthood he created and loved for Christ (all Christs) was beyond doubt. Here was a giant.

There is a lesson in this for a church establishment, which seems at times to have barely contained and tolerated one of its finest assets. Flair, imagination, contagious loving, the bending and bucking of stagnant systems are not sins.

They help transform the drab reality of many lives and bring the spark of the Incarnation to what for many is a sterile and pompous institution. Such creative priesthood is too often met by threats and suspensions, rather than encouraged as a complement and embellishment of the hard and sincere graft of the more conventional priest.

We're going to miss you, Tom, old troubadour, friend, joker, preacher, rock'n roll singer (move over Elvis), footballer, balladeer, lover of life, song writer, counsellor, laugher-at-himself, deep thinker, binder of wounds, carrier of others' crosses, I could go on.

Faults, I don't want to know. Love is blind, they say.

May the Lord console your mother and father, sister and brothers, all others who loved you, Tom, all those you loved and especially she whom you loved best.

Somewhere, a guitar is strumming.

Feicimid arís thú, Tom, le cúnamh Dé.[*]

Pádraig Standún expressed all our feelings of sorrow and loss. I missed Tom a lot, as did the people of the parish and most of all his own parents and brothers and sister and family circle. He was a great character and will always be remembered in the folklore around Moville and Derry. I had not seen him as much during the previous two or three years when I was in the US, but I had hoped to renew our friendship when I returned to Ireland.

In September 1982 Bishop Duffy appointed me to the curate's

post in Irvinestown, County Fermanagh (Devenish parish), which is next door to my native parish of Ederney. The famous island of Devenish lies within the parish boundaries. I knew many people living there, some had moved in from Ederney and others were at school with me in Enniskillen. We had always been big rivals in football. However, I looked forward to going to Irvinestown parish. I tried to approach every situation humanly and compassionately. My interest in the broader political situation had grown immensely over the previous few years and I was becoming increasingly involved in trying to highlight injustices. I brought this resolve back from America and had established good contacts with human rights workers in New York, London and Belfast.

I threw myself into the parish work as quickly and as enthusiastically as possible, becoming involved in all the parish activities and preparing children for the sacraments. We were busy fundraising for the renovation of the parish church. However, I was determined to make as much time as possible available for human rights work, which I knew to be more important than anything else I could do at that time in a parish.

I discussed with Mary Nelis from Derry the idea of a church-based justice group to focus immediately on the abuse of women prisoners. Mary was all for it, as were some others from Belfast, Fermanagh and Tyrone. The first meeting of the Community for Justice was held in Omagh on 30 June 1983. Those who attended were Billy Gallagher (RIP), Tommy Murray (RIP), Francis Martin, Joan Shortt, Maria Droogan (RIP), Mitchel McLaughlin, Mary Nelis, Noelle Ryan, Fr Des Wilson, Fr Alec Reid and Cormac McAleer from Creggan, County Tyrone.

We decided that our group should first focus attention on, and campaign to end, the dreadful practice of strip-searching of women prisoners in Armagh jail. We came in for criticism and abusive remarks from unionists and indeed from some nationalists. I felt very strongly that the nationalist people were not helped by the divisions on the nationalist side and I said this in the course of an RTÉ discussion programme some time in 1985. I appealed to the SDLP to unite with Sinn Féin to work for a just and lasting peace. Seamus Mallon of the SDLP, who was interviewed after the programme, ridiculed my suggestion and made disparaging remarks about me. Since my interview was pre-recorded, I had no right of reply. This taught me to be careful in future about taking part in pre-recorded programmes on RTÉ.

When Ronald Reagan visited Ireland in May 1984 I went to Dublin to join in the protests against what the US government and army were doing in South and Central America. Reagan symbolised the US empire and its savage policies against the poor and the native peoples in the Americas. I had just returned from America and wanted to show solidarity with the people in South and Central America who were victims of Reagan and the White House policies. I was pleasantly surprised to see so many other priests and religious present at the protest, most of whom had been on the missions.

Some of the bishops, and also Cardinal Ó Fiaich, took a principled stand and refused to meet him. I thought the Reagan visit might be the beginning of something new in the church in Ireland. It did mark some kind of new development to see so many priests and nuns taking a stand for justice, even if it was in relation to South and Central America. However, few of those protesting took a stand on the violation of human rights in their own back yard – in the six counties of north-east Ireland.

It gave me some hope that, at last, things were beginning to change, that the social gospel was becoming accepted in Ireland. Reagan was symbolic of all that was wrong with the world. He did not get a rapturous welcome like John F. Kennedy in June 1963. Reagan was closely associated with state terrorism and 'the Contras' in Central and South America, and had done nothing about the poor and homeless African-Americans and Latin-

Americans in his own country. He was also a close ally of Margaret Thatcher.

In 1984 the Community for Justice began organising public meetings to encourage debate about the future. The first meeting was in Derry, in the Guildhall, on 28 June 1984. The topic was 'The Church and Republicanism'. The speakers on that occasion were Bernadette McAliskey, Mary Nelis and Des Wilson, who challenged the existing attitude of the church to republicanism. Bernadette humorously reminded us that the official church, no matter whose side it was on, will always 'go home on the winners' bus'.

One of the few senior churchmen to recognise the political realities in the north was Cardinal Tomás Ó Fiaich. I spoke to him on a number of occasions and knew that he could not garner much support from most of the hierarchy for taking a strong stance on human rights issues. One issue that Cardinal Ó Fiaich did speak out about was the strip-searching of women prisoners, condemning the practice as the 'humiliation of women'. After this, I invited Nobel Peace Prize winner, Seán MacBride, to speak at an anti-strip-searching meeting in Enniskillen. We had some difficulty securing a venue as none of the hotels in the town would give us a room. Eventually, we rented the Irish National Foresters hall. There was a good crowd of nationalists and republicans from Fermanagh present.

In October 1984 I organised another public meeting in Belfast called 'The Search for Peace'. Along with others, I felt it was time for an open debate about the meaning of the word 'peace' in our situation and for republicans to reclaim the word, which had been hi-jacked by the 'peace at any price' brigade. I spoke about this to Des Wilson and Mitchel McLaughlin. Des always took a broader and longer view of things. He demanded a peace settlement that recognised basic rights and which offered the Irish people a modern democracy and guaranteed equality for all citizens. Mitchel

McLaughlin too was positive about discussing the issue in public and was willing to take part.

About one hundred, mostly republicans, turned up for the meeting in the Conway Mill. The guest speakers were Mitchel McLaughlin, representing Sinn Féin, Dan Berrigan, SJ, the peace campaigner in the US, Herman Verbeek, a priest, pacifist, MEP and member of the Green Party in the Netherlands and Des Wilson. Not much gender balance on the platform but there was in the audience, and there was plenty of food for thought from all the contributors. Gerry Adams, who supported the idea from the beginning, was present, and made his thoughtful contribution from the floor. I thought the best talk that night was given by Mitchel McLaughlin, who suggested that peace meant different things to different people – but for republicans it was tied up with justice and equality. Herman Verbeek spoke about the world situation and the dangers of global capitalism.

It was clear to me from that meeting that some Irish republicans had indeed been thinking a lot about how peace might be achieved by political means in the Irish context. They were keeping an eye on developments in South Africa and Central America. I knew also from my contacts with some republican prisoners that a debate taking place within the jails. In a sense 'the peace process' was already under way but the war was to drag on for another ten years. All these preliminary discussions were important to get a consensus within the republican movement about the way forward. There had to be all kinds of preparations and guarantees built into any genuine peace process that was going to have any chance of succeeding. Republicans felt they had given too much and lost too many of their people to settle for anything less than a genuine peace process in which they were fully involved.

I discussed the issue of conflict resolution in a broader context during 1985 when I was invited by a priest of the Columban Missionary Society to take part in a workshop in Navan, County

Meath. The workshop was for a group of missionaries, most of whom belonged to the Columban missionary order based at Dalgan Park, who were interested in the ongoing conflict in the north. Mary Nelis, a community worker and human rights activist from Derry, was another speaker. I knew that she would bring a dose of reality to the proceedings. Mary had a great interest in liberation theology and did not pull any punches when it came to the role of the official church in supporting the status quo. The discussion was revealing. The Irish-born missionaries were critical of our 'pro-republican' interpretation of the northern conflict, accusing us of taking a pro-IRA stance rather than making a 'Christian response'.

However, the people from other nations present could empathise entirely with what we were saying. The contributions of the Irish made me wonder about the role of Irish missionaries in many war-torn places in the world. What kind of witness were they giving? I know that some Irish-born missionaries were quite radical about the situations in which they worked in the Philippines or South Africa, but why could they not apply the same principles to the situation in Ireland? It has always puzzled me.

A month after the workshop in Navan I received this letter from one of the participants from the Philippines which confirmed my scepticism about some of the missionaries:

Dear Joe,

It's always the same anywhere I go, once I share my peasant background, my views seem to be rejected by those from a rich background. So, to be heard, I need extra energy to assert myself, to be angry sometimes to drive home my point. Society doesn't take the poor seriously until the poor run amuck (this is the other extreme, of course) or until the poor insist strongly that they are not different from the rich, that we have the same blood vessels and muscles, all of us rich and poor. But only people who have felt the pain of being hungry, broken down, isolated and rejected – only they will understand what it means to be poor and struggling for justice and peace .... It was a very well planned and well managed workshop but in the sense of finding the genuine Christian attitude to poor people in the course of the workshop, I did not find much. The First World's condescending attitude to the poor was marked .... Our struggle will go on, we will never surrender.

Sincerely,
Francia.

This woman understood where Mary Nelis and I were coming from but she could not deal with the condescending attitude of those in the group who challenged us and who had no real experience of oppression and state violence in Ireland. My contention was, and is, that oppression and state violence is the same everywhere – in Ireland, the Philippines, South America – it is always the same for those on the receiving end.

Under the umbrella of the Community for Justice, we continued to lobby on the issue of strip-searching and the abuse of prisoners. On 19 August 1985 we arranged a meeting with the Bishops' Commission for Justice and Peace at their offices in Booterstown, Dublin. We wanted them to convey our concerns to the Irish bishops' conference since the bishops had refused to meet us. Our delegation consisted of community worker Noelle Ryan, Seánna Walsh, an Irish language activist and former republican prisoner, Cormac McAleer, a Sinn Féin councillor in Omagh, Des Wilson and Briege Brownlee, also an ex-republican prisoner.

Shortly after the meeting started, Cormac McAleer rose to his feet to set out our demands. While speaking, however, he was interrupted by a member of the Irish Commission for Justice and Peace (ICJP) and told to sit down and shut up. Cormac was the only elected person in that room. Des Wilson was incensed that we should be treated like this and said that we would not tolerate insulting or bullying behaviour. He said that we had to put up with enough of that at home and announced that he was withdrawing from the meeting and invited us to join him. We all got up and left the room. The ICJP members sat in stunned silence as we gathered our papers and left. The walk-out made the evening news.

Shortly after, I wrote to the bishop of Galway, Eamon Casey, seeking a meeting. I thought that because of his record on El Salvador he might be willing to take up our concerns with the rest of the Irish bishops. However, he sent back a short note stating that he would not meet with us, using the excuse that we had walked out of the meeting with the Commission for Justice and Peace. We never sought to meet with the commission after that.

I was now fully convinced that the only way forward was the inclusion of Sinn Féin in all discussions about the political future and the resolution of the conflict. The party represented a large section of the nationalist community and was becoming more involved in local politics. From the beginning, I was opposed to the flawed Hillsborough Agreement of 1985 because it excluded Sinn Féin. There could be no lasting peace if Sinn Féin was not involved. It was as simple as that and yet it took the Dublin government a long time to accept this.

Some will argue that a priest cannot be an Irish republican because within republicanism there has been what is known as 'the physical force' tradition. I would also argue that within republicanism there is also a pacifist tradition. At certain times in our history and in the history of other oppressed peoples some believed that the only way forward was by taking up arms. Circumstances dictated the type of resistance that was needed. In the colonial situation, the colonial power will often make it impossible for the oppressed to achieve freedom by peaceful means. We saw that in Ireland and in every country in the world, including India, where the British had invaded and controlled. I understand why some people feel that there is no other way than armed resistance. However, there will always have to be a negotiated settlement. When the time was opportune, republicans chose a peaceful strategy.

In the aftermath of the 1981 hunger strike I realised, as did many others, that Sinn Féin was growing in strength and would become in time the most influential force on the nationalist side in the six counties. I felt that through a peaceful democratic strategy Sinn Féin could help to bring about the new Ireland that so many have desired and worked to achieve. I pursued a peaceful strategy alongside those who took up arms. This was risky for me in many ways because it was often perceived as total support for the armed strategy. Over the years some people criticised me for not taking a 'more balanced' approach to the issue of violence, accusing me of only being prepared to condemn the British and unionist violence while saying nothing about IRA violence. This was not true and was a deliberate attempt by some to undermine my arguments and presentation of the facts about RUC murder and British collusion with unionist murder gangs.

I understand the pain and suffering caused by IRA actions as much as I do the hurt caused to republicans and nationalists by British crown forces and unionist death squad actions. Of course I do, and I can only offer my deepest sympathy to all who lost loved ones and those injured in this long war. I did my best on several occasions to bring about a cessation from the IRA and my appeals were always treated seriously. However, there were many reasons why the IRA was not ready or willing to lay down their arms until finally doing so in 1994. The main reason, I suspect, was that the British showed no willingness or desire to end their war against republicans and nationalists and that MI5 had invested too much in the war to see it all ended very quickly.

As the war in the six counties escalated, I felt I had to make a moral judgement and a finer analysis of the situation to maintain my credibility as a commentator and a human rights activist. From a moral or ethical perspective I had to make a clear distinction between state violence and republican violence. They were not the same and they were not equal. They never are in a situation where a colonised people are in conflict with the state/government. Politically and morally they were not the same. I defined the primary violence as that of the British state/crown forces /unionist murder gangs and IRA violence as secondary, a response to a situation of institutionalised violence and tyrannical government.

Just weeks after the signing of the Anglo-Irish Agreement, I was invited to speak at the annual Kilmichael commemoration in west Cork in late November 1985. I saw this as an opportunity to counter the pro-British propaganda in the Irish media. The Kilmichael commemoration is a major event in the republican calendar and affords past and present republicans the opportunity to meet and remember. I met two survivors of the 1920 ambush, Jack O'Sullivan and Ned Young. The IRA flying column was led by the legendary Tom Barry. Three republicans and eighteen British auxiliaries were killed. It has been described as a 'decisive battle' in the war waged against the Black and Tans in west Cork. Soon after Kilmichael, the British government decided it was time to seek a resolution rather than a victory.

The day began with a memorial mass celebrated by an old friend from Maynooth days, an Canónach Mícheál Ó Dálaigh. I knew that the large audience in Kilmichael was anxious to hear about the feelings of the grassroots nationalists in the north. I told them that the people I knew and talked to did not think too much of the Hillsborough deal – and that they believed Charlie Haughey was right when he rejected the deal and stated that the six counties was 'a failed political entity'. The people I spoke to at the Kilmichael meeting were a bit unsure about the deal considering the hype that Hillsborough was getting in the media and considering that Mr Paisley was leading a revolt against interference by Dublin in the internal affairs of the six counties. This gave the agreement credibility in some quarters and raised some doubts about Mr Haughey's response.

I said at Kilmichael that the Anglo-Irish Agreement was fatally flawed since it ignored a large section of the northern nationalist population – those represented by Sinn Féin. I expressed deep disappointment at the Catholic hierarchy's total support for the agreement and argued that the British government could not be a force for peace in this country unless it was seriously trying to disengage from Ireland and making this known. The effects of British rule in the north were plain for all to see – the daily abuse of power, northern nationalists being murdered and harassed by the British and their agents in the unionist death squads and the RUC/UDR. My comments met with warm approval in Kilmichael. The people of west Cork understood the reasons for struggle. However, the Dublin media had a different agenda. The heading in the *Irish Independent* the next day was 'Priest Raps Hierarchy'. They did not make it clear what I was rapping the hierarchy about. The *Irish Times* gave the talk fuller treatment on the front page, quoting at length from the speech. I was quite surprised at the amount of publicity I received in a paper not noted for its sympathy for the strong nationalist viewpoint.

Shortly after this, I heard that there were rumblings in the parish, in Irvinestown, about the fact that I had gone to Kilmichael and said some harsh things about the Anglo-Irish Agreement and those who supported it. A group of 'respectable' Catholics (mainly associated with the SDLP) held a meeting to seek to have me removed from the parish. They decided to start a petition, but there were so few willing to sign it that their protest fell through. However, it did not stop them from trying by other means.

I had already annoyed Seamus Mallon of the SDLP on an RTÉ programme when I called on him and the SDLP to engage in discussions with Sinn Féin to seek a united nationalist way forward. I had come to this conclusion while in the US and took this opportunity to float it in public. As it happened others had been thinking along the same lines. Mallon criticised me in the strongest terms for failing to condemn 'the men of violence'.

'It was a disgrace for "a man of the cloth" to refuse to condemn the Provos,' he thundered angrily. I was not given the right to reply after his outburst on the RTÉ programme. I never thought highly of him after that.

I sensed at that time a change of attitude from some of the 'leading lights' in the parish who were also key personnel in the local SDLP. They expected the priests to support them and to promote their interests at all times and they were somewhat taken aback on realising that I was not like all the other priests they had known, who were strong supporters of the SDLP. I could sense growing hostility towards me among a certain section but it did not bother me unduly. I knew I had as many supporters as detractors. And anyway, I felt I was doing my duty as a priest, speaking out about injustice, censorship, the abuse of prisoners and of those detained by the RUC. I did not really care who I annoyed or who I was aligned with for adopting this stance. I was telling the truth and was always mindful of the gospel dictum: 'The truth will set you free.' Des Wilson repeated this piece of gospel wisdom on many occasions.

I continued to make public pronouncements against the British and their collaborators and to define the primary violence in our situation as the British presence and British military support for an undemocratic political system. I was sick and tired of hearing about the need for balance in public utterances, the need to always condemn the IRA as well as the British government and its forces. For God's sake, I thought, the two were not the same. The people who denounced me, especially in the Catholic community, had another agenda. Some people were unable – or unwilling – to make the distinction. They just wanted me to condemn the IRA. Surely there were enough clergymen doing that already. I was trying, in my own way, to awaken consciences to another kind of violence that seldom was highlighted, the suffering of the prisoners and those who were selected for harassment by the RUC, the British army and the UDR.

In August 1986 I had an opportunity to say some of these things to priests of my own diocese when we had a week-long assembly of all the priests and the bishop near Newry, County Down. The purpose of the meeting was to discuss 'the role of the priest today'. Although the clergy in the diocese of Clogher all live and work along both sides of the border, in Fermanagh and Monaghan, there was little or no discussion of the conflict nor of the plight of the Catholic people in the six counties, who were then clearly at the mercy of the British, the RUC, MI5 and unionist death squads.

My only explanation is that it would have caused too much friction among the clergy and so it was better ignored. A proposal was made towards the end of the assembly, that we, the priests of the diocese of Clogher, should make a public statement condemning the 'men of violence'. This came out of the blue. I knew what was meant by 'the men of violence', and it was not the RUC and the British army. Before long, I was on my feet. I said I did not think this was a good idea for many reasons. There had been many condemnations over the years of 'the men of violence' and these had not made any difference in terms of ending the conflict. It was wrong and futile to be selective in condemnations and we had not thought enough or talked enough about the whole issue of the causes and kinds of political violence in our country. There was a history that had to be taken into account in understanding the current phase of the conflict.

The proposal was put to a vote and was lost. My arguments had won the day and I was very pleased about that. However, I was not convinced that the clergy of the diocese would ever do or say anything to challenge the official church policy on the north. The official church was still anti-republican, and there was not a hope of persuading the clergy to take a stand for justice as this would align them too closely with republicans. It was safer to remain allied with the 'moderates', the SDLP. This would be more acceptable to the British government on whom they depended for funding for schools.

The reality of the situation was already clear to me. The official church in Ireland is the church of the well-off, the respectable. Did not Cardinal Daly on many occasions call on the people not to vote for Sinn Féin? Did he not refuse to meet Gerry Adams, when he was an elected leader? Did he not do his utmost over the years to discredit Sinn Féin as a political party? Did this church not refuse to allow a funeral mass to republicans?

One of the most depressing aspects of the church in Ireland that I have seen is the way that middle-class Catholics who have come up the ranks from ordinary working-class backgrounds turn their backs on their past and on their own people. They fall into the mould, into supporting the establishment, and look down on the working-class who did not have their opportunities. Indeed they resent the working-class taking the initiative and setting up their own economic enterprises. These are the middle-class Catholics – some attached to the Knights of Columbanus – that will reaffirm that they have made it in society. I understand that it is the same in all former colonies.

In September 1986 I was asked to testify in court in the Hague on behalf of two escapees, Gerry Kelly and Bik McFarlane, whom the British wanted extradited back to the six counties. Bernadette McAliskey and I were to testify on the same day. These men had escaped from Long Kesh in the 'great escape' of September 1983 when thirty-eight republican prisoners broke out. Having made it safely out of the country, these two men arrived with some friends in the Netherlands. Bik, a former student for the priesthood and a good folk singer, had been O/C of the republican prisoners during the second hunger strike in which the ten men died. Gerry Kelly had been in prison in England and was transferred back to Long Kesh. They were eventually arrested in the Netherlands and held in prison awaiting trial to be extradited back to the six counties.

When I was asked to testify I was on my own in the parish but decided to take a risk and go to the Netherlands. I was told it was important. The day before I was set to go, an elderly man in the parish died. I did not know what to do. I had to move fast. I went to talk to the daughter of the deceased and asked if she would mind postponing the funeral for a day, that I had been called away on urgent business. She, being the only close family member, said that she would not mind at all. In the court I asked the judge, through our lawyer, if I could make my submission first as I had to catch a flight that afternoon, for the funeral the next day in Irvinestown. The judge was very accommodating and allowed me to go first. After the funeral the next day, I told the daughter of the deceased about 'my urgent business' in the Netherlands. She laughed and said that she knew Gerry Kelly when he worked with her in Belfast, before he went off to see the world. She was glad I was able to offer him any help I could. It's a small world.

I was still very much involved in the campaign to end the strip-searching of women prisoners in Armagh jail and that meant attending plenty of meetings throughout the north. I was on my way to a meeting one evening in County Derry when I was stopped just outside Irvinestown by the RUC. They delayed me for almost an hour on the road, and then took me back to the barracks to search my car. By that time it was too late to attend the meeting. The organisers were not surprised at what had happened, as it was not unusual. It was clear to me that all our phones were being tapped and they knew my movements at all times.

As MY PROFILE continued to rise, I was invited to speak at a number of commemorations in the south remembering dead heroes from the Tan war. These provided a platform for people from the north to speak out about the situation. In October 1986 I spoke at a republican commemoration in Kilfeackle, County Tipperary, to remember the Irish patriot, Seán Treacy, who was shot in Dublin by the Black and Tans on 14 October 1920. In my address I stressed that we were one people and one nation, and that the struggle today was the same as the struggle in which Seán Treacy gave his life at the age of twenty-three. I stressed that the struggle for a new and just Ireland began in one's own local place and that the people in Tipperary and Cork had a role to play in bringing about justice in the whole of Ireland. The twenty-six counties at this time was a depressed place with high unemployment and large numbers emigrating to find work. I wanted to draw attention to this reality and to place the responsibility for changing this situation on the people and the political parties in the south.

It was on that occasion that I first met the late John Feehan, publisher of Mercier Press, Cork, who was also a guest speaker at the commemoration. After a short conversation he asked me if I would write down my thoughts about the church and that he would publish my book. I was delighted to be asked. I found the task daunting since I was already busy enough in the parish while at the same time attending meetings around the country. The most I had written until then was a few pamphlets, a few letters to the papers and an occasional article.

In due course I set about putting some thoughts on paper. I was interested in the historical role of the Catholic church and its relation to republicans and the Fenians and to the rebels of 1916. I was interested in exploring the possibilities of a liberation theology for Ireland. I wrote about my difficulty with the approach of the Irish bishops to British violence in Ireland.

The Irish Catholic hierarchy collectively failed to state unequivocally that internment was immoral. There was no statement from the bishops' conference following the murder of thirteen unarmed civilians by British paratroopers in Derry on Bloody Sunday. There was no joint pastoral condemning the unjust Diplock court system, which replaced internment without trial. There were no condemnations by the Catholic hierarchy of the alliance of the British army and the UDA, which led to the breaking of the IRA ceasefire in 1972.

The Irish bishops failed to call for a public inquiry when people accused the SAS of killing Catholics. Nor did they call attention to the partial manner in which justice was administered and sentences handed down. The Catholic hierarchy was silent about the Ulster Workers Strike and silent also when the Dublin government passed the Offences against the State (Amendment) Act. This act established 'special courts' where the mere opinion of a garda superintendent was accepted as sufficient evidence to have citizens sentenced to long prison terms. There was no statement of moral outrage when the editor of *An Phoblacht*, Eamonn Mac Thomáis, was given a twelve month jail sentence for possession of a document, allegedly illegal yet freely available in every newspaper office in Dublin. They failed to call for a public inquiry into conditions at Portlaoise prison even after the *Irish Times* in an editorial (3 Feb. 1975) stated: 'Conditions in the prison by all available accounts are inhuman and there is general agreement that they have been made still worse by recent disturbances.'

Catholic bishops were reluctant to say or do anything that might in some way be seen to give any advantage to the IRA or even show any understanding of their cause. Bishop Cahal Daly was the most vocal opponent of the IRA. On one occasion he said: 'The need for security operations in Northern Ireland is incontestable, and should not be contested. The population in both communities should be willing to accept the unavoidable inconveniences which security entails, however irksome and frustrating these inconveniences spread over so long a period certainly are.'

Following Bloody Sunday, Bishop Cahal Daly called for prayer. The only words permissible to the Christian, he proclaimed, are: 'Father forgive them for they know not what they do.' He had other words for those who bombed the British army base at Aldershot some weeks later.

If you follow this narrow 'revisionist' doctrine, violence is what some people or groups carry out against the government or state.

If you try to understand violence in a broader context it puts the emphasis on institutional and state violence while seeing the violence of armed insurrectionists as a response to that primary violence. State violence is a concerted and sophisticated kind of violence against the people and includes discrimination, torture and assassination.

I aired some of these views on an ITV documentary broadcast in Britain as well as in Ireland. I was given complete editorial control, which was most unusual at that time. I thought the programme was well produced and that I said all that needed to be said about the unjust partition of the country and the dire consequences leading on from that. Unfortunately it was broadcast at 7.00 a.m. in the morning which meant that few people actually saw it.

While based in Irvinestown during the 1980s I became more aware of the secret and sinister works of the British in Ireland. It was also clear to me that Protestants in the UDR and RUC were sacrificed to protect the identity of British agents in the IRA. At this time, I was not *au fait* with how British intelligence was operating in Ireland nor how the British colluded with loyalist paramilitaries in killing Catholics – including human rights activists like Pat Finucane. I was not aware of the extent to which MI5, MI6, the RUC's E4A and Echo 3 units, MRF, the Force Recognisance Unit or any of the many other secret agents were involved in operations in Ireland – especially in the twenty-six counties. We had an inkling that things were not right when the case of the Littlejohns became public. We had also heard something about Kincora and Sir Maurice Oldfield – but it was not clear to me how they had such power.

However, after 1984 more of the truth about their operations was uncovered and disclosed by John Stalker, Constable John Robinson, Colin Samson, Colin Wallace and Fred Holroyd, whom I met in New York. I did not know that 'the Badger' who lived in Monaghan was a British agent within the garda special branch.

This was all totally outside my ken, as well as my wildest dreams. However, I am now a bit older and wiser about the way the British were operating in Ireland – especially within the garda síochána. It was a shock to my system when I first heard and read about the extent of these secret operations and how they could arrange to have people killed. It was frightening.

The IRA stepped up their campaign in the early months of 1987. Twenty-two RUC stations were attacked, and a number of RUC and UDR men killed. In April the lord chief justice, Sir Maurice Gibson (seventy-four years) and his wife were killed in an explosion near the border at Newry on the main Dublin–Belfast road. In 1977 he had said that 'shooting may be justified as a method of arrest'. In 1984, he acquitted three RUC men of the murder of three IRA men.

On 8 May 1987 the IRA planned another attack – this time on Loughgall RUC barracks in County Armagh. Loughgall was the place where the Orange Order was founded. It was also the centre of the 'murder triangle', where thirty Catholics were killed between 1972 and 1975. Up to forty SAS men, acting on a tip-off, were lying in wait near the RUC barracks and opened fire on the vehicles carrying the IRA volunteers. Eight volunteers were shot dead – and one civilian passer-by killed – by the SAS. Some of those killed were shot again after being badly injured. It was the biggest loss the IRA suffered since an attack in Clonmult, County Cork in 1921 by the Black and Tans. The east Tyrone brigade spokesman made a statement shortly afterwards:

> We attacked Dungannon courthouse a few days ago (7 May) and the Loughgall attack was part of the IRA's plan to hit areas which remained untouched. We want to show that there is no normalisation and the SAS action proves we are in a war situation. We have always maintained that; they have always practised it but never admitted it.[*]

On the evening of 8 May 1987 I was attending a céilí in Irvinestown

---

[*] Raymond Murray, *The SAS in Ireland* (Mercier Press, Cork, 2005), p. 37.

when I heard that the SAS had ambushed an IRA unit in County Armagh. Paddy Shanaghan from near Castlederg was at the céilí and asked if I had heard the evening news, that eight members of the IRA were shot dead by the SAS, who had received a tip-off. It was only the next day when the names were released that I discovered that one of those killed was Jim Lynagh from Monaghan, whom I first knew when he was a young boy at school in the early 1970s. I knew some of the others killed from various meetings. I felt very sorry for the families for I knew the kind of pressure they would be under from the British and the media – and indeed the church authorities.

I went that evening to Monaghan. There was a rally organised in Old Cross Square and I was asked by Caoimhghin Ó Caoláin to give out the rosary through a loud hailer from an upstairs room. There were more than one thousand people present. The family of Jim Lynagh asked the priest in charge in Monaghan if I could be the main celebrant at the funeral mass. He refused. They asked him if I could concelebrate and he conceded to this request. The priest himself was the main concelebrant and gave the homily. In the homily, there were no references to the circumstances surrounding Jim's killing. As Gerry Adams said at the graveside, 'You would think he died of pneumonia. .

I attended several of the funerals of those killed at Loughgall. Huge numbers attended, showing yet again the support on the ground for these young republican volunteers.

The British, especially after the signing of the Anglo-Irish Agreement in 1985, intensified the harassment in nationalist areas throughout the six counties. The gardaí continued to do likewise in the twenty-six counties. I was receiving numerous reports about harassment near where I lived – in places like Castlederg, Strabane, Cookstown, Stewartstown, Lisnaskea. I also received complaints about the gardaí in Ballyshannon, Bundoran and other places in Donegal. I was busy taking statements from people who were being constantly harassed as well as attending meetings about this issue. The RUC and British army were clearly under orders to make life even more difficult for those with republican inclinations, and were acting on all kinds of information coming from very dubious sources.

The harassment of Catholics took different forms: arrest and detention 'on suspicion' meant that the person arrested was held for up to seven days, during which time they were beaten and threatened. There were the early morning house searches. There was harassment at UDR checkpoints and border checkpoints by the British army. They were especially tough with women who travelled across the border and who they suspected of being couriers. And there was the intimidation and harassment of prisoners who were often subjected to the degrading practice of strip-searching. The visitors of nationalist prisoners in Long Kesh, Crumlin Road and Armagh jails were also harassed on their way to and from these places.

I collected statements from people who suffered all the various kinds of intimidation and harassment and published them in broadsheets called the *Intimidation Files*. One town where nationalist people suffered was Strabane – a strongly republican town with high unemployment and many social problems. However, the Strabane people are resilient and good-humoured and were able to withstand that vicious campaign against their community by the RUC and British army. There was an informer working for the RUC in a senior position in the republican movement. I knew this man very well and never suspected for a minute that he would betray his own people. The informer is probably the most detested person in Irish history.

A number of us had called a public meeting in Castlederg in March 1987 to talk about the increase in harassment of nationalists in that town and in the surrounding countryside. Local solicitor John Fahy addressed the meeting, recounting numerous instances of harassment and intimidation by the RUC. Up to one hundred people attended, and many shared their experiences of intimidation by the RUC. One local man who spoke that night was Dermot Hackett, who worked as a bread delivery man. He complained that he was constantly harassed by the RUC and the UDR. He described in detail how he was stopped by the RUC and his bread van searched on a regular basis. Sometimes they took the trays of bread out of the van and placed them on the road. All of this was having a profound effect on his health. He felt he was being singled out and he did not know why – other than that he was a Catholic in business.

About one month after that meeting, Dermot Hackett was shot dead by a pro-British death squad. He was on his way from Castlederg to Drumquin, County Tyrone when he was stopped and shot at point blank range. The UVF admitted the killing and many years later a loyalist called Michael Stone claimed that he carried out the murder. He also said he had seen police files about Dermot Hackett and that was why he was singled out for assassination. (Stone attacked the mourners in Milltown at Mairéad Farrell's funeral, killing three men.)

Following the funeral of Dermot Hackett on 23 May 1987 I sent a statement to the local paper (*The Ulster Herald*) on behalf of the Community for Justice, stating that I had received complaints from a number of people that the RUC harassed mourners and had taken photographs of them. The report in the paper read: 'The attitude of the RUC to the nationalist people of Castlederg is despicable. They think they can do what they like but there is no way these people can continue to intimidate the people like that and we intend to highlight the harassment more and more until it is stopped. Fr McVeigh added that Mr Hackett was one of many people in the Castlederg/Aghyaran area who had been selected for "intimidation and harassment" by the RUC and British army.'

After this, my harassment by the RUC, UDR and British soldiers began in earnest. I had been harassed before but not in the very deliberate and systematic way that began then. Within a week I was being followed and stopped by the RUC. This continued for a number of years. I was harassed at checkpoints along the border and at checkpoints that were set up on lonely country roads at night. A few priests who looked a bit like me and were also a bit overweight were often hassled because the British thought they were me. The UDR and the RUC were even more vindictive than the British.

On one occasion around that time the UDR stopped me on the main street of Lisnaskea. One of them asked for my ID and insisted on calling me 'boss'.

I said my name was not 'boss'.

He asked me what I wanted to be called.

I said: 'My name is Father McVeigh or Reverend McVeigh, take your pick.'

He said he would never call me 'father' since I was not his father! And, as far as he was concerned, I was not a reverend for he did 'not believe in my religion'. He asked me to open the bonnet and the boot of the car and to step out. My car was stopped in the middle of the main street. Meanwhile, a long line of traffic had formed while all this was going on for at least fifteen minutes. He told me he had read my comments in the paper and that what I said about the UDR was not good. He said something like 'You would be happy to see us all killed.' I said I would not and that I had never said or suggested such a thing. I said I would like to have a further conversation with him out of uniform and unarmed some time. I did not hear from him again.

I made many complaints about my own harassment but the intimidation continued. Of course, I was not the only one being harassed. It was a common occurrence for young nationalists going to or coming from Gaelic football matches or dances to be stopped and held for hours. On many occasions, police and British soldiers assaulted the young people – just because they came from a certain village or area. I always advised any victims of these assaults to make a complaint to their lawyer and to their local priest. I believed that it was important to have them all recorded.

# 16

# Assassinations, Intimidation and the Enniskillen Bomb

Some time in the summer of 1987 I was asked to meet a man from Derry called Eddie McSheffrey. Eddie asked me to record that he had been beaten and tortured while in RUC custody some days earlier. At the end of October 1987, Eddie McSheffrey and another member of the IRA, Paddy Deery, were killed in a premature explosion in Derry.

Just months before this tragedy, the bishop of Derry, Edward Daly, issued a statement saying that he would not in future allow republican funerals in any church in Derry, a ruling that incensed the people. This was to be the first test case, and it was not clear if the coffins of the two republicans would be allowed into St Eugene's cathedral. The local Sinn Féin people asked me if I would say a funeral mass in the grounds of the cathedral if they did not gain admittance, and I agreed. This was covered in the Sunday papers the day before the funerals, with one front page headline proclaiming: 'Rebel priest to say funeral mass outside cathedral'.

On Monday, 2 November 1987, the feast of All Souls, I went to Derry prepared to say the mass in the cathedral grounds if the coffins were not permitted inside. As it turned out, the priest saying the mass that day agreed to allow the coffins in; I think the bishop and the local clergy had been embarrassed by the news report in the Sunday paper and were forced to climb down. There was a huge gathering of mourners, and a massive RUC presence around the cathedral and at the entrance gate. Some of them recognised me and began shouting sarcastic remarks at me. On the way to the cemetery from the cathedral, the RUC attacked the pallbearers and the funeral procession, knocking the coffins to the ground. It was a disgraceful scene, a sight I will not forget.

On 8 November 1987, only a few days after the funerals of Eddie McSheffrey and Paddy Deery, came shattering news. I had just finished saying the 11.30 a.m. mass in Irvinestown when the parish priest told me that a bomb had exploded in Enniskillen, ten miles away, with many people dead and injured. I listened to the news on the radio. A bomb had exploded at the cenotaph in Belmore Street, killing eleven and injuring many more who had gathered for the Remembrance Sunday ceremony.

I was upset, and wondered what could have happened, as I did not believe a bomb would have been aimed at civilians. I went to Derry that evening to see Mitchel McLaughlin, a leading member of Sinn Féin. I had known Mitchel for many years and we shared the same concerns about bringing about peace based on justice. I found him just as upset as I was and he had no hesitation in saying that this was totally wrong and should not have happened. One of the local Sinn Féin politicians I felt immediately sorry for was Paul Corrigan, who was the elected chairman of Fermanagh District Council at the time. He was faced with a hostile press and dealt with it the best he could. It was a very stressful time for him, his wife and family.

I prayed at mass the next day for the victims and their families and expressed my sorrow and sympathy on behalf of our community. I kept a note of what I said:

1.  We are deeply shocked and saddened by what happened in Enniskillen on Sunday. This tragedy is the latest in a long list of tragedies in our country.

2. Our hearts go out to the families of those who were killed and injured.

3. We must pray for all the people and ask God to comfort them and heal the wounded.

4. We must pray for a just and lasting peace in this country that will bring an end to this violence and all other forms of violence.

5. During this month of November we pray for all who died in Enniskillen and all those who have died because of the 'troubles' in our country.

One of those injured in Enniskillen was Gordon Wilson, who used to own a drapery shop in the middle of the town. I knew him to see as I had occasionally been in his shop. He gave a moving account of how his daughter, Marie, had died and he said that he was prepared to forgive those who had killed his daughter and injured him. I could understand the grief and anger of the victims' families. However, the media was certainly playing on it. They had their own agenda – as always.

The Catholic church leaders also felt compelled to issue a statement to be read at all masses the following Sunday. The three archbishops, Cardinal Tomás Ó Fiaich of Armagh, Archbishop Morris of Cashel and Archbishop Cassidy of Tuam, signed it. I read the statement and was not too happy about the wording of parts of it – especially the part that sympathised with the RUC. As far as I was concerned, the statement contained all the flaws and weaknesses of previous episcopal pronouncements. It was long on moral indignation but short on analysis and context. I informed my bishop about my difficulties with the statement. When I read it the following Sunday I made it clear at the beginning that the statement was written by the three archbishops.

This statement, and others emanating from bishops and priests, forced me to think a bit more about the church's response to the ongoing conflict and the almost daily deaths that resulted from it. I discussed the church's attitude to violence with Des Wilson and others during the next few months and early in the new year, 1988, Des Wilson and I issued 'An Open Letter to Irish Catholics', which was critical of the attitude of the bishops to the conflict as revealed in all their statements over the previous fifteen years. We called on the bishops to condemn the institutional violence, which was the root cause of the violence of the IRA. We questioned the bishops' support for the partisan RUC in their statement after Enniskillen.

On 7 January 1988 the *Irish Times* devoted an editorial entitled 'Excuses' in response to our statement. This editorial, which referred to us as 'Rev. Wilson' and 'Rev. McVeigh', was a complete misrepresentation of what we had written. We certainly were not making excuses for Enniskillen. We were stating that we felt it was time for a fuller debate on the issue of violence in our society. We wanted to open up the debate about the causes and kinds of violence which needed to be addressed by the church leaders if the British government was to be forced to act in a responsible manner.

Because of the gross distortion of our views in the *Irish Times*, we asked for a meeting with the editor, Conor Brady. Instead, we were granted a meeting with the editorial board, consisting of Conor Brady, Dick Walsh (RIP) and Eoin McVey – a distant cousin. Mr Brady told us that in the editorial they were responding to comments from Protestant readers about our statement in January 1988; they said they had received complaints from some Protestants who worked in the paper. Our letter said nothing that could be construed as offensive to Protestants. We were concerned, above all, about the unbalanced response of our own church leaders to the whole question of violence in our country and the repercussions of that for trying to find a resolution and an end to all violence. We felt that this was no way to seek a just and lasting peace, that it only further alienated those who believed in armed struggle.

After about half an hour with these three men, we knew we were getting nowhere. They were entirely unapologetic about the editorial. Des collected his papers and said we were terminating the meeting. The three *Irish Times* people had nothing to say and we had no time to waste. We left as quickly as we could and went back to the real world. My distant cousin is even more distant ever since.

It is often said that the first casualty of war is truth. This I know from my own experience in the north of Ireland. You could say that the distortion of the truth about the situation in the six counties began in 1972 with the British response to Bloody Sunday in Derry and with the Widgery Report into that cataclysmic event. The British government, we learned then, will go to any lengths and any expense to defend their position and their 'honour'. The war I lived through since Bloody Sunday became a propaganda battle. The media – Irish and British – were willing agents of British propaganda. Much of what has been published over the years was written to defend the British government, its disgraceful record on human rights and its complicity in the murder of Irish citizens.

According to the propaganda, the civil rights activists, republicans, and those who were aligned with them in any way, caused all the trouble. These were the real troublemakers, the reason why there was no peace.

This book is my eyewitness account of those years. It is recalled from notes and from memories. I am writing it in the hope that my memoir will contribute to the countering of the 'official' British account of what happened.

I understood my role, as a priest, to stand with the people against the reign of terror inflicted on them by the British state and to counter the endless British propaganda. It meant challenging the British and it meant speaking out and confronting the traditional alliance of church and state. There was no other way to be a priest and to witness to the gospel, as I understood it. There was no other way to be a follower of Jesus. I did not indulge in the frequent condemnations of the IRA that the church leaders practised. I felt that that was counter-productive and in my experience it did not persuade anybody to give up arms.

Over the years, some people have criticised me for not taking a more 'balanced approach' to violence and I have been accused of not condemning IRA violence. I have been a constant target for some critics in the letters columns of the newspapers and in many anonymous letters sent to me, most of which have been abusive. I try to deal with the issue of violence as honestly as I can in this book. It is a huge issue for people in Ireland and throughout the world.

I have always found it strange and indeed dishonest that some people when referring to the conflict in our country should put all the blame on the IRA without any reference to the British role in the war. I believe the British had made armed conflict inevitable by their resistance to the demand for basic human rights in 1968–69. As far as many young people were concerned the British openly declared war on the Irish people on Bloody Sunday in Derry. After that, many saw no other way to bring about change than to join the IRA and take on the British. That is a matter of historical fact. All the deaths that ensued must be seen in this context – and all of them must be regretted. There is no hierarchy of victims.

I applaud those republicans who made an effort to bring about an end to the armed conflict, who took risks for peace and who still seek to resolve the outstanding issues by political means. I regret, like everybody else, that this did not happen sooner but there were many factors at play. We all know that 'violence begets violence' and we know from experience here and in the Middle East how difficult it is to break the cycle of violence.

Some would like to exonerate the British of all responsibility for the conflict and the violence here. Introducing statistics is simply an attempt to distract from the root cause of the conflict and the necessity to place the responsibility for the conflict where it belongs.

Until the British government acknowledges its culpability for the war and the violence then it is meaningless to apportion blame on the IRA alone. Furthermore, it does nothing to move the situation forward towards a complete resolution of the problem and the restoration of Irish independence and national self-determination. The British are still here and it is now up to all Irish politicians who say they want a united Ireland to work together to remove the British colonial apparatus by peaceful political means.

There is no way to understand the twenty-five-year war without first recognising the historical background and the context. Britain's malign role in Ireland for centuries needs to be understood. When they could not hold the whole country, they devised partition and propped up a corrupt unionist regime in the six north-eastern counties for fifty years. A much more honest analysis is necessary to show the context in which the IRA came into being. I believe it is necessary to state the truth if we are going to understand what took place and if we are to avoid armed conflict in the future.

ON THE EVENING of 21 February 1988, as I drove home from speaking at a commemoration in Dunloy, County Antrim, I heard on the news that a young man had been shot dead by a British soldier, at the permanent British checkpoint in Aughnacloy, County Tyrone. I learned later that night that he was Aidan McAnespie, shot as he walked across the border to a Gaelic football match. I had met Aidan on a few occasions and I knew his sister, Eilish, very well. At the funeral mass in Aughnacloy, attended by many from the world of GAA, Cardinal Ó Fiaich denounced the murderers of Aidan McAnespie in the strongest terms.

Another SAS operation in Gibraltar almost two months later on 6 March 1988 resulted in the deaths of three Belfast republicans, Mairéad Farrell, Seán Savage and Danny McCann, who, it was alleged, were on an IRA bombing mission. They were shot without warning or any attempt at arrest. It has been alleged that these killings were carried out with the help of the Dublin authorities. There was now close cooperation between Dublin and London in the all-out onslaught on the IRA. The Gibraltar killings were to have unforeseen consequences that led to more deaths.

I had known Mairéad Farrell and her family for a long time and I had visited her in prison. Her mother came from County Leitrim and I knew her uncle and cousins, who lived in Fermanagh. I went to the funeral in Belfast on 16 March 1988 and helped to carry the coffin along part of the way to Milltown cemetery.

At the cemetery I was talking to two journalists, Fionnuala O'Connor and Mary Holland, beside the hearse when I heard the first grenade explode. This was followed by several more explosions. There was panic. Gerry Adams and Martin McGuinness, who were standing at the graveside, told everyone to get down and stay down, which most of us did. I was petrified but I could see some people running after the man who was throwing the grenades into the crowd. As he retreated, he began shooting with a revolver at those pursuing him. He shot three men dead in the cemetery where I was standing that day. Michael Stone had made his way to the funeral and mingled with the mourners before carrying out his dastardly deed. I admire the brave young men who went after him while he continued to fire his pistol. Suddenly, an RUC patrol appeared out of nowhere on the M1 motorway, arrested Stone and took him away.

That day was to have severe repercussions for the nationalist community in the six counties. At the funeral, some days later, of one of those killed in the cemetery, Caoimhghín Mac Brádaigh (thirty years), a car travelling at high speed along the Falls Road approached the funeral cortege. The crowd, many of whom had been in Milltown cemetery a few days earlier, not knowing what was happening, stopped the car and seized the two occupants whom they quickly identified as British soldiers out of uniform. In the panic that followed, members of the IRA shot them dead. The picture in the papers next day of Fr Alec Reid kneeling over the body of one of the stripped soldiers was harrowing. Alec Reid, who belongs to the Redemptorists based in Clonard, Belfast, has seen his fair share of trouble in the Falls area of west Belfast. As is well documented he went on to play an important role in bringing the leaders of Sinn Féin and the SDLP together. He had been involved over the years in trying to settle all kinds of disputes and internal rows within republican groups.

All of these killings by the British, the loyalists and the IRA were weighing heavily on me when I was invited to speak at a debate in the Oxford Union on 28 April 1988. I accepted the invitation, as I did not often have an opportunity to put my point of view to an English audience. I had a good idea of what I wanted to say about their government and their colonial policies, which in my opinion were the root cause of all the violence in our country. I felt this was not being said often enough by the SDLP or the Catholic church leaders who had immediate access to the airwaves in Britain and Ireland. The Oxford debate was: 'That British troops should be returned to the mainland'. The title and the use of the word 'mainland' reflected the bias of the organisers and I said so. The speakers for the motion were Kevin McNamara, MP, Seamus Mallon, MP and me, while those opposing were Rev. Martin Smith, MP, Brian Mawhinney, MP, the British secretary of state in Northern Ireland at the time, and retired British army commander, Major Farrar Hockley.

I argued the case for a British withdrawal from Ireland, which

I described as Britain's 'first and last colony'. The others on my side
waffled. Mallon hardly spoke to me. He was a very different man
from John Hume, whom I had met several times over the years
and who was always courteous. Even the Rev. Martin Smith, who
was on the opposing side, had the good manners to engage in
conversation with me when we met beforehand. The Labour MP,
Kevin McNamara, remained aloof and uncomfortable beside me.
I said to him before the debate began, 'I hope you will support
what I am going to say.'

'It all depends on what you say and how you say it.'

It is little wonder we lost the debate as there was no clear message from all the speakers on our side. I made my position clear
that the British had no right to be in Ireland. The unionists argued
about the rights of the majority in Northern Ireland as well as
putting forward the well-worn 'bloodbath theory' if the British
were ever to leave. I knew that there were many among the packed
audience who supported my arguments. I met Brian Mawhinney
the next morning at breakfast, and I asked him, politely, if he had
learned anything from the debate. He said he had not. He then
asked me if I had learned anything. I said, 'I did not hear much
that I had not heard before.'

The following night I was invited to speak at a public meeting
in the Mansion House, Dublin. Other speakers included Irish
language activist Gearóid Ó Carealláin from Belfast and the
writer, Ulick O'Connor. It was a good open discussion and I was
more relaxed than I was in Oxford. It was much easier to speak
at home in Dublin with a mostly friendly audience and open-
minded platform speakers.

In the winter of 1988 I was invited by a Protestant clergyman
who was then producer of religious programmes for the BBC to
take part in a pre-recorded discussion about violence. I accepted
on condition that this would be a conversation, that I would not
be badgered and that I would be allowed to make my arguments

without constant interruption. Given my limited experience of interviews for the BBC and RTÉ I thought this was not too much to ask if we were going to deal in a mature way with this serious subject. I was told that the interviewer was to be Dr Anthony Clare, a professor in Trinity College, and that he would be approaching the interview in a conversational rather than a confrontational way. With that understanding, I agreed to take part.

At the last minute I was told that Dr Clare had withdrawn and was to be replaced by a man from RTÉ called Andy O'Mahony. I had known of Mr O'Mahony but had never met him. O'Mahony was unfriendly from the start. Before we began to record, he took long gulps of air and sighed. He seemed to be psyching himself up for battle. It was a bit like the sounds that the New Zealand rugby team make before a match. He began by introducing me as an outspoken priest who was unwilling to condemn the IRA. I stressed at the beginning of the interview that condemnations were not getting us anywhere. There had been plenty of condemnations and I asked what had they achieved? I felt that it was necessary even at this stage to analyse the conflict and the reasons for the violence if we were to bring about a consensus in favour of both sides being involved in dialogue.

But O'Mahony was not interested in pursuing this line of conversation. All he wanted to know was why I had not condemned the Enniskillen bomb. I said that I abhorred the Enniskillen bomb as much as he did and that it was wrong. I said that the condemnation thing was a game which the media played to discredit certain people. 'But you didn't condemn Enniskillen?'

'No I did not condemn it. The hierarchy had condemned it so that was good enough for me.'

'But you have much to say about the British and the RUC violence.'

'Yes, because my church is not so vocal about this violence – the primary violence in our situation.'

'Yes, but you could also condemn Enniskillen.'

At this point, I was becoming exasperated. I stopped the interview and said that I had not agreed to be subjected to this kind of badgering.

The producer said, 'OK, let's start again.' So we started again, and following the introduction O'Mahony was asking me again about why I had not condemned Enniskillen. I let it go for a while but he kept on with it so I stopped the interview again.

We started a third time, but this attempt took the same direction. In the middle of it, I got up and walked out of the studio, straight to my car and home. I felt I was not going to be bullied and harassed in an interview, which I was told was to be conversational in order to tease out the main issues around the ongoing violence in our community. I was getting enough harassment on the roads from the crown forces without looking for more in a BBC studio. I could see that this programme was intent on making me out to be someone who supported Enniskillen and the killing of Protestants. I was not going to allow them to do that.

I had always stressed that my chief concern was the bringing about of peace with justice. To do that we had to look at the underlying causes of the violence. Condemnations of the IRA were not enough. I felt that after nearly twenty years of conflict it was time to think about different approaches and to emphasise the need for justice and dialogue. It was not enough to call on the IRA to stop. There were two sides to the conflict.

When discussing the violence there was not enough talk about the activities of the British agents and the collusion of the RUC with loyalist killers. It is now clear in light, of later revelations about British agents within the IRA, that many people were killed to protect these agents. In the Strabane/Castlederg area a number of Protestants in the UDR were allowed to be killed by the IRA to protect the British agents working within the organisation.

The collusion of the British with pro-British loyalist killers is now well documented. On 12 February 1989 a number of armed men arrived at the home of Belfast solicitor Pat Finucane and shot him at point blank range. It was well planned and the assassins had a free run to and from the house. In recent years, a leading loyalist confessed to his part in the killing and said that he was a police agent. It was always believed by the family that this was a clear case of collusion between the crown forces and loyalist killers. (Almost to the day ten years later, Rosemary Nelson, another leading human rights lawyer, was killed by a booby trap bomb.)

Two days after the killing of Pat Finucane, John Davey, a Sinn Féin councillor elected to Magherafelt Council, was murdered, also by British agents. I had known John for many years and had often appeared on the same platform with him at meetings and commemorations. He was a seasoned campaigner for justice and human rights.

The Berlin Wall came down in 1989, a watershed year in world history. Gorbachev had come to power in the USSR and immediately began dismantling the Soviet Union. The days of empire were numbered.

It was also the year that Cardinal Tomás Ó Fiaich died suddenly while on a pilgrimage to Lourdes. He had been part of my life for almost twenty years. While I had my differences with the Irish Catholic hierarchy, I always thought that Cardinal Ó Fiaich was a decent man who tried his best to do what he could for the people caught up in a war that was forced on them.

I had been reflecting on the role of the church in the conflict in Ireland and the constant outbreaks of violence against the British and I put my thoughts on paper. These were published in 1989 in a book called *A Wounded church* which outlined the history of the church's collusion with the state and focused on the role of the bishop of Down and Connor, Cahal Daly, who was soon to become archbishop of Armagh in succession to Cardinal

Ó Fiaich. Daly had long been an outspoken critic of Irish republicans. In the book I tried to deal with these hostile and one-sided
arguments in more detail. I was critical of the role of the official
church and I specifically challenged Bishop Daly's stance in relation to the conflict and his one-sided approach, which placed him
in opposition to republicans. The church had become authoritarian and unwilling to hear the views of ordinary Catholics or even
ordinary curates. It had become clericalised in spite of the pronouncements of the Second Vatican Council calling for openness
and transparency. This ultimately resulted in the cover-ups about
child abuse by priests and religious.

Veritas bookstores (owned by the Irish hierarchy) withdrew
*A Wounded church* from their shops after only a few weeks, in the
process giving me lots of free publicity, which helped the sales
immensely. John Feehan of Mercier Press was furious with Veritas. I had spent about two years writing the book and it had been
with the publisher and printer for about six months or a year. I
too was annoyed at the decision. I asked Fr Martin Tierney of
Veritas for an explanation and he told me that they had many
complaints about my criticism of Bishop Cahal Daly.

AROUND THIS TIME, British soldiers started hanging around outside my house in Irvinestown. I felt it was a deliberate tactic to
annoy me and to draw attention to me. One day they came to the
back door. A soldier was holding out rosary beads: 'Hey Padre,
we found these, Padre.' I told him to keep them and use them
and closed the door in his face. He was not amused and knocked
at the door again. The soldiers sauntered around the back of the
house for a while before I went out and told them, in a loud voice,
to get off the church property. I am sure my reputation hit rock
bottom out in St Angelo, where the British and the UDR were
based. I also knew if they wanted to get me it would not matter
where I was. When they could shoot people like Pat Finucane

and John Davey, I was convinced they would shoot anybody or arrange to have anyone shot, at any time. It was without doubt the time when I felt most in danger and fearful that I might be assassinated.

I had no regrets about the public profile I had adopted since returning from America. It was the only way possible for me, given my commitment to human rights. I would definitely have had regrets if I had not taken the public stance I took at that time. However, it was not without its difficulties and dangers. On more than one occasion, I felt I was in serious danger.

One of these was on a night in March 1990 when I was returning from Drumquin having called on my cousin, Colm McGrath, who was seriously ill. Between Ederney and Irvinestown I was stopped at a UDR checkpoint. I saw two UDR Land Rovers across the road. Luckily I was not travelling too fast. I was asked for ID, where I was coming from and where I was going. I told them I was coming from Ederney, which was the last place I had been. They asked me exactly where I was coming from. I felt I was being harassed and refused to say. They went to the back of my car and were joined by others. I could hear them having a conversation about what they should do. I became very afraid. Then after about three or four minutes I heard a car coming at great speed and I knew these guys could hardly have time to signal the car to stop with their red light. I instinctively started my car and drove up the road as fast as I could. I knew that the car was going to crash into me if I did not move forward. The car did indeed smash into one of the UDR Land Rovers and when I stopped my car all I could hear were screams. I drove to my cousins further up the road to call an ambulance. I was shaking from shock.

At a subsequent court case in Enniskillen I was called as a witness on behalf of the young driver, who had by then recovered from his injuries. He told the court that he had no warning that there was a checkpoint, which was situated just as he turned the corner, and he crashed into a vehicle which was across the road. I said that the young man had not an earthly chance of stopping given where the UDR checkpoint was situated and confirmed that he had no warning. The judge said that according to the law a driver must always drive at a speed which allows him or her to stop in an emergency. He found the driver guilty of dangerous driving but admonished the UDR men for setting up checkpoints on dangerous bends. One of the positive results of the court case was that I discovered the identity of the UDR men who had stopped and interrogated me that night. On making some enquiries I was told that they had a reputation for being hostile to Catholics and were sectarian in outlook. I have wondered since if that car crash saved my life that night in 1989.

The harassment by the RUC, UDR and the British army continued. It became so bad that I decided to take all three organisations to court to sue them for damages. Séamus Treacy, a lawyer in Belfast (now a high court judge) who worked for Madden and Finucane, offered to take on my case for free. 'We will put a stop to this harassment,' he assured me. 'We will make them pay for their bad manners.' All I had to do was make a statement and wait for the case to come up. As it happened, the case was settled out of court and I received a nice cheque – for a sizeable sum – in the post a few days later.

# 17

# People Power – Opening Roads, Boycotting Banks and Opposing Censorship

At my bishop's request I moved back to the parish of Garrison/ Belleek in September 1990. I was glad to be staying in Fermanagh, a most scenic part of Ireland. Not much had changed in the parish since 1974. Some of the older people had moved on to their heavenly reward to make way for another generation. The scenery was still beautiful around Lough Melvin but not many people came to visit. The place was cut off because the roads were all closed. Farmers were greatly inconvenienced – as were many people with family living on both sides. I immediately identified this as a major social issue and organised some meetings. We joined in the wider border roads campaign, which had started in counties Monaghan and Tyrone. The roads, we were told by the Northern Ireland Office (NIO), were closed for 'security reasons'.

A few unionist politicians like Ken Maginnis began using the phrase 'ethnic cleansing' to describe the IRA tactics along the border. The British army, at the behest of hard-line unionists and as part of a campaign to isolate the six counties and pretend that it was a viable entity separate from the rest of Ireland, had closed the border roads. It was similar to the tactics used by the Israeli government in isolating the Palestinians. In a country where people had interacted for centuries, however, they were hardly likely to succeed. There were too many social, industrial and trade connections along the border and between north and south.

A small number of local farmers – some from the south and some from the north – came together and set about removing the obstructions and filling in the roads to make them passable. In Garrison our actions brought us into conflict, not only with the British and RUC, but with some people who felt that we should leave things as they were. The British had blocked all the roads between County Leitrim and Fermanagh for almost twenty years. Out of fifty border roads in Fermanagh, only five remained open, and on each of these there was a permanent British military checkpoint – stopping and delaying people coming and going from work or social events.

Most people around Garrison just accepted the situation and thought that nothing could be done. Many in the neighbourhood were forced to make long detours to get to work or to their farms in the south. Neighbours were cut off from one another. If this was intended to stop the IRA, it was downright stupid. Peter Robinson of the DUP suggested at one stage that the whole border should be sealed with a high wire fence like that which the Israelis built.

To re-open the roads required heavy machinery and people who could operate these machines. It also needed heavy work with picks and shovels. As soon as they were re-opened, the British army closed them again. This cat and mouse game went on for months, even years. The people were now determined to keep the roads open at all costs. They were making a statement and were not going to put up with this further denial of their basic right to travel in their own country.

However, not everyone in the parish was in agreement with our tactics. On 27 June 1993 we met with strong opposition from a group of locals in Garrison and Rossinver who felt we should leave the roads alone. This group, which included SDLP people in the north and members of Fine Gael in Leitrim, had some kind of interest in keeping the roads closed. They held a protest against us, which was their right. However, our group greatly out-numbered them and the extra publicity their protest generated did our cause no harm at all.

I could see that this kind of non-violent resistance by the people was effective in attracting publicity and in raising the morale of the local community. We needed more opportunities for people to show their power.

A CAMPAIGN TO highlight job discrimination against Catholics began when a group of people, including Des Wilson and Oliver Kearney, came together to form Equality. Our first task was to publish an update about anti-Catholic discrimination in the six counties. The Fair Employment Commission had been camou-flaging the situation since it came into being a few years earlier. We set about discovering the true situation and published our findings in the *Directory of Discrimination*. Most of the research was carried out by Oliver Kearney, who had been working on this issue with another small group for many years. As a result of his efforts he lost his job with the Housing Executive.

We then set about using the boycott tactic and chose the Nort-hern Bank as our first target. They were not the only discrimi-nators against Catholics – but they were among the worst. We called on people to boycott the bank, and after a year it began to make an impact. Other banks and institutions were afraid that they were next; they did not want any bad publicity.

We had been following the progress of the MacBride Principles campaign in America, in which some members of the Equality group had played a very active part. The campaign, which began in 1986, was modelled on the Sullivan Principles campaign to raise awareness about the oppression of Africans under the apartheid system in South Africa. The MacBride Principles, a set of guide-lines named after Nobel Peace prize-winner Seán MacBride, re-quired American companies based in the six counties to increase representation of under-represented religious groups, ban pro-vocative emblems from the work-place, abolish discriminatory re-cruitment criteria and develop appropriate training programmes. The state legislatures that backed the principles included New York and Massachusetts, and cities which supported included New York, Chicago and Detroit. The British put a big effort and a lot of money into opposing this campaign.

The official Catholic church in Ireland was opposed to the MacBride Principles campaign, and sent a number of priests to the United States to state its position. Cardinal Cahal Daly, the senior churchman in Ireland, went out of his way to oppose the campaign. The great concern among senior churchmen was a loss of control in the working-class areas of Belfast and in other large towns.

Those speaking out against human rights violations were seen as 'fellow-travellers', 'sympathisers' or 'crypto-provos', as we were once called. Condemnations of the IRA were frequent, and after 1989 the archbishop of Armagh, Cahal Daly, also took to con-demning Sinn Féin and appealed to the people not to vote for them. 'A vote for Sinn Féin,' he said, 'was a vote for violence'. Gerry Adams refuted this argument and asked to meet with Daly. The request was refused.

Many of us were aware of the injustice and the negative effect of censoring republican opinion in Ireland, and on 22 June 1993 a number of people met to discuss the continuing policy by the Irish government and RTÉ. A Working Group Against Censorship was set up comprising Des Wilson, Noelle Ryan, Anna Barron, Ber-nadette Ní Rodaigh, Tom Cullen, Teresa Brady and Fr Maurice Burke. Our aim was to put pressure on RTÉ and the government to stop the censorship of nationally minded people and republi-cans, especially the elected members of the community.

We were very serious about taking on RTÉ. We planned a boycott of products advertised on RTÉ and in the *RTÉ Guide*. They did not like it. At first they ignored us, but after a while realised we were serious and had some power. We had a similar experience with the Northern Bank when we called for that boycott. We wrote letters to government ministers. We had a fair hearing from the minister for communications, Michael D. Higgins of the Labour party. He finally had the good sense to abolish the censorship legislation and allow access to the nationalist and republican viewpoint on the airwaves.

One man who did his best to oppose censorship in the twenty-six counties was Derek Dunne, a native of Longford who lived in Dublin. We needed journalists and writers to help with our peaceful non-violent campaigns – but they were hard to find. Only a handful were willing to risk their livelihood by reporting favourably on our campaigns. One of these was Derek Dunne. He came to stay in my parish house in Irvinestown and spent many hours helping me with my writing.

I was deeply saddened to hear of his untimely death in 1991. Derek was a true champion of the oppressed people of the north and will never be forgotten for his work on their behalf when few other journalists were prepared to do anything to make known the truth. To do so then was to put your prospects of permanent work in jeopardy. Derek did not care about that, so long as he could make the truth known. He devoted his life to exposing the oppression in the six counties. He was a writer and a campaigning journalist – talented and unselfish.

I was asked to celebrate Derek's funeral mass in Longford town, where he was born and reared. Christy Moore sang a most moving song, 'Old John O'Dreams' at the end of the mass. Christy was another man who always showed his concern for what was happening to the people in the north. Derek Dunne will be remembered for his generosity with his time and talents, his empathy with the plight of northern nationalists and his courage during his short life. He wrote a thoroughly researched the well written pamphlet about the Birmingham Six which helped to highlight that great injustice.

Derek also wrote a classic book about the escape from Long Kesh in 1983, *Out of the Maze* and wrote numerous articles about the political situation. He was outraged with the hypocrisy in this so-called Christian country. As someone so aware of the constant misreporting of the conflict in the six counties, I was grateful to Derek for his serious reporting of the situation. His investigative journalism is a monument to his integrity, sincerity and professionalism.

The Irish National Congress (INC), a group based in Dublin, were concerned about the truth of what was happening in the north. They also campaigned against censorship and against the convictions of the Guildford Four and the Birmingham Six and provided a platform for speakers who were not allowed on RTÉ because of censorship. In June 1993 I was invited to speak at an INC-organised meeting in Dublin along with Canon Nicholas Frayling, a former Anglican dean in Liverpool archdiocese, and Brian Murphy, a well known historian and a monk in Glenstal Abbey, County Limerick. I once again confronted the issue of the failure of the church to stand with the people who were being harassed and intimidated. Nicholas Frayling courageously confronted the activities of the British in Ireland. I admired him greatly and wished we had an Irish canon who would do the same.

In November 1993 I was invited to speak in Kilmichael, County Cork for a second time. I saw it as another opportunity to confront British propaganda, especially in the Irish media. Around this time, I read in the Sunday papers that a Fine Gael/Progressive Democrats TD, Michael Keating, had issued a statement calling for me to be 'defrocked' by my bishop. I had not known of anyone to be 'defrocked' in the last hundred years and thought it would be

interesting to know what it involved. I was not to find out, however, as my bishop had more sense than to listen to the ranting and
raving of the politician.

# 18

# The Darkest Hour

While the war continued there was, at last, some good news on the political front. It was announced that the leader of Sinn Féin, Gerry Adams, had held talks with SDLP leader, John Hume and they intended to continue talking in spite of opposition from some in their own parties. This was the first piece of good political news for many years. I always believed that some kind of united nationalist approach was needed if the IRA was even to consider calling a ceasefire. I felt that such an approach, backed by the Irish in America, was bound to put pressure on the British and the unionists to come to the negotiating table. We now know that the British maintained contact with the republican movement for many years and were aware of developments in republican thinking. I knew there would be difficulties and challenges for both Gerry Adams and John Hume as a result of their effort. Not everyone in the SDLP was in favour of Hume meeting with Adams or with both men publishing joint statements. Adams was also in a precarious position. He did not want to see a serious split in the republican movement – so he had to tread carefully and keep people informed of progress.

On 9 November, 1990 the British secretary of state in Northern Ireland, Peter Brooke, delivered a speech in which he declared: 'The British government has no selfish, strategic or economic interest in Northern Ireland: our role is to help, enable and encourage.' This statement was well received in republican circles. So too was the news of the resignation of Margaret Thatcher the same month. John Major, as the new leader of the Conservatives, became prime minister. There was no hope of progress while Thatcher was in Downing Street and the arrival of Major and the statement by Brooke opened up new possibilities.

In 1992 a leading member of Sinn Féin, Jim Gibney, was the guest speaker at the annual republican Wolfe Tone commemoration at Bodenstown, County Kildare. He took the opportunity to talk to the republican grassroots about the need to build the peace process, which began with the Hume–Adams meetings and the IRA/British contacts.

The outcome of the long war between the IRA and the British was becoming clear – a stalemate. The IRA had become even more daring, and in February 1991 they fired a mortar bomb into the garden of 10 Downing Street, a few yards from where the prime minister, John Major was meeting his Gulf war cabinet. Another IRA bomb at the Baltic Exchange in London in April 1992 caused chaos in the city and a huge loss of revenue for the British exchequer. On 24 April 1993 the IRA attacked the Nat West tower in the centre of London's financial district at Bishopsgate. More than at any time in the previous thirty years the pressure was on the British to seek a settlement – one that included Sinn Féin and the IRA.

Even while the IRA campaign continued, Sinn Féin leaders and others, including the leader of the SDLP, were making efforts to find some kind of a breakthrough in the political stalemate. Gerry Adams held another series of meetings with John Hume to discuss the possibilities and conditions for a cessation of the IRA campaign. The taoiseach Charles J. Haughey and his successor Albert Reynolds encouraged this strategy.

I was greatly encouraged by the political moves and felt that we, who had been involved in various justice campaigns, had an obligation to use whatever power and influence we had to encourage the movement within nationalism and republicanism for dialogue and negotiation. In 1993, a few of us formed a campaigning group, Clergy for Justice. The first meeting was called by our friend, Fr Maurice Burke, a retired member of the African Missions (SMA) who lived in Dublin. A number of clergy in the Dublin area and two from the north attended the inaugural meeting. It was difficult to find priests who were willing to become involved. Maurice Burke spent twenty years in Nigeria and another twenty in a parish on Staten Island, New York. He had a deep interest in Ireland and kept in close contact with events in the north. Soon after he returned to live in Santry, Dublin, the special branch of the garda síochána raided and searched his home. This was the climate in which human rights activists had to work at the time. Maurice was the best-informed man I ever met about the British secret services and their agents.

In May 1993 our group of priests together with some victims of British violence had a meeting with the new papal nuncio, Emmanuel Gerada. We felt it was time to increase the pressure on those with influence to speak out against the British repression in Ireland. Some of us had met the previous papal nuncio, Gaetano Alibrandi, several times, once during Bobby Sands' hunger strike. The group which met the new nuncio in 1993 included P. J. Carragher, whose son Fergal had been killed by British soldiers in Cullyhanna on 30 December 1990, and Mr and Mrs McAnespie, whose son, Aidan, was killed by a British soldier on 21 February 1988. We left the papal nuncio in no doubt about the seriousness of the situation for the nationalist people living in the north and about the British policy of shoot-to-kill. He expressed a degree of disbelief at some of the stories we told him about British army harassment. When P. J. Carragher related the story of the British army raiding his home, taking down a picture of the pope and standing on it, the nuncio was visibly perturbed.

We gave him plenty of documented evidence of insulting behaviour by the British, RUC and UDR towards Catholics, including a number of priests.

We reserved our criticism of the Catholic hierarchy for the end of the meeting. It was pointed out that, time and again, people asked for help from the Catholic bishops abroad but were told that they could not intervene unless requested to do so by the Irish bishops. We told him about how Irish bishops, priests and religious blocked the campaign for the MacBride Principles in America. We wanted the papal nuncio to know about the abuse and intimidation of the ordinary Catholic people because we doubted if he would hear the whole story from Cardinal Cahal Daly. Daly was not known for his sympathy for those Catholics at the receiving end of state violence.

Many tragedies during the long war received attention in the world press. The killing by the IRA of Louis Mountbatten on 27 August 1979 and the killing of 18 British soldiers in Warrenpoint, on the same day hardened British government's resolve. The response to the hunger strike of 1981 and the success of Sinn Féin afterwards made the IRA more determined. The Enniskillen bomb in November 1987 brought the conflict once again to the attention of the world. Then there was the killing on 24 October 1990 of Patsy Gillespie and five British soldiers by the IRA. Patsy Gillespie was forced to drive a bomb from Fort George British army base where he worked as a cook to a British army checkpoint near Derry city. The following day I was in Dublin with Oliver Kearney and Des Wilson of the Equality group to highlight discrimination at an exhibition in Buswells Hotel. The late John Wilson, the tánaiste in Charlie Haughey's government (and a cousin of Fr Des), came along. He talked about the latest news from Derry. He was clearly upset about the Patsy Gillespie tragedy and wondered what was coming next. It was clear to me that the situation was now an issue of serious concern for the government in Dublin.

With no let up in the IRA campaign, the pressure was on the British political establishment for a change of policy. Some people in high places in the London and Dublin political establishments were already convinced that it was time for a change of approach. We know that contact with the IRA had been ongoing about the conditions for a ceasefire. Twenty-three people died in the last week of October 1993. These included the victims of the IRA bomb on the Shankill road, the UVF shootings in the Rising Sun bar in Greysteel outside Derry City and the two brothers Gerard and Rory Cairns from Bleary in County Down killed by the UVF.

There were many more funerals of victims of the UVF during the months of May and June 1994. On 18 June 1994, the UVF killed six men who were watching the World Cup match between Ireland and Italy in a pub in Loughinisland, County Down. The killings were relentless. I remember feeling the fear and foreboding at that time more than at any other time before that.

On the morning of Sunday, 7 August 1994 I was in Pomeroy attending a commemoration for Patrick McElhone who, twenty years earlier, had been taken from his home and shot dead by British soldiers, when I heard about the shooting of Kathleen O'Hagan at her home about five miles away. I went straight to the house and found Paddy, her husband, in a shocked state. The younger children were taken away to a neighbour's house. The oldest boy of nine or ten years was there, telling us about 'the bad men' who shot his mammy. It was a heartbreaking scene.

Kathleen O'Hagan, thirty-four years of age, the mother of five children and expecting another, was shot dead by the pro-British UVF in the early hours in front of her children. When Paddy, her husband, came home from the local pub he found the children all gathered around their mother, who lay dead on the floor.

I had known the O'Hagan family for about six years since their house was raided and the floors dug up with pneumatic drills by the RUC in September 1988. On that occasion Paddy was taken to Gough barracks in Armagh for interrogation. The British army sealed off the house and farm for three days, during which time nothing was found. Paddy was released without charge. I was asked at that time by Councillor Cormac McAleer to come to their home to take statements and to give the family a bit of moral support. Kathleen was a young Irish mother concerned for her children. The destruction of her lovely home by the RUC from Omagh caused her great distress.

Her funeral on 9 August 1994 was one of the saddest I ever attended. It took place in the small parish church of Broughderg, near Greencastle in County Tyrone. A number of us had a confrontation there with the local parish priest who at the end of mass thanked the RUC. A local woman, Fidelma McAleer, was so incensed that at the end of the burial service she took the microphone and stated that she and all the people she knew in the parish wished to be dissociated from the parish priest's remark. She was warmly applauded in the cemetery.

(Tragedy and suffering were to continue for the O'Hagan family in the years after that. One of the little boys, Thomas, aged five, died in a fire in a shed beside the house on 19 August 1997. Their father, Paddy, died of a heart attack on 11 March 2002 and another boy, Niall, died as a result of a motor-bike accident.)

After the O'Hagan killing I felt very dejected. Nobody knew who might be next. I was hoping against hope that the peace process might soon move us all forward into a new political situation that would bring an end to the violence. I was not very optimistic given the recent spate of killings by British/loyalist death squads all over the north. They appeared to be able to carry out these killings without fear of being caught or brought to justice. The situation was out of control.

# 19

# A Ray of Hope

On the first day of September 1994 I was in Glasgow visiting some relatives when I heard on the news that the IRA had called a cessation 'of all armed actions'. I could hardly believe it. My initial reaction was one of immense relief and a certain amount of disbelief. I was a bit apprehensive, of course, wondering would the British, as before, take advantage of the situation to humiliate republicans or would they seek an honourable settlement? These questions ran through my mind that day and the next day as I made my way home. This was big news and I wanted to be around for the reaction.

The unionists were taken by surprise and did not know what to say since they had based their political lives opposing and attacking the IRA. They were not sure if the British government had already done a deal with the republican leaders. The British Conservative prime minister, John Major, relied on the unionists to stay in office. While Major was a different kettle of fish from Margaret Thatcher he made it clear he was not enthusiastic about talking to Sinn Féin. His 'stomach would churn' if he had to talk to Gerry Adams. While he said this, British officials were engaged in talks with Irish republicans behind the scenes.

John Major wasted that opportunity for an honourable settlement. This is what I expected would happen. I had learned a long time ago that you could never trust the British to do the honourable thing. They do not seem to have that precious quality that is so necessary for human living and for civilised politics. They do not keep their word.

However, the thinking at the time in the republican family was that even if we do not trust the British, we must trust ourselves. Morale was high; Gerry Adams had prepared the ground well, having held talks with John Hume, and with many others who might influence the British government, including representatives of the Dublin government. He also kept the republican base informed about what was happening. We in the Community for Justice and Springhill Community House had several meetings with him and other Sinn Féin leaders. They told us about the new political strategy aimed at forcing the British to cut a deal.

The response from the Dublin government under Albert Reynolds was more positive than from the British. As each day passed, confidence among republicans grew; they were on television and radio now putting forward their case. They were travelling to America and all over Europe to win friends and influence leaders. As far as I was concerned the right decision had been made – and it was a courageous one in the circumstances. The main loyalist paramilitary grouping soon afterwards also declared a ceasefire. All of the paramilitary groups were under pressure to cease all military actions. Already there was a more relaxed atmosphere.

Within Ireland and in many other countries where there had been ongoing and seemingly intractable conflicts, 1994 was a year of hope. South Africa held its first ever democratic elections, with ANC leader, Nelson Mandela, becoming president. I felt that if a new beginning could happen in South Africa it could happen anywhere – even in Ireland, where our conflict was often described as 'intractable'. However, there was still terrible conflict and mass murder elsewhere. In Rwanda the United Nations and the world leaders stood idly by, while there seemed to be no end to the killing of innocent people in places like Bosnia and Croatia that year – and international governments did not seem to care.

In November 1994 I was invited to America to speak at a number of events. I told people about the hope we now had in Ireland for a peaceful and prosperous future. I was not aware that one of the organisers of the trip was opposed to the IRA cessation and was part of small group of Irish-Americans who continue to criticise Gerry Adams and the Sinn Féin leadership. Anyhow, I continued conveying a positive message: the opportunity now existed for a new beginning that would lead to the unified Ireland that we all dreamed about. I stayed with a priest in New Jersey, of Irish-Italian extraction. He was kindness and hospitality personified.

SINCE FIRST MEETING Carolyn Forché in 1979 I had often thought about visiting El Salvador – another country where the poor had suffered greatly in the recent past, with more than 80,000 people (mostly poor country people and those living in favelas in the cities) killed during the ten-year war (1975–1985). The US backed the corrupt government forces, which were attacking the rebel FMLN and the poor people with whom the FMLN lived. Since the 1992 FMLN ceasefire the people of El Salvador were also trying to build peace and come to terms with the trauma they had been through. I wanted to go there to see for myself and to visit the tomb of one of my heroes, Archbishop Oscar Romero. A friend of mine, a Franciscan friar, had been working there all during the war and was lucky to survive.

In July 1995 I embarked on the short trip to El Salvador. I felt more relaxed about travelling so far away since the IRA ceasefire. I flew to New York and on to Miami. On the plane from Miami I was sitting beside a well-dressed older man from El Salvador who was smoking a large cigar. He had all the appearances of being a wealthy man, one of the privileged few of that unjust country. I tried to have a conversation with him. He had broken English and I had hardly any Spanish. I gathered from him that his family owned a coffee farm. He was happy that the war had ended and there was now peace – even if it was a little shaky. I had heard that fourteen families, who own the best land for coffee growing and sugar cane, own this small country of five million people about the size of the province of Connacht. Coffee is the chief industry and El Salvador is one of the chief exporters of coffee in the world, mainly to America. The people work on the coffee farms for a dollar a day. Their bosses are among the wealthiest people in the world.

I arrived at the dilapidated San Salvador airport on 19 July 1995 and was met by my Franciscan friend, Ciaran Ó Nuanáin. There were armed guards everywhere. It was still a heavily militarised zone and reminded me of home. Ciaran had visited me in Fermanagh a year or so before and had accompanied me to a border roads opening between Garrison and Rossinver in County Leitrim. He was not at all comfortable – a man who had survived a most brutal war in El Salvador. Maybe the presence of so many armed police and British on the Leitrim/Fermanagh border reminded him too much of El Salvador.

The local people in the parish where Ciaran worked were just wonderful – warm and friendly. I saw at first hand the trauma, but also the enthusiasm, of a people coming out of war. I began to see liberation theology in action – the close identification of the people with the church and the clergy and of the clergy with the poor. Many catechists in each parish helped people to read and reflect on the bible in the political/social context in which they lived. The parish had a rather basic health clinic where children were vaccinated and which gave out whatever medicines they had available to sick children.

The people had no money. Most could not afford to go to McDonald's – except perhaps for a big occasion like first communion or confirmation. Housing conditions were very poor and hygiene almost non-existent. This was the reality of the third world that I had heard and read so much about. It was great to see the fantastic work that some priests and religious were doing there, in raising awareness and empowering the people. Ciaran is not interested in handouts, he believes it undermines the people's struggle and prevents their empowerment. I have many happy memories of the short time spent in El Salvador and the people I met. Ciaran kept reminding me that the theological process in the basic Christian communities was important for liberation, a simple process of prayer, reflection (on the situation) and action; prayer, reflection and action – over and over again. This was liberation theology at work.

On 21 July I went with Ciaran to the tomb of the martyr Oscar Romero. Ciaran knew the caretaker of the cathedral and we were allowed access to the basement where the tomb was located. It was a large tombstone placed at the top of a very expansive space – underneath the main floor of the cathedral. There was no furniture, just a huge empty space – quiet, peaceful and sacred. It was a very special moment when I stood in silence and thought about the great man who was laid to rest there some fifteen years earlier. The cathedral was closed to the public since it was destroyed in an earthquake in 1986 (more than 1,200 were killed). It was considered unsafe to enter but I was not going home without visiting Romero's tomb. The diocese could not afford to repair this huge cathedral. However, the new archbishop (a member of Opus Dei) appealed to some of his rich friends for financial help, and the cathedral reopened for the pope's visit the following year (1996).

The people in El Salvador regard Romero as a saint, and are not waiting for Rome to canonise him. He is their saint because he took their side and opposed the military repression of the people. In his radio broadcasts he called on the military to lay down their arms. These broadcasts, it is thought, made him a target – someone in a position of authority who had to be silenced.

The people of El Salvador were trying to rebuild the infrastructure and the economy against all the odds. I saw the squalid
living conditions, the armed guards everywhere. I experienced
the hustle and bustle in San Salvador, the lightning, thunder and
rain, the earthquake that measured 4.5 on the Richter scale. That
scared the life out of me. I remember the sadness in the eyes of the
country people whom Ciaran brought me to meet. They had been
traumatised by the violence they witnessed and experienced.

Despite their poverty, those who had survived the trauma went
about their work – small jobs they could find in the church or
the community. I was reminded that poor people throughout the
world – who comprise the majority of the population – have so
much in common. They have not lost their humanity and their decency. These are 'God's chosen people'. They are not any nationality
or ethnic group.

I returned home from even more convinced that liberation theology in action is the only hope for the church and that the true
mission of the church is to stand with the oppressed. The people
in El Salvador were blessed to have had a charismatic leader like
Oscar Romero. I was convinced that the official Catholic church in
each country needs to be at the forefront in defending the human
rights of the poor if it is to become a credible witness of the gospel.
With the rise of neo-fascist parties throughout Europe – in France,
Austria and Belgium in recent years (mainly in relation to racism
and immigration) – the church needs to take a stand on human
rights and the dignity of the people. One of the most powerful
metaphors in Catholic teaching – we are all created in the image of
God, redeemed by Jesus and inspired by the Holy Spirit – is powerful in proclaiming the need for respect of human rights.

One of the greatest needs in Ireland or anywhere else is to
make known the truth about what is happening, something you
will not find in the media, which is controlled by big business. I
was even more convinced of this having visited El Salvador and

seeing the great work being done there by priests and religious in disseminating information and progressive political ideas.

In 1997 I began to publish a newsletter, *The Irish Witness*, aimed at informing clergy and religious in Ireland and abroad about political developments and the continued violation of human rights in the north of Ireland. Rosemary Nelson, a solicitor in Lurgan, helped to pay for the printing and postage at the beginning. We worked from a room granted to us by Springhill Community House in Ballymurphy. A number of people helped out – it was mainly voluntary as we did not have much money apart from a few donations. The subscriptions did not cover printing costs. Most priests and religious were indifferent, but I expected that.

In 1997 I also published a collection of my talks and writings since my return from America in 1983. Entitled *Crying Out for Justice, 1983–1997*, I decided to publish it myself as I did not think it was the kind of book a publisher would be interested in and the process would take too long. Gerry Adams agreed to launch it on 13 October 1997 in the Conway Mill. It was a more hopeful and relaxed atmosphere than we had for years. In the introduction, Des Wilson stated:

> Often, it seems, we have not only neglected but overturned the Christian message. Sometimes we have, but we have never forgotten it. That is why the oppressors are always confronted sooner or later by the real victors. In this book we can see why the oppressors always lose in the end. It is an unnecessary tragedy if we let other oppressors take their place when we have the power described in this book.

THE PEACE TALKS began in earnest in 1997–98, culminating in the Belfast Agreement in April 1998. As expected, Paisley's DUP refused to take part in the negotiations. The Belfast or Good Friday Agreement, which was signed on 10 April 1998, was described by Brendan Anderson as 'a wordy masterpiece of compromise, language manipulation, vagueness and deliberate ambiguity'.* Most

---

\* Brendan Anderson, Joe Cahill – *A Life in the IRA*, The O'Brien Press, Dublin, 2002), p. 365.

republicans saw it as 'a road map' for bringing about a united Ireland by peaceful political means and it was endorsed at a special Sinn Féin árd fheis on 18 April 1998.

Senior republicans saw this period as a transitional phase between British colonial rule and a United Ireland. I knew from conversations with republicans inside and outside of prison that they had the experience and energy to bring the process to a successful conclusion. As Joe Cahill said: 'The Good Friday agreement is not a settlement. It's not perfect, it has faults, but it's a basis for progress. It could be a stepping-stone to a thirty-two county republic. I see it as a new line of strategy.'* So did most republicans – but not all.

The Good Friday Agreement was a guarantee that the voice of Irish republicans and nationalists could never again be ignored. It has the potential to resolve our national problems non-violently through the institutions and rules established under the agreement. The potential is there for a new and unified Ireland based on consensus and democratic principles.

Conflict resolution is an ongoing and difficult process and one that requires imagination and creativity. It takes place on many levels – from the political top table to the grassroots – and with many different interested parties. We learn from places like South Africa and El Salvador, but each situation is unique with its own special issues to be resolved.

Not all those who had been involved in the IRA would accept the terms of an interim settlement. There were a small number of republicans who disagreed with the Adams/McGuinness strategy and the Good Friday Agreement which became a part of that strategy. Some wanted to continue a military campaign, believing that this was the only way to force a British withdrawal from Ireland. During the early months of 1998 there were several explosions around Enniskillen, the work of these breakaway groups.

---

* Brendan Anderson, Joe Cahill – *A Life in the IRA,* The O'Brien Press, Dublin, 2002), p. 367.

# 20

# Remembering Rosemary Nelson

How's Joe McVeigh?' was Rosemary Nelson's usual greeting. She almost expected me to say 'I'm great' no matter how I was feeling inside. She was always full of life and energy. I called often to her office in the middle of Lurgan and if she was not busy she invited me to her room for coffee and a coke. She lit a cigarette and talked about her concerns. She told me about the intimidation of her clients by the RUC and about the threats against herself. She spoke about her concern for her family.

I knew the risks involved in taking on human rights issues and in representing people accused by the RUC of being 'enemies of the state'. In the first issue of the *Irish Witness* (September 1997), I wrote with Rosemary in mind: 'The gospel is always and ever calling us as church and as individual Christians to witness to truth and justice. Witness involves taking a public stance, speaking out about the violation of human rights. Witness implies caring, standing with the people, not being afraid to be seen with the people and even being afraid and still standing up for the rights of the oppressed. To stay silent about the violation of human rights is unacceptable. Those in positions of power in the church are specifically called to speak out about injustice and the violation of human rights.'

I wrote this after several conversations with Rosemary. If ever anyone I knew exemplified the role of the committed Christian it was Rosemary. She had been a lawyer in Lurgan for more than ten years. She had taken on many high profile cases like the Robert Hamill case. She was also an advocate for the people of the Garvaghy Road in Portadown. One of the annual events that created most tension in the six counties from 1995 onwards was the Orange parade to Drumcree parish church on the outskirts of Portadown. The Orangemen in Portadown had been used to getting their own way and parading back from Drumcree through the mainly nationalist Garvaghy Road. This was seen by the residents as provocative – a purely coat-trailing exercise to taunt and humiate the residents. After the IRA cessation there was even more triumphalism, when in 1995 Trimble and Paisley paraded on the road and danced a jig of defiance at the finish for the media and their supporters.

The British government was forced by public opinion to do something about it, and so ordered that the Orangemen were not allowed to parade on the Garvaghy Road the following year. In response, a Catholic taxi driver, Michael McGoldrick, was shot dead by pro-British loyalists near Lurgan. The Orange supporters set up roadblocks, before the RUC changed the decision and allowed the Orangemen to march on the Garvaghy Road. They did the same in the Lower Ormeau Road in Belfast against the wishes of the Catholic residents. In Harrysville, Ballymena, in a show of pure bigotry, Catholics were attacked while going to church. Paisley remained silent. Northern nationalists including the SDLP were incensed with secretary of state Mayhew and the British government.

In 1997 the Parades Commission was set up to deal with contentious Orange marches. The commission attempted to facilitate a meeting between the Orange Order and the Garvaghy Road residents but the Orange Order refused to talk, arguing that their organisation was purely religious and cultural and should not be prevented from marching wherever it liked on the 'queen's highway'. The Catholics of Portadown and throughout the six counties see the Orange Order rather differently, however – as triumphalist, racist and sectarian, in the same mould as the Ku Klux Klan in the United States.

In 1998 the nationalist people of the Garvaghy Road stood firm, and through their leaders Breandán Mac Cionnaith and Joe Duffy announced that there would be no walking on the Garvaghy Road unless the Orangemen talked to them. Rosemary Nelson was the legal adviser to the Garvaghy Residents Association. The Orangemen refused to talk, and nationalists held their own protests against the intimidation. Every July they were cut off from the outside world while the Orange protest went ahead. However under the terms of the 1998 Good Friday Agreement people were to be free from all forms of sectarian hatred and abuse.

In July 1998, just a few months after the Good Friday Agreement, I was asked by Rosemary Nelson on behalf of the Garvaghy Residents Association to speak at a protest rally on the Garvaghy Road. I wanted to show solidarity and to express my sense of outrage at what had been happening there. They had suffered a lot over many years and now, in light of the Good Friday Agreement, they were determined not to be treated as second-class citizens any longer. I admired their courage. This protest march attracted a huge crowd. My message was that the days of unionist triumphalism and supremacy were numbered.

I had known Rosemary for a few years and worked with her on a number of justice issues, in particular the Robert Hamill case. Robert Hamill, a young man from Portadown, was set upon and kicked to death in the centre of the town, in full view of the RUC.

In the days following the rally I was yet again publicly criticised and condemned by some – including priests – in the newspaper columns for identifying with the Garvaghy Road residents.

On 12 July 1998, just one week after the rally, three children were burned to death in Ballymoney, County Antrim when loyalists set fire to their home. The three Quinn brothers were victims of unionist hatred, which has been drilled into sections of the loyalist people over many years. This brutal action shocked all of us who thought we could not be shocked any more. The Ballymoney incident reminded me of the film *Mississippi Burning*, about racism in the southern states of America. Racism thrives if those in power allow it to thrive. If discrimination is tolerated it will thrive. Strong legislation is needed to stop it. The legislators need to be willing to enforce the legislation and show by example their abhorrence of all forms of bigotry and racism.

One month after Ballymoney, on 15 August, a bomb exploded on a crowded street in the centre of Omagh. A group calling themselves the Real IRA (RIRA) drove a car full of explosives into the town centre. The Omagh bomb killed twenty-nine people, including a woman pregnant with twins. I knew one of those killed by the explosion, Philomena Skelton, a native of my home parish of Ederney. She lived in Drumquin with her husband and young family and was in Omagh shopping for the children, who were about to go back to school after the summer holidays. I knew her own family, the Logues, very well and I also knew the Skeltons from Drumquin through Gaelic football and music. I attended her funeral in Drumquin, another heartbreaking occasion.

There is some speculation that the RUC refused to act on the warning to protect a British agent working in the RIRA. The anger and outrage of the people showed that those who planted the bomb had no support within the republican community. Sinn Féin denounced this action and sympathised with all the bereaved. One of those who offered comfort and support to the many injured and bereaved was a classmate and friend, Fr Kevin Mullan, a native of Omagh and now parish priest in Drumquin. We were in Maynooth together for the seven years and have remained friends ever since.

A few weeks after the Omagh bomb I was invited to the US to speak in two colleges outside Boston, in the old industrial towns of Lawrence and Lowell. The other guest speakers were Congressmen Peter King, Marty Meehan and Richard Neal, as well as the Irish consul and the British consul. Who would have ever believed that I would be on a platform with a British consul, whose family happened to be from County Tyrone? Of course, the Omagh atrocity was on all our minds. I talked about the sense of outrage and deep disappointment in the whole community. I wanted to emphasise the positive so I outlined my hope for a new Ireland based on the terms of the Good Friday Agreement signed earlier that year. I wanted to reassure the American audience and the other speakers that the people who bombed Omagh had no support.

In the years since the IRA ceasefire I saw it as my responsibility to support the peace process being advanced by Sinn Féin. Since I saw it as a real chance for lasting peace with justice in Ireland and am convinced it will lead to a thirty-two county republic, I was prepared to go anywhere to talk about the significance of the process and the need for public support for those on the republican and loyalist side who were promoting it.

On 15 March 1999, while driving from Enniskillen towards Irvinestown, I heard on the news that a solicitor in Lurgan had been seriously injured in a booby trap explosion. Pat Fahy, a solicitor from Drumquin, was travelling in the car behind me and I signalled to him to pull over. He also had been listening to the radio and we both knew that it had to be Rosemary Nelson. It was surreal – the two of us sitting outside the agricultural college near Enniskillen trying to take in the news we had just heard. Later that afternoon it was confirmed that Rosemary Nelson had been killed in a booby trap bomb placed under her car. Rosemary had really helped the people of the Garvaghy Road and the Hamill family in Portadown.

Her murder by pro-British agents was a devastating blow to her husband, children, her parents and family members. It was also a dreadful shock to her friends and the local people. Breandán Mac Cionnaith was in the US when he heard the news and came home immediately – shocked and shattered.

I attended Rosemary's funeral in Lurgan and was touched by the strength of her family in this time of great loss. The reflection at the mass, 'When a Good Person Dies', expressed how we felt:

Night is coming on
The last birds fly hurriedly to their nests.
Slowly but surely darkness takes possession of the world.
However, no sooner has darkness fallen,
Than the lights begin to come on –
Below us, around us, above us, near us and far away from us –
A candle in a window, a lamp in a cellar,
A beacon in a lighthouse, a star in the sky.
And so we take heart and find our way again.
When a good person dies darkness descends on us.
We feel lost, bereft, forlorn.
But gradually the lights begin to come on
As we recall the good deeds done by Rosemary.
They spring up all over the place.
We are amazed at how much light is generated.
In this strange and beautiful light
We not only find our way
But find the meaning of life itself.

There is no doubt that Rosemary was hated by elements within the RUC and in some unionist circles. Members of a neo-Nazi group called Combat 18 gloated over her killing. Nobody has ever been charged with her murder.

The Rosemary I knew was a totally unselfish person. She taught us all a lesson about humility, persistence and commitment to justice and human decency. It was a real privilege to have known her and to have witnessed her commitment to justice and truth.

A week after her murder I was asked to chair a meeting, of nationalists and republicans in Enniskillen, about the need for a new police service and the end of political policing. There had been a hearing of the Patten Commission in Enniskillen some time before – but it seemed one-sided and did not give many nationalists who wanted to speak a chance to do so. Rosemary had been due to address the Enniskillen meeting, which I opened by calling for a public independent inquiry into her murder. During the previous three years she had told me a number of times about threats to her life and had expressed concern for her safety and that of her family and clients. She knew that her life was in danger but continued to work fearlessly for her clients. There has always been widespread belief that, because of her involvement in so many high profile legal cases and her close association with the Garvaghy residents, elements within the RUC had a part to play in her murder. Some members of the force certainly showed their deep hostility towards her during the time I knew her.

There are many victims of the war in Ireland over the last thirty years. People often ask what it was all about. I believe the war came about as a result of the denial of democracy and human rights for fifty years by a corrupt regime supported by an arrogant British establishment. The unionists and the British government refused to grant the demands for civil rights and equality, as that would mean the end of their dominance and supremacy in this part of Ireland. It took many years for them to accept the inevitable. Rosemary Nelson was another victim of their intransigence.

There were many, like Rosemary, who worked tirelessly over the years to bring about justice and peace. There are unsung heroes both in Ireland and throughout the world who devoted all their time and energy to bring this about. These are the real leaders who eventually brought us to the transformed situation we have today and to within striking distance of a final solution and the reunification of Ireland.

# 21

# The Dawn

Since 26 March 2007, and the picture of Gerry Adams and Ian Paisley sitting together with members of their respective parties, I have a real sense that the long conflict in Ireland is on its way to being resolved by peaceful political means. There will be difficulties along the way but the elected representatives of the people are now engaged in building peace, justice and prosperity for all in Ireland in accordance with the wishes of the vast majority of the people of Ireland. There is still much work to be done to bring about the kind of just society in Ireland that was envisaged by the revolutionary people of 1916.

I believe that Irish people must now work for and build a united Ireland by peaceful and democratic means. The government in Dublin and all nationalist parties have a huge responsibility to show that politics can work. The way to ensure that there will be lasting peace is to make British involvement in Irish affairs irrelevant. The unionist/loyalist parties have accepted the principle of consent and have pledged to work the institutions of the Good Friday Agreement, including the all-Ireland dimensions. As Gerry Adams, the Sinn Féin president, stated on that momentous occasion in March 2007, the two traditions of Orange and Green are now preparing to work together for the good of all the people of Ireland. Rev. Ian Paisley agreed to lead his party, the Democratic Unionist Party, into a power-sharing arrangement with Sinn Féin.

This would have been unthinkable even a year before. Although he has now decided to retire from his role as first minister, the principle of power-sharing as the way forward has been established. There is no going back. After much soul-searching and many difficult moments, all the pieces of the jigsaw are now in place to progress the situation in a way that does not threaten anybody.

The seeds for this settlement were sown many years before when some people within Ireland decided that the only way to end the war and move forward was for the chief protagonists to engage in dialogue and negotiate an honourable settlement. The IRA had intensified their armed struggle and had attacked British cities and British bases in Europe. Their members died on hunger strike in 1981. They said repeatedly that they were prepared to carry on the war indefinitely. There was only one way to stop the war and that was to start talking. The meetings between Gerry Adams and John Hume prepared the way for open talks with the Dublin and British governments. The Fianna Fáil leaders and their advisers in Dublin were persuaded that Sinn Féin was serious about building peace in a new Ireland. London was still to be convinced. An Irish government led by Bertie Ahern and a British Labour government led by Tony Blair, supported by American president Bill Clinton, engaged with republicans and unionists to bring about the Belfast Agreement of 1998. It represented the first stage in a new settlement in Ireland between Orange and Green. After a number of hitches, the scene was set for an altogether new agreement between those who had been sworn enemies for centuries.

A new power-sharing executive involving Sinn Féin and the DUP met for the first time on 8 May 2007 and elected Rev. Ian Paisley as first minister and Martin McGuinness as deputy first minister. This was a truly historic moment in recent Irish history. After so many years of conflict and violence, the main parties pledged to work together for the good of all the people of Ireland.

One of the tragic results of British interference in Ireland over many centuries is the division of people along religious lines. That prevented the growth of a normal democracy on this island. It was the British who 'planted' English and Scottish families. They then pursued the classic colonial tactic of 'divide and conquer'. I believe that this division of our people based on religious affiliation can only be properly resolved in the context of decolonisation and the rebuilding of the Irish nation. When that happens, new political alignments will emerge on this island that will represent all the different shades of political opinion.

There is now an urgent need for a new kind of politics – the politics of nation-building in which everybody in Ireland has a part to play. In the context of the Good Friday Agreement, it is clear that the old divisions can be resolved and healing can take place. This needs to happen if there is going to be a united democratic Ireland at peace with itself.

The historic statement from the IRA on 28 July 2005 and the political changes since then afford us all a real opportunity to put the past behind us and to work together – unionists and republicans and nationalists – for a better future for all the people of this island. There are many social problems like poverty, drugs, and suicide which need to be tackled. The gap between rich and poor in 'Celtic Tiger' Ireland has widened and has been well documented by Fr Peter McVerry.

There is still a lot of healing needed on all sides and this will take some time. There is no hierarchy of suffering. Both republicans and unionists have suffered and both have a responsibility to encourage the healing process. Protestant and Catholic church leaders can make a big contribution to the healing process and to the creation of an Ireland where everybody is accepted and welcomed. They can make resources available for counselling and other services. Healing Through Remembering is an organisation that has stressed the need for telling our stories as a way of healing. I am writing this book in that spirit – not to cause hurt by recalling our troubled past but to contribute, even in some small way, to an understanding of the experience of one side of the community and to the process of reconciliation in our country.

There is a challenge to engage with those who differ from us politically and to establish common interests and common concerns. Only in this way will the feelings of fear and distrust built up over many years be broken down. We need to be honest with each other and listen to our opponents.

We should now be able to live together on this island, on the basis of equality. We should be able to work together to bring about a country that is outward-looking, forward-looking and economically sound. The most important thing now is that we make sure that violent conflict never happens again between Irish people and that we can resolve our difficulties by peaceful political means. This will require leadership and co-operation from all sides.

We are now in the process of building a new democracy, a democracy where all the Irish people, including our unionist brothers and sisters, will feel at ease and where immigrants from other countries will be made feel welcome.

It is important to acknowledge the major changes that have occurred in Ireland since the IRA ceasefire in 1994 and the peace process that evolved after that. There has been a sea-change within Irish republicanism, thanks to the highly skilled leaders who promoted a policy of generosity and tolerance along with political astuteness. Sinn Féin is now a growing political force in the twenty-six counties and has boldly set itself the task of persuading the people of Ireland, including the unionist people, that it is to the advantage of all on the island of Ireland to govern themselves free from British interference. Even though Sinn Féin is still a small political party in comparison to the other parties in Ireland it has had (and continues to have) a major influence on events on the island of Ireland. Its greatest influence will be in the creation of a new democracy.

The Belfast Agreement of 1998 provided for cross-border bodies to improve the social and economic conditions of all the people of Ireland – especially in disadvantaged border areas. That requires co-operation at all levels. There needs to be an integrated system of roadways and railways, of health services and education facilities. The people of the border areas who have been disadvantaged over many years need resources to build up small industries and create learning and recreational opportunities for all age groups. Irish elected representatives and Irish community activists working together for all the people in the spirit of the Proclamation of 1916 can achieve all of these improvements.

The St Andrew's Agreement of 13 October 2006, involving the Dublin and London governments and the political parties, offered a way out of the political deadlock. Paisley's Democratic Unionist Party (DUP) has become the largest pro-union party in the six counties. On 26 March 2007 Mr Paisley and the DUP expressed a willingness to share power and to work the Good Friday Agreement in the terms laid out at St Andrew's. For the first time we saw a more constructive Mr Paisley who was not opposed to power-sharing or to doing business with Dublin.

The churches could make a valuable contribution to the building of a new inclusive Ireland, to establishing a culture of human rights, justice and peace and a new and vibrant democracy. Our native Irish language must be preserved and promoted and be given its proper place in education and worship. All of the churches could put resources into developing a new spirituality for our times, one that is in touch with modern thinking as well as with our deep Celtic soul and the love of the natural world.

There is need for a conversation in Ireland about the kind of democracy we want and the kind of republic we want. Much of the power over the lives of nationalists and unionists in the north still resides in Westminster. Decisions about the economy are made in Westminster and imposed on the people – whether they like them or not. Only recently, in December 2007, the issue of corporation tax in the north surfaced. The northern assembly argued for a lowering of corporation tax to bring the north more into line with the twenty-six counties and attract more inward investment. The British government disagreed, arguing that it would have a negative effect on the English economy, especially in the north of England. They feared that some companies would leave England for the six counties. This kind of control is bad for everyone in the six counties and the smart unionists know it.

The future is now to be worked out through dialogue and discussion involving all sections of the Irish people. Working at building democracy is the way forward. It is the way to defeat authoritarianism, arrogance and bullying by government – all of which we have known and suffered in the past.

We need to continue to discuss the advantages of building an Ireland of equals for all the people of this island – Catholic, Protestant and Dissenter. I believe that this is a spiritual as well as a political project and it challenges all of us who live here. Could Ireland become known once again as the 'Island of saints and scholars'?

# 22

## Still Priesting

The change in attitude to the Catholic church and to the clergy in Ireland during my lifetime is dramatic. The traditional Catholic religion that I grew up with in the 1950s has almost disappeared. The numbers attending mass and the sacraments have fallen – just like other countries in Europe. Vocations to the priesthood are in steady decline; our diocese of Clogher has not had a priest ordained for ten years. Many seminaries in Ireland have closed. The Irish Catholic church is in crisis.

Some believe the change in attitude began when the story about Bishop Casey broke in 1992; for others it was the revelations about child sex abuse by clergy and the abuse of children by nuns in the Magdalene laundries. Some trace it back to the pope's visit in 1979 while more say it coincided with the arrival of the 'Celtic Tiger'. But the reasons for the decline in religious practice in Ireland and the disillusionment of young people with the official church are complex. The cultural revolution that has taken place in Ireland in the last twenty years has to be a major factor. Irish society has changed beyond all imagining.

The child abuse revelations had a big impact on Catholic consciousness. Many were shocked by the way the trust of the people was abused and how the bishops and church authorities handled many of the cases. The Ferns Report declared that 'bishops placed the interest of the church ahead of children' in dealing with clerical child sexual abuse. People ask what kind of church were the bishops protecting? Was this the kind of church Christ intended?

Many of us who studied for the priesthood in the 1960s were full of enthusiasm and hope because of the changes introduced by the Second Vatican Council (1961–64), its emphasis on human dignity and human rights and the important role of the laity in the church and in the world. However, many people, both clergy and laity, became more than a little disillusioned with the Catholic church in Ireland because of the rowing back to the old authoritarian ways. Instead of involving the laity, the church in Ireland remained a clerical church. Instead of becoming a church of the poor and marginalised, it continued to support the status quo and maintain a close comfortable relationship with the government.

Some say that the present crisis is an opportunity for building a new church and creating a new spirituality – if people are encouraged. Perhaps the new church will need to be built from the bottom up, through the growth of small Christian communities engaged in prayer, reflection and action for justice. I think we could learn from the experiences of the church in countries like Brazil and El Salvador. If there is to be a new kind of politics – the politics of compassion and justice – then people need to be empowered. People need to realise their own power and that can happen in small groups when people reflect on their faith and discover the call to action for justice.

For me, one of the joys of being a priest is being able to connect and identify with other men and women throughout the world who give their lives in the service of the oppressed and who are committed to working for justice. I find it a source of pride to be associated with so many wonderful and compassionate people, who are answering the call to work with the poorest of the poor in countries all over the world. I include many of my contemporaries in this group. The energy, the passion and the commitment of all these people is admirable, and is a clear witness to the gospel of justice and non-violence in the world today. Some have made the supreme sacrifice and given their lives for the gospel and the people they served.

During my life as a priest I met all kinds of opposition, criticism and suspicion from within the church and outside. However, I was determined to stick to my decision to take the side of the people rather than the institution and to speak out about injustice. I thought often about Oscar Romero and about Carolyn Forché's encouraging words after she returned from El Salvador – about the role of the priest as 'the voice of the voiceless'. I was determined to keep the focus on British repression and the violation of our basic human rights by the British and the Irish governments. I was not surprised that my motives were often misrepresented and that I was subjected to all kinds of criticism and abuse – especially from 'true Catholics' and 'true Christians'.

I often feared for my life. I knew there were some ruthless and well armed people about who did not like me or what I stood for. I was even more afraid of bringing trouble upon my family. I did not want them to be hurt or isolated because of my public profile. I knew that they might not share my strong political beliefs and feelings, though they might suffer for them. Unionists, nationalists, members of the Dublin and British governments, UDR men and politicians all attacked me. One DUP politician who was born and reared beside me described me as 'a papish agitator'. A local Free Presbyterian minister had many nasty things to say about me – in his pulpit and in his newsletter, *The Burning Bush*. He even made up stories about me in an attempt to destroy my reputation in the parish and in the local community. As a result I received threatening letters and phone calls from a group called Ulster Resistance, closely associated with Ian Paisley and Ivan Foster.

I had often to be mindful of those words in the gospel, 'Be Not Afraid'. Those are the words of someone who knew all about fear and threats. I have indeed lived through turbulent times, a long war and the long search for a just and lasting peace in this country. In recent years I have seen the dramatic social and economic changes in Ireland – especially in the twenty-six counties, the new wealth and the industry, the new roads, new buildings and new houses. I am constantly reminded that not all have benefited from the new wealth and that the gap between rich and poor is increasing because of the unjust way wealth is distributed. The churches in Ireland have a vital role to play in challenging this reality.

Many times over the years I thought about why I remained a priest. I always wanted to celebrate our faith with the people – especially those who felt alienated from both institutions, church and state. I wanted to be with people, especially at key moments in their lives. It is very satisfying to be part of a celebration that lifts people's spirits and gives people a deeper appreciation of their dignity as human beings. I felt that I was called repeatedly to live my life in solidarity with the people.

In spite of the difficulties and my own failings, I have stayed in the priesthood for more than thirty-five years. I made the original commitment to live a life of service to the people and I saw no good reason to give that up. Each disappointment or crisis – however painful – was an opportunity to renew that commitment. Each mistake was an occasion for learning and moving on.

One of the lessons I learned in my life is that you cannot sit on the fence – that is, if you care about the world we live in and about how your sisters and brothers are being treated unjustly. Every human being is called to take sides and to act against injustice. You cannot be neutral where there is injustice and the denial of human rights. We should have learned from the experience of the Nazi concentration camps, that Christians couldn't be silent in the face of bad government and the abuse of power. We all could learn from the example of people like Franz Jaggerstatter, the Austrian farmer who defied the Nazis and went against the advice of the clergy and refused to join the Nazis. As a priest you cannot sit on the fence when the people you are called to serve are under attack from the forces of the state, when the rich and powerful oppress the poor. You have to take sides and you have to speak out. You cannot just say, 'I will make some representations quietly behind the scenes.' That is not the public witness that is called for in the gospel. You have to take the consequences of making a public commitment to serving Christ. That is what conscience means to me – taking a stand for what you believe to be right.

Another lesson I learned in my life is that we need to be gentle with ourselves and with each other and with the planet earth. According to Wayne W. Dyer, 'Living with a spirit of mercy and putting it to use each day is the way to tame our more base and primitive instincts while nurturing love and compassion. We need to be gentle with ourselves.' He goes on: 'If you are unable to give yourself authentic compassion you will never be able to give it to another, any more than you can give love to another if you do not love yourself.' With regard to caring for the earth we have now a choice – either to become agents of transformation or carry on destroying the environment. Each person has a part to play.

IN 2002 I suffered a heart attack, which was a life-changing experience. I was forced to slow down and take things a bit easier. Since then, I have had an opportunity to read more books and attend all kinds of seminars and talks. I have had the privilege of working at the St Patrick's Pilgrimage centre on Lough Derg during the summer and autumn months. Meeting people there and hearing confessions is very rewarding. It is my hope that, as my health improves, I can return to full time parish ministry.

# Epilogue

My story began in 1945, the year the Second World War ended. Sadly, it was not the end of war or the end of preparing for war. There have been wars in every decade since then in many different parts of the world from Vietnam to Palestine, from the Balkans to Pakistan, from South Africa to Ireland, from Iraq to Afghanistan. It is estimated that there have been more than 140 wars since 1945. Millions have died in these conflicts, which were caused mainly by the greed for power, control and the unwillingness of those in power to grant justice and basic human rights, share power or give up territory that does not belong to them. The military-industrial complex continues to have huge influence on governments and is able to get whatever money it needs to expand its power and influence.

My story is about a personal experience of war – a war that I believe was forced on the Irish people. War is never glorious. It causes untold suffering, sadness and sorrow. That is my experience and that is what I have witnessed. The terrible thing is that those with political and military might have no sense of the evil they are doing when they force war on people who do not want it. While we now have hope for a peaceful future in Ireland there is still much work to be done to build a culture of human rights and equality.

A key issue for all people of faith is how to bring about justice and lasting peace in our world where the prevailing ideology favours the idea that might is right. The rich and powerful are prepared to spend any amount of money on weapons of mass destruction to maintain supremacy and control of oil and other rich mineral reserves. They have most of the world's media on their side. For more than a decade the western powers have declared 'a new world order'.

The US government's war on 'terrorism' after the Al Qaeda attacks on September 11, 2001 has brought the world to a very dangerous point in history. Human rights are now systematically ignored in Guantanamo and other detention centres around the world.

One American writer and human rights activist, Barbara Olshansky, states: 'I believe that we are living in a time that history will judge thoroughly and harshly. The terrorist activities of recent years will be much discussed for decades to come, but I wager that the years following the September 11 attacks will be viewed largely within the context of the United States' use of unprovoked military force to promote its ambitions for empire. And why not? The hallmark of post September 11 America is a country governed by politicians who seek unchecked power to pursue their global 'war on terror' and who express a chilling disregard for human rights and the rule of law in that pursuit. It is a government that ignores the concerns expressed by many nations about the use of power and resists the scrutiny of the United Nations human rights experts. Our government undermines its own moral credibility, casts aside its role of advancing human rights in the world, and makes us all much less safe by committing humanitarian and human rights law violations in the name of national security. Through our unprovoked aggression, our indefinite executive detention of prisoners without due process, and our torture and abuse of them, we model and legitimise repressive conduct for nations around the world. When the world wants to know will our actions match the vision and rhetoric of the Founders of this country?'*

It saddens me that the Irish government has supported American

---

* Barbara Olshansky, *Democracy Detained*, Seven Stories Press, New York, 2007.

foreign policy by providing facilities at Shannon airport. Amnesty International has voiced its concerns. The Irish churches are silent.

A huge challenge facing radical Christians and human rights activists comes from those Christian fundamentalists who support military intervention and the death penalty. Today many in leadership positions in the churches are ambivalent about the use and sale of military weapons by the major powers in the world. There was no great outcry from church leaders against the US government's military intervention. While there are some prophetic voices – like Roy Bourgeois, John Dear and Dan Berrigan – working to end militarism and the oppression of the poor, the official church line is to support the super powers. It is surely time for the churches to make a radical break with the militarists – liberal and conservative.

Faced with all the forces of reaction and militarism, what is needed most of all is a prophetic imagination which 'connects the religion of God's freedom and the politics of human justice.' That is another way of describing liberation theology.

The way forward for the Christian churches, it seems to me, is to adopt a liberation theology approach – to oppose the use of military intervention and to promote the gospel of non-violence. There should be continuous tension between the reign of God and empire. I have been inspired by the writings of liberation theologians and by the re-reading of the scriptures, especially the prophetic books and the gospels, from the viewpoint of the oppressed. The Christian churches should refuse to cooperate in any way with governments that inflict war on other nations. The Vatican should be absolutely clear about its opposition to military conquest and military intervention by the superpowers.

Some people grow up believing in their own power and privilege, which leads them to abuse power on a grand scale as we have seen with Hitler, Mussolini, Franco and many other dictators and oligarchs. There is now an ideology of 'exceptionalism' – a belief among a section of the political/military establishment that they are exceptional among the nations. It is an extension of the old belief in 'manifest destiny'. Now, instead of conquering a continent, the most powerful state in the world promotes a policy of 'a new world order'.

I am pleased to have many friends in the United States who do not share this outlook and who are as opposed to US foreign policy as I am. Some of them are involved in civil disobedience to make their opposition known.

It is a great scandal that there are fundamentalist Christians who support the use of military might against the poor – often 'in the national interest' or ' in the interest of national security'. The manufacture of deadly weapons continues often with the excuse that they are needed to maintain peace. War continues to affect the lives of millions and life goes on in war torn zones. Those who claim to follow Christ have a special responsibility to join in the search for justice and lasting peace. This is why I stress the need for prophetic imagination. We live in the global village. My experience teaches that there are always underlying causes where there is conflict and violence and that these have to be addressed if there is to be justice and peace.

The great spiritual writer, Thomas Merton reminded us many years ago that in order to create a new culture of peace and non-violence in the world, we needed to examine our own hearts and our own attitudes. He wrote: 'Prayer and sacrifice must be used as the most effective spiritual weapons in the war against war, and like all weapons they must be used with deliberate aim; not just with a vague aspiration for peace and security, but against violence and against war. This implies that we are also willing to sacrifice and restrain our own instinct for violence and aggressiveness in our relations with other people. We may never succeed in this campaign, but, whether we succeed or not, the duty is evident. It is the great Christian task of our time.'*

---

* Thomas Merton, *Catholic Worker*, October 1961.

This is a sobering thought on which to end my story but it is one that must be heeded. Life is too precious and the situation in our world is too perilous.

# Index